POVERTY IN EIGHTEENTH-CENTURY SPAIN

JOAN SHERWOOD

Poverty in Eighteenth-Century Spain

THE WOMEN AND CHILDREN OF THE INCLUSA

UNIVERSITY OF TORONTO PRESS
Toronto Buffalo London

© University of Toronto Press 1988
Toronto Buffalo London
Printed in Canada

ISBN 0-8020-2662-1

Printed on acid-free paper

Canadian Cataloguing in Publication Data

Sherwood, Joan, 1929–
Poverty in eighteenth-century Spain: the women
and children of the Inclusa

Includes index.
ISBN 0-8020-2662-1

1. Inclusa (Madrid, Spain) – History.
2. Foundlings – Spain – Madrid – History – 18th
century. 3. Child welfare – Spain – Madrid –
History – 18th century. 4. Wet-nurses – Spain –
Madrid – History – 18th century. 5. Poor – Spain –
Madrid – History – 18th century. 6. Spain – Social
policy. I. Title.

HV1245.M32I53 1988   362.7'32'094641   C88-094548-6

This book has been published with the help of a grant from
the Social Science Federation of Canada, using funds provided by
the Social Sciences and Humanities Research Council of Canada.

Contents

TABLES vii

FIGURES ix

PREFACE xi

Part One The Institution

1 The Balancing Act: Income and Expenses of the Inclusa 3

2 The Human Resources of the Inclusa 34

Part Two The Wet-Nurses

3 Rural Poverty and the Inclusa 51

4 Urban Poverty and the Inclusa 71

Part Three The Infants of the Inclusa

5 The *Expósito* as Bastard:
Illegitimacy and the Enlightenment 95

6 The *Expósito* as Victim: The Mortality in the Inclusa 125

7 The *Expósito* as Patient: The Medicalization of the Inclusa 150

8 Infanticide and the Inclusa 174

NOTE ON SOURCES 211

NOTES 215

INDEX 235

Tables

1.1 Expenses for straw goods and labour 13
1.2 Price of oil per *arroba* 15
1.3 Bales of textiles for pay-days and admissions to the Inclusa 17
1.4 Admissions of infants with alms from parishes and individuals 23
1.5 Sources of income of the royal treasury 31
3.1 Rural occupations of husbands of wet-nurses, 1700–99 57
3.2 Population of the city and province of Madrid, 1717–23 to 1797 66
3.3 Rural and urban addresses of wet-nurses of the Inclusa, 1700–99 69
4.1 Principal occupations of husbands of wet-nurses in Madrid, 1700–99 75
4.2 Patterns in occupations of husbands listed by urban wet-nurses 76
4.3 Addresses of nurses taking out infants of the Inclusa 86
5.1 Percentage of legitimate and illegitimate admissions of infants to the Inclusa (June–December 1700–1800) 111
5.2 Numbers of *incluseros* assumed legitimate/illegitimate (1700–1805) 113
5.3 Percentage of admissions to the Inclusa presumed legitimate/illegitimate 115
6.1 Mortality of infants and number of nurses 134
6.2 Occupations and mortality rates: urban/rural 138
6.3 Admissions by sex to the Inclusa, 1700–99 138
6.4 Deaths within the hospital, 1764–87 140
6.5 Deaths within the hospital, 1791–1801 140
6.6 Deaths within the hospital, 1800–05 141

6.7 Total deaths based on *entradas* for June and December of decade years, 1700–90   143
6.8 Total deaths based on annual summaries, *entradas*, 1787–1802 146
6.9 Fate of infants abandoned to the Inclusa, 1700–99   148
7.1 Diseases causing deaths of *expósitos* in 1802   163

Figures

1.1 Admissions to the Inclusa and the price of wheat in New Castile, 1700–99   6
1.2 Admissions to the Inclusa and alms received with infants, 1700–99   22
3.1 Towns from which wet-nurses came, 1700–99   52
3.2 Rural occupations of husbands of wet-nurses   56
3.3 Rural and urban wet-nurses of Inclusa, 1700–99   58
4.1 Occupations of husbands of urban wet-nurses, 1700–99   73
4.2 Changes in proportions of occupations, 1700–49 and 1750–99   76
4.3 Addresses of urban wet-nurses of the Inclusa   83
5.1 Average monthly admissions to the Inclusa by decades, 1700–99   118
5.2 Monthly admissions to the Inclusa above and below the mean, 1700–99   119
5.3 Ratio of new-borns to overall admissions, 1744–1800   122
6.1 Admissions and mortality of infants of the Inclusa, 1700–99   126
6.2 Monthly deaths of infants above and below the mean, 1700–99   144
6.3 Monthly admissions of infants above and below the mean, 1700–99   145
6.4 Mortality of infants of the Inclusa and the price of wheat, 1700–99 147

Preface

Poverty has been a permanent feature of every known civilization. The paucity of material goods and the primitive nature of the productive processes have meant that in every society some people have been forced to suffer deprivation. Women and children, because of their relative powerlessness, have always been among the most dispossessed. The feminization of poverty is not a recent phenomenon.

The eighteenth century offers a particularly advantageous perspective from which to study poverty because it was in that century that a transition was made from the traditional, paternalistic attitude toward poverty (which accepted its inevitability) to a more modern approach derived from the progressive and humanitarian ideals of the Enlightenment. In this new view, poverty and the poor were to be eliminated. Some enlightened thinkers and officials came to believe, contrary to what Christ had said, that the poor need not always be with us. A study of a foundling hospital, the Inclusa of Madrid in the eighteenth century, provides the opportunity to examine both the older and the newer approaches to poverty, especially as they dealt with women and children.

Poverty in the Old Regime is a difficult phenomenon to study. Royalty, nobility, and intellectuals have left behind records of their activities. The poor in this pre-bureaucratic age tended to pass through this world largely undifferentiated and unrecorded. There was one institution, however, that maintained a scrupulous record of at least some of the poor from the cradle to the grave. The continuous and unbroken records of the foundling hospital in Madrid, from its founding in 1572 to the present day, provide the kind of written and statistical documentation that would satisfy the demands of even the most rigorous and positivistic of modern researchers. In these records, the lives (brief though they were) and deaths of the poor were punctiliously recorded. In this area, at least, the grim reaper kept score.

Because these archival records give us equally well-documented information about the wet-nurses who were hired to care for the abandoned children, they provide information about the lives of both women and children, the most oppressed of the poor.

The records of the Inclusa reveal Old Regime attitudes toward the poor and the practical means adopted to alleviate their condition. By the end of the eighteenth century, under pressure of rising rates of abandonment and deteriorating economic conditions, both philosophy and methods had shown themselves to be woefully inadequate. At this point, the hospital came under the management of a group of noble-women, the Junta de damas, or women's wing of the prestigious Royal Economic Society of Madrid. Under the influence of Enlightenment ideals, the Inclusa was totally reorganized and an attempt made to put its administration and finances on a rationalized, modern basis. The records of the Inclusa, therefore, enable us to contrast the older and newer approaches toward poverty.

There have been numerous studies of foundling hospitals, but to my knowledge this is the only study of the foundling hospital of Madrid using its archives for the critical period of the eighteenth century. France has pioneered in demographic studies and in the nineteenth century produced many statistical works with interesting data on foundlings. Inquiries by B. Remacle,[1] and by Jean-François Terme and J.B. Monfalcon,[2] contained the material for early histories such as Léon Lallemand's *Histoire des enfants abandonnés et délaissés: Etude sur la protection de l'enfance aux diverses époques de la civilisation* and *La question des enfants abandonnés et délaissés au xixe siècle.*[3] More recently, local archives have been plumbed by Jean-Claude Peyronnet for Limoges,[4] and Janet Ruth Potash for Lille and Lyon.[5] The Hôpital des Enfants-trouvés in Paris has been extensively researched in studies by Claude Delasselle,[6] Nicole Sergent,[7] and in a recently published book by Rachel Ginnis Fuchs,[8] while George Sussman has concentrated on the wet-nurses who took out the Paris foundlings.[9] Several works on the poor have treated the foundling problem with sensitivity, in particular, Olwen Hufton's *The Poor in Eighteenth-Century France*,[10] J.-P. Gutton's *La société et les pauvres: L'exemple de la généralité de Lyon 1534–1789*,[11] and Cissie Fairchild's *Poverty and Charity in Aix-en-Provence, 1640–1789.*[12] There have been two histories of the London

xiii Preface

Foundling Hospital, one in 1935 by T.H. Nichols and F.A. Wray[13] and a recent study entitled *Coram's Children*[14] by Ruth McClure. In Spain there was a great deal of contemporary interest in the topic at the end of the eighteenth century. Much of this literature focused upon raising public consciousness and leaned heavily upon a vocabulary of 'death,' with titles such as *Destrucción y conservación de los expósitos* by Antonio Bilbao y Durán,[15] and *Causas prácticas de la muerte de niños expósitos en sus primeros años* by Joaquín Xavier de Uriz, administrator of the foundling hospital in Pamplona.[16] Official government concern with the problem is evident in the work of the highly placed bureaucrat Pedro Joaquín de Murcia, *Discurso político sobre la importancia de los Hospicios, casas de expósitos y hospitales que tienen todos los Estados y particularmente España*.[17] Numerous general works on social welfare have made reference to foundling hospitals. One recent book by Jacques Soubeyroux on Madrid has devoted a chapter to the expósito.[18] There have also been local studies of the foundling hospitals in Valladolid, Santiago, and Seville.[19] There is much excellent work being done by medical historians in Spain for the eighteenth century that has discussed child care.[20] But the most interesting accounts of early paediatrics are to be found in the writings of the doctors themselves. In particular two works by the doctor of the Inclusa Santiago García have been especially relevant.[21] Antonio Carreras Panchón has studied the mortality figures for foundlings in *El problema del niño expósito en la España ilustrada*.[22] Paula de Demerson's detailed and fascinating biography of the Countess del Montijo[23] provided much information on the role that the Junta de damas played in the administration of the Inclusa at the turn of the century. I owe to Valentina Fernández Vargas my discovery of the archives of the Inclusa, which no one had used up to that point.[24] Claude Larquié has since published articles about the wet-nurses of the Inclusa in the seventeenth century.[25]

The Inclusa of Madrid was exceptional in many ways. The institution gave its name to all the foundling hospitals in Spain and the colonies of the New World. It is the only hospital in which a group of enlightened women were able to gain complete control of an institution and to apply the new methods of the Enlightenment to its administration. It also had the advantage of gaining the sympathetic attention and support of the highest officials of the state, the king, the queen, and the king's first minister, Godoy. Unfortunately, for reasons discussed later, this support and the changes put into effect by the coterie of noblewomen were unable to remedy the plight of the poor. Perversely, in 1804, in the midst of the new reforms, conditions for the poor were such that 100 per cent of the infants abandoned to the Inclusa died.

Foundling hospitals were in difficulties all over Europe, but in some ways Spain remained unique. As the problems facing the government and the economy grew, foundlings in Spain were not any better off than those in any other country in Europe, but there was never a sense that they were a responsibility to be shirked. This attitude was in marked contrast to views prevailing in England and Ireland, where the treatment of foundlings marks a black page in the history of decent people. There, attitudes toward the foundling represented an extreme individualism that saw the primary function of government as protecting the rights of the propertied classes. The workhouse and foundling hospital provided relief for more fortunate and influential citizens from the public nuisance of beggars, and especially beggar children. Some areas in the west of England and Wales found it economically viable to pay women to make the trip to Dublin with their foundlings in 1770.[26] Other parishes regularly employed a 'lifter' whose specific task it was to remove foundlings to other jurisdictions. In England it was not unusual for pregnant wretches on the point of delivering to be transported over the boundary to a neighbouring parish. In Spain, responsibility for the foundling was assumed to be just and reasonable. But as in all foundling hospitals everywhere, there were problems in fulfilling that responsibility.

In an age of progress and enlightenment, the history of the Inclusa presents an anomaly. For enlightened reformers it seemed possible at last to make the world a better place for all, even the poorest and weakest of the poor. Nevertheless, conditions for the poor did not improve. The records of the Inclusa have provided a unique series of documents from which to reconstruct the lives of the women and children of the poor who were associated with the hospital in many aspects. They have made possible a history that focuses on the Inclusa but illustrates the problems – in all their complexity – faced by women and children of the poor in Madrid in the eighteenth century.

I owe much gratitude to the director of the Diputación Provincial del Instituto de Puericultura, Dr J. Matos Aguilar, and his secretary, Carmen Jímenez, who have been gracious in a way that only the Spanish can be. My thanks also to the archivist of the Real Academia de Medicina, Antonio Vallejo de Simon. The project started as a doctoral thesis supervised by William Callahan of the University of Toronto, xv Preface

who has been both mentor and friend. The maps and charts were done by Ross Hough of the Department of Geography at Queen's University with funds from the Arts Research Council. Bruce Bell of the computing services was also of assistance. Advice and instruction on the use of statistics was given generously by Professors Louis Broekhoven and Mario Creet of Queen's University. Ellen Friedman of Boston College provided much encouragement. I am also grateful to Thomas E. Cone jr, MD, for his helpful comments on the paediatrics of the eighteenth century. Lydia Burton has been a patient and painstaking editor. In particular, I would like to thank the archivist of the hospital, the late Sor Irène, a member of the same order of Sisters of Charity who were brought in by the Junta de damas to the Inclusa in 1800. Her warmth and generosity cannot be overstated. I only regret that the trials of scholarship meant that she did not live to see published a history of the institution to which she and so many women had devoted their lives. This study was aided by a grant from the Social Sciences and Humanities Research Council of Canada, the Advisory Research Committee of Queen's University, and the Social Science Federation of Canada.

Finally, I would like to thank my family – three little girls, now three young women – who were, on occasion, dumped unceremoniously with babysitters and camp counsellors in a friendly but foreign country while mother photographed sources, and a husband who was unfailingly generous with love, support, and encouragement. This book is dedicated to John.

PART ONE

THE INSTITUTION

1

The Balancing Act:
Income and Expenses of
the Inclusa

Paternalism defined relationships between the authority structures of church and state in the Old Regime and their subjects. The king was the father of his people; the pope, as Christ's representative, was the Holy Father. The church described its members as the family of Christ, and the state considered its subjects as children owing loyalty and obedience in return for fatherly concern. In a special way the poor qualified as children, entitled as such to 'charity' – literally love and protection from both church and state. The Inclusa depended upon the state, the church, and individuals who saw the poor in the terms laid down by these two institutions.

The Old Regime had developed an elaborate system of charitable institutions in order to mitigate the harsh conditions of everyday life for much of the populace in a pre-industrial society. It was taken for granted that the poor would always be there. They were part of God's plan for the salvation of more fortunate brothers and sisters. Their role was twofold: to provide examples of the inscrutability of providence in an insecure world, and to provide opportunities for generosity and benevolence on the part of the wealthy. Thus, the poor were there for the benefit of both donor and recipient of charity.

Hospitals for the old, the sick, the orphaned, and the destitute were originally under the aegis of religious organizations. The Inclusa of Madrid began as a project on the part of a group of lay individuals and friars of the Order of St Francis. The confraternity was dedicated to Our Lady of Sorrows in the chapel of la Victoria, on the calle de San Jerónimo, just around the corner from the Puerta del Sol. (Her statue, or a replica, is still there.) One of the charitable endeavours of the order was a modest asylum consisting of twelve beds for poor, convalescent priests. In 1572 the group extended its activities to take in foundlings who had been abandoned at the portals of churches and convents or on stairways of private dwellings, or left on deserted street corners.[1] As early as 1587 the hospital expanded and took over houses in the neighbourhood of the square, along the calle del Carmen and the calle de Preciados.[2] It was during this period that a soldier returned from the Flemish town of Enkuïssen with a picture of the Virgin and Child which he donated to the hospital. Tradition has it that the name Inclusa derived from a corruption of Enkuïssen, but its hold in the popular mind must surely have come from the welcoming connotations of the word 'Inclusa' and the function of the institution as a home for the unwanted. By 1615 the confraternity found that its work had outstripped its resources and the Inclusa was incorporated as one of the royal hospitals of Madrid.[3] The confraternity itself was abandoned in 1651, its work for poor priests forgotten, but the institution continues to function today as a paediatric hospital under the auspices of the Diputación Provincial del Instituto de Puericultura in calle O'Donnell.

One of the redeeming features of the Old Regime was its welfare system, and concern for the foundling was evidence of the benevolent paternalism of the Hapsburg and Bourbon monarchies. But in Spain the foundling hospital had another association with paternalism. The honour of the family was dependent upon the sexual purity of the female who was under the protection and surveillance of the male. The role of the foundling hospital was both to uphold this honour and reinforce this form of patriarchy by caring for abandoned and illegitimate infants. It was a shelter where an unwanted infant could be brought, baptized, and sent out to nurse. If the child died, and it was taken for granted that many would, at least it died after a Christian baptism and did not leave the parents a legacy of guilt for a crime of infanticide. The Inclusa was to provide for the honour of the mother (or more to the point, the honour of the mother's family) and the soul of the child. The illegitimate infant had no place in the family strategy of traditional Spain. By means of the foundling hospital, the king assumed the duties of a surrogate father, provided for the infant a surrogate mother in the wet-nurse, and thus preserved the honour of the family.

How well the Inclusa fulfilled its function of caring for the newborn once baptized was directly connected with its finances, and these registered like a barometer the fortunes, good and bad, of Madrid's poor. Institutions like the Inclusa were important to the government as a means of moderating somewhat the impact of these ups and downs on the poor, who might otherwise take out their anger on those in power. For instance, the Inclusa functioned as a safety valve for social unrest in times of crop failure. The finances of the Inclusa illustrate how the government attempted to deal with the threat offered to the stability of the regime by the victims of poverty. Infants flooded the Inclusa every time the price of grain went up (fig. 1.1). This function of poor relief periodically put considerable strain on the resources of the hospital. However, good years followed bad. With the recurrence of a bumper crop, the pressure was off everyone and the Inclusa had a chance to recuperate, regain its strength, and rebuild its exhausted treasury.

Despite these periodic crises, a cursory glance at the account books of the Inclusa for the century gives an impression of remarkable stability, almost stagnancy. The awning of the patio was put up in March and taken down in September for many decades by members of the same family. The matting on the floors was put down in the fall and taken up in the spring. Crockery purchases were made in September at the fair in the Plazuela de Cebeda; coal was delivered in May or June; the year's supply of honey came in February; and paper was delivered for the record books in December. Regardless of wars, inflation, rising population, and urban expansion, the pattern of the day-to-day life of the institution remained, on the surface, unchanged for a century.

But in reality the picture of stability was deceptive. Supplies were becoming more expensive as a result of inflation, while at the same time and for the same reason the financial reserves of the Inclusa were declining in value. Even without additional demands on its resources, the Inclusa would have had trouble. Instead, by the end of the century, it was being flooded by infants requiring more nurses and more supplies. The *gastos* (account books) can be read as both an example and a symptom of the trouble facing the Old Regime as it tried to come to grips with the issue of poverty.

An examination of the financial arrangements of the Inclusa brings to light difficulties experienced by church, state, and ultimately all classes of society in eighteenth-century Madrid as they interrelated with the Inclusa. The institution's administrators were churchmen and important bureaucrats, and its benefactors came from the highest ranks of the nobility, even from the royal family. Suppliers were merchants, both well-off entrepreneurs and small artisans, and its staff ranged from affluent to destitute.

The political problems plaguing the government in the eighteenth century provide a background against which the Inclusa and its

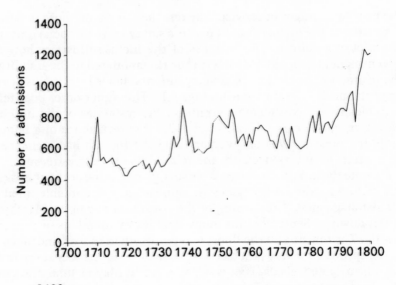

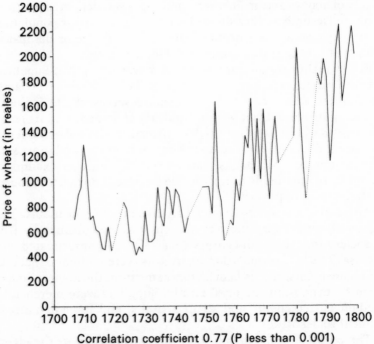

Correlation coefficient 0.77 (P less than 0.001)

FIGURE 1.1 Admissions to the Inclusa and the price of wheat in New Castile, 1700–99

company interacted. In 1700 the last of the Hapsburgs, Charles II, was
replaced by a Bourbon, Philip V. The new monarch surrounded himself
with capable administrators and prepared to restore the dimmed lustre
of Spain and to rival, if not equal, the Bourbon court of his grandfather
in Paris. Though Spain was at war more often than not in the first half of
the century, sweeping reform in public finance, the maintenance of a
stable monetary policy, good crops, and a unified kingdom set the stage
for an economic upturn in second half of the century. But by 1789 the
optimism of the early years was being put to the test. A series of disastrous harvests had caused grain prices to rise steeply; wars with Britain
and France disrupted trade with the Indies, and markets collapsed.
Mounting expenses for the wars of the French Revolution put the government in debt and destroyed the credit of the state bonds (vales reales),
which had been promulgated to encourage investment in government
projects and were responsible for fuelling much of that economic
expansion.

Enlightened reformers saw Spain's problems rooted in the framework
of the Old Regime, pointing out that the numerous privileges based on
class and wealth were ultimately destructive of the good of the entire
nation. They pin-pointed the inequities of the tax system that exempted
those best able to pay and undermined the stability of the whole structure. The inherent weaknesses in tax arrangements coupled with the
increasing costs of armies and welfare exposed the need for a radical
revision of the regime if the Bourbon dream of a new Spain was to
become a reality. Because the Inclusa depended for its funds on the
government, on the generosity of the wealthy noble class, and on a
network of charitable organizations (many connected with the church),
its mode of operation provides useful insights into the complicated
economics of the Old Regime in Spain as it tried to deal with the poverty
that threatened its foundation.

The records on which this study of the poor is based can be compared
to the papers of an extended family where no one had taken responsibility for arranging the archives over centuries. To dig into the treasury
of the Inclusa is to enter a morass, an underground of entangled and
contradictory grants, regulations, exceptions, and privileges phrased in
legalistic and bureaucratic terminology of daunting complexity. One
aim of this brief survey is to illustrate the complicated nature of finances
for institutions like the Inclusa, as well as for individuals and individual
families in the Old Regime. In many ways the Inclusa itself functioned
like an extended family.

In addition, the *gastos* record the everyday, commonplace items needed to run the hospital, and in the process make it possible to describe the Inclusa's physical setting and day-to-day routine.[4] Expenses necessarily focus on the housekeeping aspects of the hospital. The prosaic data of the *gastos* place the institution in its physical surroundings and show how its finances involved Madrid's powerful as well as its poor.

EXPENSES OF THE INCLUSA

The Inclusa was situated at the Puerta del Sol, the heart of Madrid, where even today colourful throngs of people are to be found. To pause is to become the object of the solicitations of the blind lady selling raffle tickets, the cripple with the tobacco consignment, the noisy news-vendors, and the gipsy with her infant who is far too old and healthy-looking to be lugged about, but is conveniently dosed with soporifics. Under a sign that cheerfully proclaims this to be the site of 'The cheapest shoe store in the world,' the tourist pushes through the throngs that are present at all hours and in all weather. A momentary respite from the wheeled traffic can be found at the fountain in the centre where the eighteenth-century favourite 'Mariblanca' has recently been reinstalled. With luck and a certain agility, the other side of the square can be reached and the streets that lead up to two of Madrid's most famous modern department stores, El Corte Ingles and Galerias Preciados, names that evoke a painting of Velasquez. Between the calle del Carmen and the calle de Preciados the visitor's attention may be caught by a window crammed with fans, flamenco and bullfighter dolls, lace mantillas, and tooled leather goods. This souvenir shop stands on the site of what was once the most famous foundling hospital in Spain – the Inclusa of Madrid.

The accessibility of this location may have saved the lives of many infants, for the child could easily be left by someone disappearing into the crowd of passers-by, and it was convenient for women to come and offer their services as wet-nurses. But from the viewpoint of artistic merit, travellers claimed there was absolutely nothing worth describing about the hospital and its chapel.[5] Engravings of the period give us some idea of the building's appearance in the eighteenth century. It was four or five storeys high, of brick, since limestone was expensive and had to be brought a distance of five or six leagues. The windows were barred with iron grille work and embellished with small balconies, and the roof was of red tile. One can still see houses in the older section of Madrid around Lavapies that look very much like the buildings in the Puerta del Sol in the eighteenth century. The doorway opened into an open courtyard, with a well or fountain where infants were often surreptitiously left. The turnstile arrangement that was a feature of many founding hospitals was not installed in the Inclusa before the nineteenth century. Probably there was laundry drying on the narrow balconies surrounding the area. From the outside there was nothing to distinguish the building of the Inclusa from the rest of the neighbourhood.

Deeds in the files of the hospital record the gradual expansion of the hospital. The earliest reference cites a house in the calle del Carmen bought from a carpenter, Pedro de Roblado, and his wife María Lopez, and purchased by the Confraternity of Our Lady of Sorrows in 1553. In the next few years the confraternity bought up a number of houses along the calle del Carmen, calle de Preciados, and Puerta del Sol. These holdings encompassed an area extending from the stairway of a cheap tavern to the front of a public passageway in the calle del Carmen, then through a cross-way to the calle de Preciados. The total purchase price came to 1400 ducats.[6] The original Inclusa could not have been very prepossessing. By means of legacies and further purchases the hospital continued to expand along the calle del Carmen in the sixteenth century. A bequest in 1598 brought half a house in the street and three altar-pieces: one of the Virgin and Son, one of St John the Baptist, and one of St Joseph. Because very early in its history the patronage of the Inclusa was expanded to include St Joseph as cohort to the Virgin Mary, it is possible that this tradition originated here.[7] The next year the other half of the house was bought from Miguel de San Martín, who kept a cheap tavern.[8] In 1634 more houses along Carmen and an alley-way sixteen feet long and seven feet wide were acquired in the Puerta del Sol.[9] Following these acquisitions, expansion concentrated in the calle de Preciados, where another inn and three houses became the chapel in 1669. Subsequently a generous bequest from Luisa de Oliva, widow of the first secretary of the Council of Peru, brought more houses in this street and the Puerta del Sol.[10]

The titles of these holdings indicate that the neighbourhood was one of cheap eating-houses, taverns, and inns. Nor were the buildings on the square itself impressive. Thirty-six houses were bought and demolished in one short block to build the Post Office in 1768.[11] The hospital and chapel of the Inclusa must have been an improvement over the shabby string of lodging-houses and haunts frequented by the lowest element of Madrid that characterized the area until well into the eighteenth century, but I have no information as to exactly when or how this motley assembly of houses became the hospital.[12] As infants kept coming, more and more space was added – like a growing family. In 1769 there was a deed for 'some houses' in the calle de Preciados 'for the expansion and ventilation of the hospital.'[13] Finally, in 1785, six additional houses were incorporated simply to accommodate growing needs.

Space, light, and air remained a problem as long as the hospital was located in the square. In 1760 Don Antonio Zorraqúin, a prominent cloth merchant and one of the founders of the commercial corporation called the Five Major Guilds, planned a redevelopment project that meant adding on storeys to some houses in the calle del Carmen opposite the Inclusa. The administrators took legal measures to block the scheme, arguing successfully that such construction would interfere with the light and ventilation of the hospital.[14]

If the architecture of the Inclusa was not impressive, the same held true for the interior. Sums laid out for daily expenses reveal that furnishings were simple in the extreme. The rectory had varnished tables, at least one trimmed with a ribbon border set in with traditional heavy tacks; outside of the chapel, paint was not very much in evidence. There were benches, and low, wooden backless *silletas* rather than chairs. Roughly hewn, these had a kind of clasp in the centre so that they could easily be carried about to serve as a work-bench, dining chair, or nursing stool depending on the need of the moment. Though exceedingly practical contrivances, they were far from comfortable. Bolsters and cushions were the only concession to ease in the sturdy, sober, but not unattractive furniture of the period.

Walls were of rough plaster, coated with lime, with few hangings or decorations – a cross, a mirror, perhaps a few religious pictures. There is no mention of glass panes in the windows before 1740,[15] and it was 1780 before screens of woven straw were replaced by glass in the nurses' quarters.[16] The floors were of tile, glazed and patterned with the attractive mosaics still seen in even modest Spanish homes. From September to June they were covered with matting meant to cut the chill and damp and to deaden sound, though one observer claimed they served only to keep the dirt warm.[17] The first sign of spring was the tossing out of these mats with their collection of winter mud, crumbs, and vermin.

The first room of the hospital the child was brought to was the admissions office, where details of the infant's brief history were recorded on a page with the name. The page number then went on a lead plate fastened about the neck to make the infant officially a child of the Inclusa. (This procedure was more humane than the practice of the Real Hospital of Santiago, which employed a surgeon to 'mark,' i.e. cut, the new-born's arm.[18]) The infant was then deposited in the nursery and given a temporary wet-nurse until the next woman arrived from the streets of Madrid or some dusty country road to take on the charge of keeping the baby alive on a long-term basis.

Information about the furnishings of the nursery comes from the mattress maker who supplied fresh straw each year. In the nursery in 1710 were two mattresses, each twice as large as those on the nurses' beds, and here fourteen to twenty infants were tossed together. In 1740 there were twice as many infants on the same size mattress.[19] Nevertheless, they were better off than the denizens of the Dublin foundling hospital where 'infants scantily clothed in what they or their fellow foundlings had worn on admission, were put in straw-filled cradles said to be swarming with bugs.'[20] Certainly they were better off than the infants of the hospital at Rennes who were put in an attic where they froze in winter and stifled in summer, and where at one time as many as 150 were tossed three, four, and five together on a straw mattress.[21] One of the first measures taken by the Junta de damas when the organization of charitable women took over the hospital in 1799 was to put two nurses to a bed with two or three nurslings, and to replace the straw mattresses with woollen ones, which could be kept clean by frequent washing.[22] This was an important measure from the viewpoint of hygiene and one not instituted in British hospitals before 1861.[23]

Despite an improvement in bedding facilities, overall sanitation remained primitive. The measures used were largely a matter of ventilation and vinegar.[24] Fortunately the wall-to-wall matting did not extend to the nursery. Instead there were small round mats that could easily be swept out and aired. In addition, about a peck of lavender per month was scattered about the floor of the nursery to try and counteract the nauseous combination of sour diapers and sick children.[25]

The expense accounts with their minutiae of items of everyday life reveal how a household functioned in eighteenth-century Spain. Bills from masons, carpenters, and suppliers of straw goods and cooking utensils make it possible to reconstruct what the kitchen looked like and how it operated. In this one room of the hospital, conditions most resembled those in the average home. There was the usual collection of coal-tongs, garlic-cellars, pitchers and pots of brass and copper, an iron pan, an oil jar, and other odd bits of crockery. Like the furniture, utensils were built to last. But little attention was paid to serving dishes before 1799 when the *damas* raised the standards of table service.[26] One can only conjecture that prior to this effort, everyone ate out of the same pot. However, the eighteenth-century kitchen did have an equivalent to our ubiquitous plastic items. Straw goods were cheap and could be replaced easily. Esparto grass brought in from the surrounding countryside on the backs of mules was sold to a weaver who worked it into wide rolls with a multitude of uses, or shaped it into baskets, fans, bolsters, dusters, brooms, dustpans, dishes, bowls, and even 'glasses' of fine straw. Straw purchases were made in the September fair in the Plazuela de Cebeda where all the thrifty housewives in Madrid stocked up for the year. In 1710 three-dozen brooms, three rush baskets, six window screens, a dozen round mats, fans, and brushwood sticks to scour and stir were bought.[27] In short, almost any item for the kitchen that did not have to hold water or go over the fire was constructed of this useful material.

The largest outlay for woven goods was for the rolls of matting that provided shade for the patio in summer and cut the chill from cold floor tiles in the winter. Matting was one of the few concessions to the climate in a Madrid household. It was put down in strips leaving a margin of about one foot next to the wall. In 1760 the Inclusa gave out a contract to a master weaver to supply the household with all its straw goods.[28] In 1789 the franchise holder was a woman who may have been the artisan's widow, but since she was termed *maestra* it is possible that she qualified on her own. Pictures of street vendors often depicted a woman peddling straw goods. The prices took a sharp upturn in 1770 by 241 per cent, though labour costs to put down matting in the fall and take it up in the spring hardly varied over the century (table 1.1). As a gauge of the physical expansion of the Inclusa, it took six rolls of matting to cover the floors of the chapel, offices, and rectory in 1710, and thirteen rolls in 1790.[29]

The main attraction of the kitchen was neither its colourful appearance nor the aroma of the perennially simmering *puchero*. Travellers of the time suggested the only way to keep warm in Madrid was to make friends with the cook and sleep in the kitchen.[30] The focus of the room was the hearth or open fireplace, for stoves did not come into general use in southern Europe before the nineteenth century, and in some rural areas not before the twentieth. In France in 1720, the development of a

TABLE 1.1
Expenses for straw goods
and labour (in reales)

Year	Straw goods	Labour
1700	118	30
1710	127.50	30
1720	125	32
1730	70	28
1740		
1750	58	38
1760	164	24
1770	560	24
1780	601	24
1790	718	
1800	800	32

SOURCE: *Gastos*, 1700–1800

lowered mantel, a narrower and deeper hearth, and a curved shaft had
made it possible to heat a whole room and cut down on smoke as well,
but in Madrid one had practically to sit in the fireplace to stay warm.
This hearth had a raised brick or stone base and an ample chimney shaft
that left room for benches often built right into the wall.[31] From the
overhanging edge of the mantel hung a black dipper of oil that contained
a piece of cotton for lighting the lamps. The mantel also provided a
useful shelf for the pottery jars and pitchers of the region, with their
attractive blue designs. In the chimney itself was a heavy iron chain
attached to a notched ring that allowed adjustments in height, and
hanging from it was a black cauldron that kept water permanently hot.
Cooking was done in long-handled copper utensils, which, when not in
use, were burnished to a sheen and hung from hooks in the walls. In
many kitchens the traditional yellow and blue tiles of flowers and birds
lined the walls to shoulder height. In all, it was a gay, warm, and
colourful room in contrast to the rest of the house. One can imagine
the nurses and their charges enjoying a snack around the hearth with
the *madre* whose private account book or *tandas* provided for these
extras in the days before the pace became frantic and the atmosphere
desperate.

Outside the kitchen, heating facilities were meagre or even dangerous. What heat there was came from a charcoal-burning brazier. This
was a brass bowl fitted into a low wooden frame; it was customary for
the nurses to sit on cushions on the floor and tuck their feet under it. A

more elegant version, often of beautifully wrought brass, was placed on a high wooden tripod in the homes of the wealthy. Probably as much heat was generated by proximity and conversation as from the brazier. The charcoal, often of poor quality, was a genuine menace in a household of infants. For safety's sake it was to be lit in the open air and stirred until soot and dangerous gases burned off. Braudel has noted that such fumes caused many deaths among the poor in Paris.[32] The use of charcoal in the Inclusa may have been a measure of economic necessity, as in other poor households, but it also posed a threat to the health of new-borns.

Not only was the brazier inefficient and unsafe, the process of ensuring the supply of coal was complicated and wasteful. It was delivered once a year by the wagon load or *carro*[33] to the hospital, though the poor bought it by the *arroba* of twenty-five pounds, and the very poor (who lived from one day to the next) by the pound. Once delivered it was piled up in a make-shift shed and then sorted through for pieces of usable size. This procedure was referred to as 'cleaning' the coal, because it had to be sprinkled with water to keep down the dust. In 1760 only 834 *arrobas* were salvaged out of 900.[34] Some years a labourer was paid to sift through the coal again in December. Coal was expensive because the mountains around Madrid were exhausted and coal had to come from long distances.[35] Fortunately, after 1728 a government subsidy ensured a supply free of any charges except for delivery and piling it up.[36]

An eighteenth-century household of the poor used oil for lighting and cooking. The oil came in huge hogskins from one of 256 shops, or it could be purchased by the *panilla* of a quarter of a pound from one of the numerous street vendors.[37] The primitive technology was to refine the greenish liquid by pouring it into a frying-pan and heating it till a piece of bread turned black. This burned off contaminations and the oil was then poured into jars for cooking. Travellers scorned the domestic product, but the Spanish, like other mediterranean nations, were addicted to its use. In fact, such was the prejudice against butter that it had become associated in the popular mind with causing leprosy.[38] The process of preparing this oil for consumption must have exposed the new-born to considerable pollution in the setting of the hospital.

Oil-burning lamps were another source of treacherous and unpleasant fumes. But their presence on the outside of the institution is evidence of a gradual improvement in the condition of the streets of the time. In 1700 there were only two lanterns: one at a stairway leading to the

TABLE 1.2
Price of oil per *arroba* (in reales)

Year	Hamilton	Inclusa
1700	30.83	32.35
1710	20.41	29.41
1720	24.95	38.43
1730	15.00	28.00
1740	24.12	42.00
1750	32.00	54.94
1760	22.00	
1770	34.37	38.00
1780	37.50	43.00
1790	42.00	50.40
1800	46.50	66.50

SOURCES: E.J. Hamilton, *War and Prices*, 246–57; *Gastos*, 1700–1800

admitting office, the other at the door of the rectory.[39] Then, in 1765, the government appointed an official to see to the installation and upkeep of lamps at the doors of all buildings and billed landlords annually for the service. That year eight lamps illuminated the outside of the Inclusa.[40] As the hospital expanded, so did the number of lanterns. In 1785 there were ten for the hospital alone and six for its holdings, and by 1790 eighteen lamps brightened the neighbourhood at the expense of the Inclusa.[41] From this account the Inclusa was particularly well lit by night; whether this was to make it easier or more difficult to abandon an infant is impossible to say.

Oil was an important item in the household budget. There have been estimates that the average person consumed between 7.5 and 8.5 litres per year in the period 1750–1820.[42] Literary sources are even more generous. According to Romea y Tapía, writing in 1763, a well-off householder with an extended family of nine persons, including servants, would use 20 *arrobas* or over 50 litres per person per year.[43] For this reason the price was controlled by local judges and supplied by government monopolies. This procedure kept the prices within the reach of the average consumer, despite inflation, at least until the 1790s. However, the Inclusa paid consistently more than did those outside Madrid, supporting the thesis that transportation costs were an important factor in making the capital more expensive than its surrounding area.[44]

Supplies for the inmates – clothing for the infants – never became a complicated matter for the Inclusa. The child often arrived wearing no more than a ragged shift covered with a shawl, to the tattered ends of which might be pinned a note. Unless wrapped in bloody rags, which was sometimes the case, or in lace and finery, which was unusual but not unheard of, the baby went out with the nurse dressed as it had come in. The expenses listed for outfitting an infant were minimal – just tapes for bonnets, or a few yards of serge or heavy cotton. In 1780 forty yards of blue cotton were purchased, which could mean an attempt to provide uniform dresses or simply that the hospital was saddled with more older infants.[45] On another occasion, there was a considerable outlay to outfit the infants in 119 shifts, 13 neckcloths, and 3 skirts and dresses.[46] Still this could only have made a difference to a fraction of the babies passing through the Inclusa. Obviously, as with the rest of the poor population, dress could not have a high priority.

Nurses left with a blanket and a few linens. These were renewed at the pay-days of Pentecost and Christmas, but the nurses were expected to account for them when a child was brought back, or if it died. There are numerous references to nurses being docked pay because they could not produce the linens again. It was assumed that missing clothing had been sold – another sign of the desperate poverty of the women hired as wet-nurses by the Inclusa.

Textiles called for only a token outlay of funds thanks to government subsidies. Bales of cloth arrived monthly from the customs-house where they were stamped, tagged, and given to porters who brought them to the Inclusa for three reales each. Most of these bales were heaps of *talegas y quiebras* – literally odds and ends – from the royal textile factory. These scraps of cloth were not large enough to sell, but useful to soak in milk or water and stuff into the mouth of a hungry infant, or to throw into a crib as bedding, or perhaps to be patched together for diapers or shawls. The blankets and linens, in contrast, came from some distance. They were described as *cordellates*, a term usually assigned to the cheap peasant cloth from Aragon.[47] After 1720 all the needs of the Inclusa were supplied by the nearby royal factories at Brihuega or San Fernando. When they were shut down in 1783, the biennial quotas came from Sigüenza, a town about forty miles north of Madrid. The distance added ten reales to the cost of each bale.[48] Table 1.3 shows how the number of bales per year increased with the numbers of infants under the care of the Inclusa.

If a child managed to outgrow diapers and wraps, and graduate from the Inclusa at age seven, he or she was sent to the orphanage,

TABLE 1.3
Bales of textiles for pay-days and
admissions to the Inclusa

Year	Bales	Admissions
1730	6	526
1740	4	617
1750	9	809
1760	7	693
1770	7	685
1780	13	748
1790	20	849
1800	36	1202

SOURCES: *Gastos*, 1700–1800 and
Entradas, 1700–1800

Desamparados, or to a group of religious ladies known as the *beatas*. As
an entrance requirement, a dowry was required of the child, which
consisted of two blouses or shirts, one pair of shoes, socks, belt, a comb,
and sufficient serge material for a dress or suit. The box containing this
gear cost double the contents, and was made of large, ill-squared planks
held together by nailed iron bands; it would serve as a cupboard as well
as a suitcase for the few possessions of a lifetime.[49]

Bedding linens did show some improvement over the century. Straw
mattresses covered with coarse hopsacking, sheets of hemp or sailcloth,
and blankets of dull, reddish-brown flannel were on the nurses' beds in
1730. By 1780 the sheets were linen, doubtless still very coarse, but an
improvement over hemp. The refined touch given by bedspreads is first
listed in 1783, and that same year the beds were painted green and
matching tables put into the nurses' quarters.[50] With the new administration in 1799, there was a quantum leap in quality of living style, at
least for the twelve nuns from France who came to administer the
hospital. Twenty-four new sheets were purchased for 100 reales, and
forty yards of blue ticking from France for mattresses at 6240 reales.[51]
The new woollen mattresses for the nursery came to only half what had
to be laid out for the fancy French ticking. The Junta de damas opened up
a new era for the Inclusa in many ways.

Discussion of bedding inevitably leads to laundry arrangements.
Fortunately the importance of soap and water was recognized. The
administrators were given a supplement for their laundry costs, the
nurses were supplied with a ration of soap and were expected to keep
themselves and their charges clean, an the laundress took care of

household effects and the infants' diapers. The laundress of the Inclusa might count herself more lucky than some in Madrid because she had facilities at hand and did not have to go down to the river bank. However, to judge from the regularity of plumbers' attentions to such matters as 'repairs to the pipes for water flooding cellar,' new pipes, tiles, and taps, these facilities were far from dependable. As the hospital became more crowded, such problems could be seriously disrupting. In 1790 and again in 1795 there were stretches of time when the Inclusa was without water altogether and a street porter had to be paid to haul linens to the banks of the Manzanares and back.[52] Even without complications, there was not enough space to dry the linens for thirty or forty infants in the fresh air, and the fumes and steam from the laundry room were considered harmful to the infants' health. This was an important reason for moving the hospital to larger quarters, according to the doctor of the Inclusa.[53]

The water supply for laundry provides a final example of the way in which the resources of the Inclusa were being overtaxed. Bills show that the plumber was at least twice as important to the Inclusa as the locksmith, glazier, or carpenter. His tip was sixteen reales at Christmas, when other tradesmen were given only eight reales. In 1770 this tip rose to thirty reales and in 1778 to fifty, while others continued to receive only eight.[54] Plumbers set the pace for other trades as early as the eighteenth century. In 1760 a water-main had been built in response to the new municipal regulations of Charles III.[55] But by 1790 it was inadequate for the needs of the Inclusa. In 1790 and again in 1795 labourers had to cart laundry to the river and bring back water to the hospital.[56] At the end of the eighteenth century, the Inclusa could no longer depend on its water supply and a move to new quarters had become inevitable.

But this need for a change in its physical surroundings was only one example of a breakdown in its operation, and laundry was just one symptom of serious underlying problems. In the past these had been dealt with on a day-to-day, piecemeal basis, typical of an old-fashioned institution. Occasionally lump sums were doled out to the laundress to compensate for rising soap costs; or nurses had to be recruited to act as part-time laundresses, with minimal success; but there was no consistent policy. In the *gastos* we see the progressive exhaustion of the resources of the Inclusa as the hospital struggled from one crisis to the next, getting weaker with each one.

The façade continued to hold up, and the routine of everyday life presented in the *gastos* remained unchanged for a century. Nevertheless, maintaining that façade was becoming increasingly difficult. Year after year the administrators turned in desperation to the government for additional funding. But the government itself was in financial straits, making it less and less responsive to the pleas of the institution. The problems of the Inclusa in the Puerta del Sol epitomized the troubles facing the Old Regime at the turn of the century. Though at first glance the pages of the *gastos* in 1700 might seem interchangeable with the pages in 1799, the Inclusa was engaged in a losing battle against rising costs and declining income. It, like the government and much of the population, was getting poorer.

Turning to the sources of the institution's income, it becomes even more clear how strains on the economy in general affected the Inclusa. Here we see in microcosm the complicated and delicate nature of the structure that made up the Old Regime, as the Inclusa, like many families, attempted to maintain a balance between output and income.

INCOME OF THE INCLUSA

Though the difficulties at the end of the eighteenth century were overwhelming, the financial troubles of the Inclusa date from its earliest days. Jerónimo de Quintana, writing in 1628, pointed out that 'the Inclusa is often responsible for nursing as many as 1300 infants a year from Madrid and the surrounding towns. This runs to 18,000 ducats a year while the hospital does not possess more than 10,000 ducats annual income.'[57] Nor did the situation improve later in the seventeenth century. Don Leanardo de Croy listed the income of the Inclusa at 15,815 ducats and expenses at 26,678 ducats in a report on the royal hospitals in 1676.[58] The shortfall between the two figures became exacerbated whenever there was a crop failure; then a difficulty could become a disaster.

In the early years of the Inclusa, funds were collected in the simplest way imaginable – an alms box on the table of the Convent of Our Lady of Victory where members of the Confraternity of Our Lady of Sorrows held their meetings.[59] However, success soon overwhelmed both the facilities and financial resources of the brotherhood. Though it had come under the patronage of Philip II as early in 1572, this trend toward government involvement became more specific when in 1606 the government centralized all hospital services in Madrid, and in 1615 the Inclusa was incorporated as a royal hospital – thus entitled to one-sixth of the taxes set aside for hospital support.[60] The treasury also depended on private individuals, involving income from numerous chaplaincies and benefices set up by patrons. That is, in return for a specific number of masses and prayers, sometimes said by the donor's own appointee or chaplain, the Inclusa was bequeathed a sum of money or some form of income on real-estate or investment holdings. Benefactors concerned about their eternal security perceived an institution devoted to the care of the unwanted and helpless as an attractive proposition, and this kind of donation was important all through the Inclusa's history.

But the most significant source of income for the hospital was neither the government nor private funds. The Inclusa was a business, providing a service for various parishes and other charitable institutions and individuals, and it exacted pay whenever possible for nursing the infants. La Sagrada Pasión (the section of the general hospital devoted to poor women), Desamparados (the orphanage), and the various parishes of Madrid and the surrounding towns were all expected to give twenty-two reales per month for the infants they brought to the Inclusa to be nursed. These 'alms' were also given as a matter of course when someone – who could afford to pay for an infant's nursing but was leaving it to preserve the good name of the family – abandoned an infant. Honour is a strong component of the Spanish character, and it is also possible that many individuals leaving an infant for reasons of poverty, not shame, left a token amount when they brought a foundling. This explains the special arrangement made with the Brotherhood of the Refuge (Refugio), a group of charitable noblemen who went about the streets of Madrid by night collecting the sick and the homeless. Their allotment was only eighteen reales a month for the infants' support, a realistic assessment given that the infants they dealt with were completely destitute. There was an assumption that alms would be brought with the foundling, and the indigent depended on the brotherhood to fulfil this obligation. The poor in Madrid had their own code of honour.

Such funds collected for nursing made a significant contribution to the income of the Inclusa. In the early years of the eighteenth century, there were very few infants admitted to the Inclusa without sums from one source or another. In 1700, of the thirty-seven infants listed during June and December, only one did not contribute something towards its own nurse.[61] In 1710, although the year was disastrous for the poor, only 7.3 per cent were abandoned directly to the hospital without a donation from some intermediary.[62] However, as the years went on, the practice of bringing the infant directly to the hospital became more common, and the role of intermediaries declined. The Refugio had turned more to other forms of charitable works, so that despite little change in overall numbers coming from other institutions, the brotherhood's share became proportionately less. However, the most remarkable shift occurred in the role played by the various parishes. In 1700 half the infants were sponsored by a curate of one of the Madrid churches or one of the nearby towns. In 1790 only 2 of the 106 infants admitted during the months of June and December had been sent by parishes. The total abandonments passing through the hands of the parish went from 48.6 per cent in 1700 to 11 per cent in 1799.[63]

It would be interesting to know why the role of the parish as intermediary between the family and the Inclusa declined. Perhaps the midwives, relatives, and even parents wanted to bypass the local parish where moral censure might be exerted. Perhaps the parishes themselves encouraged the practice as a means of sloughing off onto the Inclusa the burden of the cost of nursing. Perhaps the poor who were leaving their infants were rootless newcomers to Madrid without close ties to any of the parishes. Or, more likely, it was a further indication of the desperate condition of a large sector of the population of the city that had begun to overwhelm the charitable resources of the parishes. The Inclusa could no longer depend on parishes to any considerable extent.

Another factor could have been related to the changing proportion of illegitimate infants admitted to the Inclusa. It is more likley that the parish curate felt more responsibility for the traditional *expósito* abandoned to save the good name of the mother and her family. In the past many of these infants were admitted with notes attached bearing the name of the curate as witness to the new-born's baptism. Under the seal of the confessional it was probable that he knew intimately the details of the lives of his parishioners and had a key role to play in the whole procedure of leaving an infant to the Inclusa. Conceivably, this personal approach was becoming increasingly impossible for curates of many urban parishes with crowds of newcomers. Possibly some unmarried women had moved to Madrid, attracted by the anonymity offered by the Inclusa. It is quite likely that the child brought from the parish was considered a responsibility of the parish, but the obligation of the parish was increasingly shirked by priest, and its intermediary role shunned by parents, as the century went on.

Whatever the reason, the income the Inclusa had received from parish alms declined dramatically over the century. By 1800 this form of

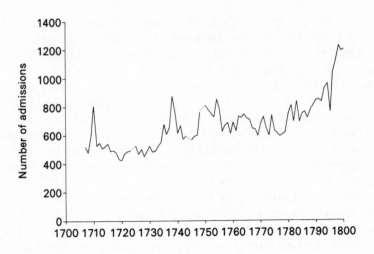

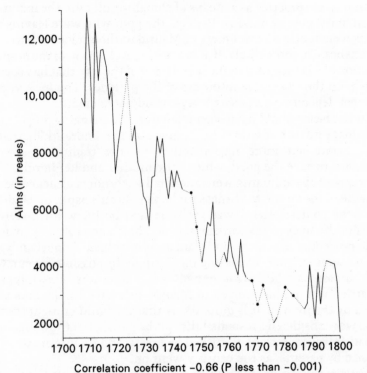

Correlation coefficient –0.66 (P less than –0.001)

FIGURE 1.2 Admissions to the Inclusa and alms received with infants, 1700–99

23 Income and Expenses of the Inclusa

TABLE 1.4
Admissions of infants with alms from parishes and individuals

Year	Admissions	With alms	Total alms (in reales)
1700	500	250	12,000
1710	804	191	11,344
1720	426	140	8,230
1730	526	111	6,290
1740	617	109	6,782
1750	809	77	4,125
1760	693	93	5,018
1770	685	48	2,638
1780	748	45	3,206
1790	849	missing	–
1789	1,194	51	4,010
1800	1,202	39	1,620

SOURCE: *Gastos*, 1700–1800

support had become as obsolete and inadequate as the collection box had been at the end of the sixteenth century. It was one further example of the transformation occurring within the welfare system and within society as a whole. Though the Inclusa was still able to exact funds from institutions, the money from parishes had been vital to the financial viability of the hospital and this income had practically disappeared by the end of the century.

Funding in the form of alms was absolutely essential to the Inclusa as infants increased in numbers. Figure 1.2 illustrates the growing shortfall as the century progressed. In 1700 exactly one-half of the infants came with alms from individuals, an important supplement to the donations from institutions and confraternities. For example, the year 1710 was one of great distress. The War of the Spanish Succession saw Madrid change hands twice and crops had been a failure two years running.[64] Though the numbers of poor leaving infants to the Inclusa were exceptionally high, still one-quarter of admissions were paid for either by parishes or by individuals. Gradually, however, a new pattern began to establish itself (see table 1.4). Conditions for the poor in 1740 resembled those of 1710, but the alms came to 8024 reales less. By 1750, another year of disastrous grain shortages, there were 809 admissions but only one-tenth contributed any support, and as the century progressed the differential between alms and infants continued to widen. This in itself could account for the financial problems of the Inclusa at the end of the century. In 1800, of a total of 1202 infants admitted, only 39 brought alms from individuals or parishes, for a total of 1620 reales.[65]

Evidently individuals and individual parishes were no longer providing even the minimal sums that the Inclusa required for paying a wet-nurse. Other demands on the parishes for charity may have precluded their ability to donate funds for the abandoned infant. Presumably individuals who could afford a donation could also pay a nurse and they would not be abandoning the infant in the first place. But this had always been the case. For whatever reasons, it is evident that the curate's role as go-between, facilitating arrangements for his parishioners and providing alms for individuals too poor to pay the Inclusa, was no longer operating on any large scale. The information in the *gastos* suggests that the traditional tie between the poor and the church, at least at the parochial level, was weakening by the end of the eighteenth century.

The income the Inclusa received in the form of alms was listed with admissions for each month and totalled for each year in the *entradas*, but other sources of income are much less easy to assess. The best source is an inventory (drawn up in 1801), as valuable for what it reveals about the complexity of finances in the Old Regime as it is for information about the actual income of the hospital.

In 1799, Don Tomás Prado y Ovejero, a lawyer of the College of Advocates, was commissioned by the Junta de damas to examine the records of the Inclusa and reorganize the papers so as to 'clarify the materials which had not been set out in an orderly fashion.'[66] Here we can see in detail the incredibly intricate and confusing set of arrangements on which the institution depended. Because the focus of this study is poverty as it affected particularly women and children in the eighteenth century, the records are interesting also for sidelights into the way in which some wealthy families used the facilities of the Inclusa to provide for unmarried daughters and nieces. For wealthy families, the poor of the Inclusa were a kind of insurance policy for their families in this world as well as the next.

Prado did his best to impose some order by categorizing the various sources of income donated as legacies under the headings of *juros* (municipal or government bonds), *censos* (mortgages on property holdings, land, or investments), wills, deeds for houses, and royal subsidies. However, the task of organizing documents, some dating back more than 200 years, to find out what income was still available was formidable. Moreover, there were gaps in the accounting procedures that made a complete summary impossible. For instance, the inventory lists wills for the period 1653–1707 only, though obviously many came to the hospital after that date. There was also some overlapping between items, so that some can be found under more than one heading. Despite these drawbacks, it is the best source available for assessing the Inclusa's income during the eighteenth century.

INCOME FROM PRIVATE SOURCES

Real Estate
We have already seen how the records of deeds and titles chronicled the physical expansion of the hospital and gave a description of the neighbourhood of the Puerta del Sol. Prado's inventory is also useful in pointing out some of the problems involved with being a landlord in the Old Regime. In the 1790s the Inclusa called in an architect to advise them on whether some holdings should be kept up or simply demolished.[67] It is obvious that the kind of house purchased or donated to the Inclusa was often of poor construction and, as we shall see, the titles were often burdened with liabilities. Though its net worth cannot be precisely calculated, it is probable that the value of real-estate holdings of the Inclusa was not considerable.

The Juros *and* Censos
One reason it is difficult to estimate the value of real estate is because the title was seldom a simple transfer of ownership. It involved loans, mortgages, and, in particular, a legal arrangement of the Old Regime called in Spain the *mayorazgo*. The *mayorazgo* is the key to understanding property ownership in the Old Regime. The *mayorazgo* was the privilege whereby a family could entail property to see that land passed on intact to the legal successor. It demonstrates the prior place given to family, and especially to the eldest son of the family. It ensured that the patrimony did not become dispersed among a number of children, leading to a loss of the holding altogether – and perhaps the disappearance of the family's claim to noble status. Instead, the land devolved to the eldest son, who passed it on to his son. Of course, the *mayorazgo* was of most concern to the nobility, not only because it had the most property to transmit, but because as a group it was vitally concerned about the title and prestige of the family name. In fact, the right to entailment had traditionally been a privilege of the nobility and the *mayorazgo* became its seal of membership. For this reason, those who

had adopted the trappings of a noble life-style and were eagerly pushing themselves up to the next level of the social strata were anxious to secure one as a formal recognition of their pretensions. Once this badge of acceptance was acquired, however, the new nobleman had to live up to it. Often this required a move to Madrid where the title holder existed on his income and no longer took any interest in seeing that his land was cultivated efficiently and productively. And, of course, property could no longer be transferred to others who might be interested in seeing that it was. In a country where so much of the land was already in the dead hand of the church, the *mayorazgo* became the symbol to reforming economists of all that was wrong with Spain.[68] However, the *mayorazgo* was very important for the finances of the Inclusa. Income from land was one of the major ways in which beneficiaries left sums to pay for masses for their souls, but this could only be managed by working around the terms of the entailment.

The means to achieve this purpose raises another Old Regime convention: the *censo*. *Censos* provided a regular income annually on the rent from a piece of property so that money could be redistributed to other members of the family, dowries arranged for daughters, or compensation given to family retainers in their old age. Thus, the women and younger sons of the family could be taken care of by means of *censos*. The type most commonly bequeathed to the Inclusa was a pension based on capital that had been secured by mortgaging all or part of the holding. It functioned as a trust fund whereby a regular yearly income was paid out on capital over a designated period, or even perpetually. Generation after generation mortgaged the same piece of land as *censos* were bought and sold, though the holding itself could not change hands because of the claim of the *mayorazgo*. As a result, some of these pieces of property had built up a long dossier of documents. There were cases where the Spanish term for property, *bienes raices*, or rooted goods, came to have an almost literal meaning. Many of these titles resembled an old tree with gnarled and twisted roots reaching deep into the earth as the number of *censos* became inextricably wound around one another. Much of the wealth of Spain was tied up in this way, and for this reason the sale of a piece of real estate was seldom a simple transaction.

Although almost half the *censos* were on real estate, they could be negotiated on any type of revenue-producing income, such as municipal taxes, the monopoly on the sale of tobacco, or the title to some office. *Censos* kept armies of lawyers and clerks occupied and made owning property in Spain in the Old Regime a matter of infinite complexity. About 76 per cent of the benefices bequeathed to the Inclusa were financed by means of a *censo*.

The basic problem for the Inclusa was that *censos* could be difficult to collect. Some benefactors hedged their donation with so many conditions that the hospital was lucky to get anything at all from the legacy. In 1630 Diego Mendez Blandór left a *mayorazgo* in favour of his wife and son, their children both legitimate and illegitimate, and descendants from any marriages until such time as his line should die out. Then, and only then, were 1000 reales of income to come to the Inclusa. In 1800 descendants of Don Diego still enjoyed the patrimony.[69] Francisco Borgia, archdeacon of the cathedral of Valencia, left a *censo* of 300 ducats to the Inclusa in case his brother had no daughters needing it for a dowry.[70] One can see why there would be problems in figuring out what the Inclusa was entitled to, let alone collecting it. The usefulness of the *censo* as a form of family strategy was undeniable, but the very flexibility that appealed to the family worked against any outsider attempting to collect a share.

For the deceased philanthropist, *censos* provided very good value for the money. A *censo* was a convenient way to finance a chaplaincy of masses. The income was payable over a long term or even perpetually, which had the advantage of reminding the hospital of its obligation when the donor was no longer there. Of course, the Inclusa remained bound by the terms of the *censo*, even though the real value of the funds might have declined considerably over the years or the money for the masses had long since been spent. For instance, in 1681 María Granados left a *censo* of 400 ducats to pay for masses for her soul.[71] In 1682 the hospital sold the *censo* for a lump sum but the obligation remained and masses were said all through the eighteenth century at the Inclusa's expense, whether Doña María's soul still had need of intercession or not. Over the years the hospital had accumulated a considerable backlog of masses and had to conscript a number of destitute, immigrant French priests in order to keep up its side of the bargain long after the original money had been dissipated.

In fact, actually realizing money on bequests could raise serious problems for the treasurer. Contested wills involved the Inclusa in lengthy and costly legislation. Widows and daughters were sometimes in competition with the foundling for support. It is likely that lawyers fees made substantial inroads into any profit either the Inclusa or the family might expect from its portion.[72]

Many of the grants listed in Prado's inventory took the form of promises with little hope of fulfilment. Others were couched in confusing terminology, leaving a degree of ambiguity that made the effort required to collect them problematic. Finally, even when income on *censos* could be realized, its value was decreasing steadily as inflation nibbled away at fixed incomes. As a result, the Inclusa had to depend more and more on the government for financial aid in order to carry on. It is obvious fom Prado's inventory that many, like the bereft widows and daughters vying with the foundling of the Inclusa, were facing serious difficulties in their attempt to stretch a fixed income to cover expenses.

INCOME FROM GOVERNMENT

As a royal hospital, the Inclusa was entitled to royal support, but like much of the money from individual benefactors this support came in a number of ways – some of them indirect and all of them complicated. The hospital was the beneficiary of *juros*, or annuities on royal income,[73] a series of tax exemptions, certain fines that were to be paid directly to the hospital, and finally a set of outright gifts or privileges. The *juros* listed in the inventory by Prado probably no longer held good in the eighteenth century. The government tended to farm out income on taxes to individuals whose claim then held priority. For instance, the report of Galdiano y Croy lists a *juro* for 1172 ducats on the taxes of Murcia that did not yield any income at all in 1676.[74] The bankruptcy of 1664 automatically wiped out the *juros* in effect before that time.[75] It seems likely that few government *juros* were of any real value, except for ones that had come to the hospital by way of legacies from private individuals, and as we have seen, those came with their own set of problems.

Occasionally the royal treasurer assigned income from a fine to the hospital. But collecting these funds could be another exercise in frustration. For instance, in 1684 the governor or the city of Ocaña was fined 500 ducats.[76] He claimed to have forwarded the money in two payments to the royal treasurer, but five years later only 300 ducats had ever reached the Inclusa. Neither *juros* nor fines were particularly remunerative for the treasury of the Inclusa.

A more satisfactory arrangement allowed the administrators to buy certain basic articles without paying the taxes levied on goods entering the city. Between 1651 and 1685 the Inclusa was allowed forty *arrobas* of wine and forty of oil annually. In 1718 this amount was changed to twelve *arrobas* of each, or conceivably this was in addition to the previous exemption. In 1798, as one of its economy measures, the government abrogated these privileges for religious institutions. A letter appealing this decision pointed out that a saving of four reales on each *arroba* of wine had meant a great deal to the individual staff members, as it had provided an annual supplement of 568 reales to their income.[77] The decision to move away from rations as a form of payment to the staff around this time may have been directly connected with the loss of this form of income.

Indirectly, the taxes on wine and oil had benefited the Inclusa because a certain proportion of these taxes (*sisas*) were allocated to the support of the royal hospitals, and, as we have seen, the Inclusa was entitled to one-sixth of this income. Cosme de Abaunza, who was commissioner in charge of the administration of hospitals in 1693, had listed these as follows: surtax of two maravédis on each pound of beef; 10,494 reales from the wine tax; 41,470 reales on taxes of wine and meat for prisoners; 10,494 additional reales on wine for prisoners. In addition, the hospital received one-sixth of the 22,000 reales related to the tax on public fountains, and one-sixth of the 110,000 reales realized from the sale of theatre tickets.[78]

Another important way that the government aided the hospital was by subsidizing coal and textiles. In 1646 the Inclusa had been rationed a supply of coal free of taxes. After 1728 the supply was extended so that the hospital had no need to buy coal at all, but only to pay the cost of delivering and unloading its supply.[79] From the beginning the hospital received textiles free of charge. As we have seen, bales of *talegas y quiebras*, or 'odds and ends,' came every month from the customs-house. Similarly, twice a year blankets and linens for the nurses and their charges were transported from the royal mills. For the Inclusa the only cost was the delivery-men's pay. Although linens and material for clothing had to be purchased occasionally, by far the greatest share of this large item of expense was borne by the government.

These exemptions were a major means of keeping the institution functioning, and it is possible that the Inclusa may have been entitled to more. For instance, the exemption from the wine tax could apply as well to property holdings of the hospital. This meant that tenants living in the houses belonging to the Inclusa were entitled to the same privileges. Catalina Martínez, guarantor of the guild of tavern-keepers, was responsible for collecting the wine tax in 1744. Being a woman who brooked no nonsense, she refused to listen to the arguments of the tenants and ordered some houses belonging to the Inclusa in the calle de Jacometrezo siezed for tax evasion. The issue came to court and it was decided that the tenants had to pay the tax, but not to the guild of tavern-keepers. It was to be paid to the Inclusa itself. Probably the matter went back a number of years because the sum involved was considerable, but if Señora Martínez had not taken the initiative, 11,000 reales would never have reached the coffers of the Inclusa.[80] Still, the procedure to exact some of these claims based on real estate, *juros*, and fines was very involved and may well not have been worth the time and trouble to collect them, especially after inflation had made such heavy inroads into real income. The protector, Josef Vilches, who attempted to restore the financial equilibrium of the Inclusa in 1784, showed good judgment in concentrating on finding new sources of support rather than dragging out old claims.

Finally, although these were not strictly government funds, the Inclusa owned shares in the royal bank and in a number of large companies that were closely connected with the infrastructure of the Spanish state. It had invested heavily in an issue of government bonds called *vales reales* and had acquired shares in the Company of the Philippines, the Royal Canal of Tauste, and the Five Major Guilds from a series of legacies.[81] These companies were only quasi-private. For instance, in 1798 the government loaned the corporation of the Five Major Guilds five million reales in order to save its credit.[82] The viability of the state was closely connected to public trust in these companies. Similarly the financial state of the Inclusa was directly dependent on the economic well-being of the monarchy. The difficulties plaguing the regime could only have unfortunate repercussions on the Inclusa as well.

In summary, it is clear that the crown and city of Madrid, despite their own financial problems, were always generous. If sometimes the support voted on paper did not materialize, the government itself had the same problem. Unfortunately, as the Inclusa required more and more help in order to cope with the influx of infants, the government was less and less able to provide it. While the economy continued to expand, the problem had been one of coaxing or pressuring the state for additional funds to cover deficits. This was worrisome but not impossible, and as long as the government enjoyed dependable sources of income, so did the Inclusa. Conversely, when the government was in difficulty, so was the hospital. The eighteenth century, overall, enjoyed

TABLE 1.5
Sources of income of the royal treasury (in per cent)

Year	From taxes	From debts	From Indies
1788–91	76.9	11.9	11.2
1793–97	55.5	32.6	11.9

SOURCE: Gonzalo Anes, *El Antiguo Régimen: los Borbones*, 290

growing population, improved agricultural production, a healthy commercial trade with the colonies, and the beginnings of industrial
development. Under these conditions, a moderate inflationary tendency could be absorbed relatively painlessly by the expanding economy.
However, in 1793 the government found itself forced to borrow on a
grand scale in order to finance wars with France (1792–95) and Britain
(1796–1802). At the same time, commodity shortages brought on by the
British blockade and the loss of French trade gave impetus to a sharp
price rise. This time the inflationary cycle was not accompanied by an
increase in the volume of trade, and the result was disastrous. However,
instead of embarking on a painful policy of making firm tax demands on
the wealth of nobles and clergy in order to remedy the situation, Charles
IV fed inflation by continuing to borrow and to issue paper money. Table
1.5 shows how the crown continued to collect its income.[83] Income
from tax revenues was also affected by the trade blockade. In 1792 the
customs service had brought the crown 183,000,000 reales; in 1798 it
was only 47,000,000 reales.[84]

Certainly there was no lack of goodwill on the part of the crown or the
city of Madrid. In 1798, the patroness of the Inclusa, Queen Maria Luisa,
showed the hospital royal generosity. Two trunks of clothing fit for a
prince were donated to the Inclusa. They were intended for a new heir,
who along with his mother, Princess Amalia, had died in childbirth. For
a brief instant one imagines the pathetic infants of the Inclusa decked out
in frills and finery of a prince of Spain. Of course, the clothing and linens
were auctioned off and brought the welcome sum of 350,000 reales.[85]

But windfalls like this were not enough to secure the financial
stability of an institution whose problems were endemic to the whole
economy and were becoming worse as the century went on. Economists
analysing the collapse of the Spanish economy at the end of the
eighteenth century point out that a revolution was taking place in the
depths of society during these years, although it did not occur in a
political sense until May 1808. Spain entered the nineteenth century

involved in a war that was to last thirty years and would almost totally destroy an economic structure over three centuries old.[86] The economic crisis of the Inclusa was one facet of a general breakdown in the whole mechanism of the Old Regime.

The close relationship between admissions and the cost of grain shows that the infants of the poor had always inundated the hospital in years of high grain prices (fig. 1.1). The parallel between the two factors is evident in the years of near famine, 1709–10, 1734, 1739–40, and 1752. During the second half of the century, the correspondence was even more striking. Economic historians have established that 1763–65, 1770, and 1784–93 were exceedingly difficult periods for the poor. The figures of the Inclusa reflected this almost exactly with high admissions in 1762–66, 1771, 1774, and finally from 1783 on. None of this is particularly unexpected. However, the difficulties facing the Inclusa were unique at the end of the eighteenth century. After 1783 the fluctuating pattern, where the numbers of admissions rose with grain prices and then fell off as a new crop released the pressure on supplies of food, began to change. It was replaced by a pattern where numbers of admissions continued to rise year after year. Poverty had entered a new phase.

Triggered by circumstances beyond control that besieged the Inclusa with a steadily increasing influx of infants, the whole structure of the institution was exposed as obsolete and antiquated. Not that abandoned children in large numbers were a new phenomenon. There had been critical years before, such as 1751 when numbers were as high as in the early 1790s. But in the past such numbers had been the result of the periodic social and economic crises that had then abated long enough for the institution to recuperate. By the end of the century, these crises were no longer subsiding. Inflation in the numbers of children and inflation of the economy were the twin blows that served to undermine the finances of the Inclusa. As expenses increased and real income declined, short-term solutions no longer sufficed. Poverty was no longer amenable to the old solutions. The financial practices of the Old Regime were no longer viable.[87] The dying infants of the Inclusa were witnesses to the failure of the institution and ultimately of the Old Regime to provide for its poor.

There was no period of recuperation for both staff and finances; instead, infants continued to come, wave after wave, year after year, exhausting the human and the material resources of the institution. Reflecting this pattern, the financial condition of the Inclusa became one of permanent crisis. It was one facet of a crisis that was to place in jeopardy the whole system of welfare of the Old Regime, and it suggests that something new was occurring in the behaviour of the poor that affected the trend of abandonments and made the financial situation of foundling hospitals like the Inclusa increasingly precarious. All indications lead to the conclusion that larger numbers of infants were abandoned and the reasons were more closely connected to economics than to the traditional concerns of familial honour. Both the institution and its clientele were in desperate straits. As we shall see, those abandoning an infant were doing so for different reasons at the end of the century than at the beginning, and the financial difficulties of the Inclusa were part of this phenomenon.

It is clear that the fortunes of the Inclusa were interwoven with the lives of the working poor of Madrid through their children. In addition, the hospital's salary rolls took in a broad cross-section of this same class from both the city of Madrid and its surrounding countryside. We turn now to the men and women who made up the staff of the Inclusa in the eighteenth century.

2

The Human Resources
of the Inclusa

The Inclusa was part of the fabric of the society of the time and its salary rolls provide a unique perspective from which to consider the poor of the Old Regime. Infants were not the only group of poor who depended on the Inclusa. Through its wage rolls, we are able to chart the progressive worsening of the real income of the working poor in Madrid in the eighteenth century. The institution's staff, administrators, and clientele covered the whole spectrum of the populace of the city and court of Madrid, from members of the nobility and clergy to its weakest and most helpless constituent – the foundling. The hospital functioned as a kind of extended family, giving support to many poor through their connection, more or less direct, with the Inclusa. There were large numbers of the poor who survived on the fringes of society, scraping a living from odd jobs. And, of course, poor women made up a large proportion of that group. Wet-nursing supplemented income for women with family responsibilities who may have had other work in addition to caring for their own new-born and an *inclusero*. The Inclusa also provided extra income for large numbers of people whose connection was only semi-official. Porters who brought the infants from the various hospitals were given tips; tradesmen received a gift at Christmas; extra workers were called in for religious festivals and feast-days. The servants of the protector, a government appointee who was the nominal head of the hospital, were always given gratuities as well as refreshments when the formal inspection took place once a year.[1] The Inclusa touched the lives of many *madrileños* in the eighteenth century.

For instance, in 1700 the procession in honour of Our Lady of the Inclusa and St Joseph involved a surprising number of people and was marked by an impressive display of largesse. Members of the Confraternity of St Joseph of the Carpenters attended with their statue, the officials of the Convent of la Victoria escorted Our Lady of Sorrows, a group from San Ginés led the assembly with the cross, and the Brotherhood of the General Hospital put in an appearance. Messages were sent out to the rural towns to round up the country nurses with their charges, and a crier went through the streets of the city to make sure all women with children from the Inclusa were on hand. The constable of the court and hospitals arranged for holy water and sprinklers that the children carried to shake at the bystanders; and there were twenty-one ushers to see that order was maintained on the route. All participants received tips and refreshments.[2] After 1720, celebrations on the feast-day were confined to the chapel and preparations were much less elaborate, but even then there were choirs, musicians, and the special preacher (plus his coachman) to pay.

Salaries and wages illustrate the familial nature of the institution during the Old Regime. The staff lived in the hospital, and often stayed on after retirement. This arrangement was particularly important for women who might have no other place to turn. The Inclusa assumed responsibility for widows and sometimes for other dependants as well. Two nieces of a deceased administrator lived on in the hospital, receiving rations – one of them for thirty years.[3] When the treasurer, Francisco Bustos, died in 1791 after thirty-two years of service, his wife, Lorenza Sarmiento, took over his place until she herself died in 1798.[4] Various menial jobs were done around the hospital from 1720 to 1770 by members of the de Rojas family.[5] There were two accountants in a row with the surname Závala. The Inclusa formed a tightly knit, extended family. Wages were low, but the Inclusa cared for its own.

Taking care of abandoned and illegitimate infants was only the most obvious function of the Inclusa. Married women who had to care for a child could supplement family income through the Inclusa. The nurses' wages, small though they might be, were important to families living on the edge of indigence, and during critical periods provided a form of social insurance for many households of the working poor. A paternalistic approach to wages was not just a formality. Though the nurses were paid officially only twice a year, at Christmas and Pentecost, advances to tide them over the months between were not unusual. As the century went on, it is clear from the *gastos* that this practice was becoming more common. Obviously there were expectations that the Inclusa could be turned to in an emergency and, by and large, these expectations were not disappointed.

The hospital's function as buffer between the poor and the harsh realities of life under the Old Regime was, however, becoming more difficult to fulfil as the century progressed. The result was that an institution that nominally served poor folk became part of the system that was exploiting them. Inflation took its toll of those who depended on wages. By 1800 the real income of the unskilled worker in Madrid was 60 per cent less than it had been in 1726 and well below the level required to maintain health and efficiency.[6] The lag between prices and wages came out clearly in the salary records of the institution. Some unskilled jobs paid only a fraction more than they had in 1700. The *gastos* also indicate that the inflationary cycle began earlier than some economists believe. According to Vicens Vives, the rise began in 1731 and a trend was clearly established by 1735. However, wages for the Inclusa rose in 1729–30, which would indicate that the inflationary pattern had already been in existence for some time. Wages went up again in 1770, whereas economists pin-point a second inflationary spiral beginning in the period 1774–75. By the 1790s the effect of inflation on wage earners had become devastating. For instance, the median salary of day-labourers rose only eight points in relation to 1780, while the coefficient of prices soared to 150.[7] That particular statistic was to have momentous consequences for the poor of Madrid and for the hospital of the Inclusa.

In the pages of the *gastos* we are given a very clear picture of the impact of this wage lag on different groups of workers. Generally speaking, the poorer you were, the poorer you became. The servant who had been paid three reales a day in 1700 was receiving three and one-half reales in 1800. The wages of the laundress went from five to seven reales, though she had to buy her own soap at much higher prices. Ironically, one of the factors that enabled the Inclusa to carry on was the low wages it could pay its staff. These workers were no less victims of the economic conditions of the time than were the infants abandoned by parents who could not afford to care for them.

The staff of the Inclusa were victimized in other ways. After 1783 infants began to flood the institution, but the number of persons on the salary lists scarcely changed over the century. The same people were expected to carry a much heavier work-load at wages that remained considerably behind the cost of living. As the century went on, they were working harder and making less in real terms.

However, in an institution of the Old Regime a pecking order and gender distinctions affected the degree of exploitation involved. The staff was made up of two groups. The first, the administration, took care of institutional matters such as upkeep, supplies, records, religious functions, and business details. It included the protector, administrator, rector, collector, sacristan, accountant, treasurer, and clerk. These, with the exception of the widow of the accountant when she took over her husband's job, were all male and were better paid than others. The second group, less hierarchical in structure and predominantly female, was directly in charge of the infants and saw to their feeding, health, and material welfare. It included the head nurse or *madre*, nurses, laundress, and after 1761, a male doctor and surgeon who had been added to the permanent staff. A third group, usually male, was not completely dependent on the Inclusa. It included part-time workers such as handymen, musicians, the constable, and preachers who were called in for feasts and special occasions, and a host of tradesmen, delivery-men, and repairmen.

Nominally, the head of the Inclusa was the protector. He was an appointee of the Consejo de Castilla and the crown paid his salary. The protector, as his name would indicate, acted as patron of the Inclusa and as a government representative. He assigned posts and arranged salaries, and his accession to power was often the occasion for looking into the administration and accounts of the institution. However, the appointment was usually a sinecure for life, and things settled back into their routine quite quickly after the new official made a few changes in staff, or called for an inventory.[8] His role was predominantly formal, and he showed up for the ceremonial occasions and the annual *junta*, or meeting of administrators. An exception was Josef Vilches (appointed in 1793), who insisted on taking his responsibilities seriously. He refused to preside over the dissolution of his empire, which was under siege by the Junta de damas of the Royal Economic Society of Madrid, and he made a creditable effort to improve the financial position of the Inclusa. But usually, the protector was head in name only.

In fact, the institution was run by three priests. The administrator was in charge, the rector was responsible for the records (though the actual transcribing was done by an overburdened clerk), and the collector was in charge of the masses and mass records. The rector's accounts (*entradas*) listed the legal status, origin, baptismal date, the date of birth, and, only too often, the date of death. Baptismal records, whose brevity provide little information about the foundlings, were also kept in the parish church of San Ginés.[9] The chaplain or collector saw to the Inclusa's obligation to say masses for its benefactors. In the early years of the century he was steward and sacristan as well. These three priest-administrators were the élite of the hospital staff.

In keeping with the hierarchical nature of an institution in the Old Regime, those in authority were in the best position to enjoy the system. It is difficult to calculate in monetary terms the actual wages of the priests because, in addition to living accommodations and rations at four reales a day, they had extra stipends for their work on feast-days. Holy Week they received forty-three reales, at Pentecost and Christmas fifty reales, and on the Feast of St Joseph twenty reales. These were the perquisits that were clearly set out. There may have been other less obvious favours such as the lavish set of meals costing 300 reales that was laid on for the administrators on the feast day in 1700. Although examples like this became rare as the century went on, until 1750 the administrator received 550 reales twice a year for his expenses.[10] As senior priest, he also had first claim on the more lucrative mass stipends: he monopolized those at twenty-two reales. His actual salary rose from eight reales a day in 1700, to fifteen in 1770, and to twenty-one in 1792, but this made up only a fraction of the real income. The salary of the rector followed closely this pattern, and he came into his own in 1801 when the administrator was dismissed by the Junta de damas who intended to run the Inclusa themselves.[11] Though accused of extravagance, the women made some cut-backs at the expense of the high-paid administrator.

The collector was the priest whose status improved most over the century. In 1700 he was not an official staff member at all, but was paid for the masses he said on a piece-work basis. He managed to eke out a living by performing the duties of steward at two reales a day and sacristan for another two reales. His situation improved considerably in 1730, when he was given a raise to six reales a day and expected to concentrate on saying the masses. Under these conditions he could pay someone else to assume the duties of sacristan-steward and still make 1000 reales a year more than in 1720. As for the rest of the staff, his wages went up in 1773, and by 1792 he was earning fourteen reales. For this he was obliged to say an average of two and one-half masses a day.[12] However, at this rate the Inclusa found itself 1275 masses in arrears of its quota by 1794. In order to clear up this backlog, the hospital arranged to farm out masses to a number of needy French émigré clerics who were only too happy to say mass at a stipend of three reales each – an arrangement that had no appeal for Spanish priests.[13] Obviously the clerics in Madrid were one group sheltered from financial problems.

Doing the actual work of keeping records were three clerks: the accountant, the treasurer, and the *oficial de libros* or book-lackey. In 1700 the accountant earned wages of nine reales a day; by the end of the century he made nineteen reales. In 1728 a second accountant, the treasurer, was added to the staff for the minimal rate of four reales, which was merely the ration stipend. When some salaries were actually cut back in 1750, however, the treasurer received a raise to six reales and a Christmas tip of twenty-four reales putting him in the same category as the other administrators. By 1792 he was being paid at the same rate as the rector and the accountant. At that point the treasurer was the widow of Francisco Xavier de Bustos, who had taken over his job at his salary – a sign that there was no discrimination from the standpoint of equal pay for equal work in the case of widows of administrators.[14] Of course, there was a rationale behind this arrangement that made good economic sense; rather than support the widow at the expense of the hospital, she was employed and paid her own way right up to the day she died, if handwriting (which became progressively weaker as the years went on) can be taken as evidence.

Most of the paperwork of the hospital was done by an overburdened and underpaid clerk. He was first hired in 1710 when the hospital began to send out letters rather than people to notify the nurses of the pay-days at Pentecost and Nativity. Under the supervision of the rector and administrator, he kept the records of the infants and of the nurses who took them out. That is, the rector and administrator signed the monthly and yearly totals that the clerk had drawn up. The clerk also shared the duties of the accountant when extra work was required for the periodic inventories and inquiries into hospital finances. Despite the fact that he ran the office, he was paid only three reales a day, the same as unskilled labourers or servants. His Christmas tip indicates he held the same status as the grave-digger or laundress, although he was entitled to supplements of oil, wine, and living accommodations. His wages went from three reales to six reales in 1770, and then to eight and one-half in 1775, where they remained even when other staff members were given further increases.[15] The clerk had been bypassed when the death of his patron Francisco Colón in 1792 left him with no one to represent his interests. He describes his situation eloquently in a letter protesting this slight:

For eighteen years I have been working without any raises in salary except when the protector, Sr. Don Joseph Herreros, granted me one *arroba* of oil and one of coal in consideration of the extra light and heat I require, for I must get up at all hours in order to record the admission of infants and therefore need to warm the office. I am often at work both day and night as assistant in both the office of the rector and the accountant. These duties involve dispatching the infants, giving out extra advances to the nurses' salaries, and clearing goods dispensed from taxes through customs. All these things have been done with care and efficiency as the rector and administrator will vouch. Therefore in recognition of my low wages and the high cost of living, I beg you to give some consideration to my request.[16]

More than a year later the administration got around to refusing his petition. However they softened the blow by conceding that in cases where 'extraordinary' work was called for, he could then request extra pay.[17] There would appear to be few hours of the day or night when the clerk was free to do extra work, but he was recompensed with eight reales at Pentecost and Christmas, and given a similar sum for the task of preparing the inventory of 1760 and 1790. It was part of the modus operandi of an Old Regime institution to dole out concessions in this paternalistic way as a kind of 'grace' or special concession, always making clear it was a one-time gratuity.

The clerk functioned as the office donkey. When his patron was no longer available, he had nowhere to turn to plead his cause or to obtain a modicum of justice. When the clerk renewed his application for a raise four years later, he was given one-half real more a day in salary and a lump sum of 640 reales in consideration of the fact that his health had broken down.[18] He had not been assigned rations until 1735, though the rest of the staff were given them in 1729. His salary raises only produced nine reales in 1799. According to Jovellanos, even the mason made six or seven reales in those inflationary times.[19] In 1800 the Junta de damas was constrained to recruit a second clerk, which surely confirmed the justice of his cause. His physical collapse indicates the way in which human resources of the Inclusa were being exhausted at the end of the eighteenth century.

But most of the real business of the Inclusa was done by women. The administrative side of the hospital dealt with figures and finances, but not directly with infants, who were in the hands of the nurses and the matron. Nurses, of course, were the mainstay of the institution, but their status and wages were low. Their Christmas tip was two reales, while the rest of the staff were given eight. The priests, in contrast, received twenty-four, and the administrator forty. From 1700 to 1770, nurses were recruited for three reales a day in rations plus a salary of twenty-two reales a month 'for decency,' which presumably meant for clothing to cover themselves. For this sum they were expected to nurse two or three infants. When a third was assigned, they were given one real a day more – or if it were an older child six *cuartos*, which was slightly less. The basic rate was supplemented by allotments of oil and wine, a stipend for soap, and a bed, or part of one.[20]

In keeping with its familial format, most of the nurses' pay came in the form of rations. These may not actually have been food, but a sum of money based on the price of food. It was theoretically the equivalent of one pound of beef, one litre of wine, and a loaf of bread, and it provided a means of calculating a living wage. However, since food prices varied from one month to another, as well as from one year to the next, it is difficult to estimate how much of that amount actually went for the cost of food. The exception is the year 1796 when, according to the protector, all of the ration stipend went on meals alone.[21]

The salary structure of an institution of the Old Regime cannot be understood without taking into account the place of rations. Rations epitomized the paternalistic format of the Inclusa. They operated as a cost-of-living index to ensure that even though wages were low, they were never below the subsistence level. It was common practice for artisans' apprentices to eat at the master's table in lieu of wages, or for servants and shop assistants to receive part, if not all, of their wages in board. All the staff of the Inclusa received rations, but they made up almost completely the salary of the matron and the nurses – perhaps a sign of their subordinate position in the hierarchy of the Inclusa, and evidence that the institution was patriarchal as well as paternal. The rest of the staff were given four reales for rations, and the nurses three, until 1770 when the amount increased to four. In January 1797 more than two weeks went by without a single woman offering her services as nurse, while the seven already in residence each had three or four infants.[22] In a panic, wages were raised to six reales a day and the various allowances for soap, rations, etc., were done away with. The measure did serve to attract nurses again and enable the Inclusa to keep its door open for the infants threatening to overwhelm the hospital.

The Inclusa, however, had never presumed to provide more than a temporary shelter and a temporary nurse until a permanent one could be found to take the child into her home. These women from the city or nearby towns earned eighteen reales a month while the child was at the breast and ten reales a month after. If the same woman took care of the child until it was weaned she was given a supplement of 122 reales – apparently an incentive to keep the child alive and healthy.[23] By 1790 the wages had gone up to forty reales for the first month, the dangerous period for the infants, then thirty until weaned, and finally twenty for an older child. The woman was expected to account for supplies of linens and blankets, and the Inclusa could refuse to pay when the child had obviously been maltreated.[24]

Reckoning the salary for a nurse was a matter of some delicacy. When the child died, it might be months or weeks before any official had to be aware of it. Defrauding the institution by collecting a salary for the care of a dead child must have been a constant temptation. The only formal contact between the nurse and the hospital in the towns of the province was provided by the curates who themselves had some sympathy with the women when it came to a conflict between poverty-stricken parishioners and a distant institution.

Not that the nurses were uniformly heartless. Despite the misery of some of these homes, the infant's chances for survival were much better with its own personal nurse. When the infant lived, it sometimes was adopted 'for devotion' after the formal term was up.[25] However, more often the child did not live to be sent back to the Inclusa and suffer the psychological damage of being abandoned twice.

If nurses were the foundation of the Inclusa, the matron, or madre, was the corner-stone. Almost every phase of the child's care came under her supervision. She chose the nurses, when there was a choice, and kept records of their pay and the condition and quality of their milk. She saw to their health, performance, morals, and behaviour and decided when one should be dismissed. One of the regular items of expense was a calendar where the date each nurse arrived was recorded to compute her pay accurately. Controlling a group of women, some of whom were suspected of having abandoned their own children so they could profit themselves from their milk, and any of whom could have found better-paying positions with private families if their quality and character had been satisfactory, called for the talents of a headmistress-cum-police matron.

Her records of petty-cash outlays on a day-to-day basis were kept in a book called tandas, or 'tickets.' Here could be found items for the nurses' quarters such as the odd stool, cushion, or chamberpot, cord and cotton for lamps, lavender for the floors, soap and snacks for nurses, and a miscellany of odds and ends for infants: bindings for swaddling cloths, herbs, eggs, sugar, honey, and wine and rum for medicinal purposes, as well as the ingredients for the *papilla* or gruel given to supplement the milk supply. In a modern hospital, she would have combined the functions of supervisor, dietitian, and personnel director, with a little of the pharmacist and doctor thrown in.

Obviously, the administration could not reward in monetary terms the diverse talents of the *madre*. It did not even try. For most of the century, her salary was three and one-half reales of rations a day, only one-half real more than the nurses and without the additional twenty-two per month. The tip of eight reales at Christmas gave tacit recognition that her status was a jot above theirs. Perhaps the administration took it for granted that holding the purse-strings would allow her to take care of any personal needs. Still, the discrepancy between wages and responsibilities is astonishing. In 1760 the injustice was acknowledged in the form of a yearly supplement of 500 reales.[26] But in 1770, when the *madre*'s rations went up to four and one-half reales, this monetary supplement was cut back to 200 reales.[27] The broad disproportion between her responsibilities and the work she performed remained. However, in an Old Regime institution there were compensations. On retirement, 'because of her years,' she continued to live on in the Inclusa, drawing the same rations as she had as an active member of the establishment.[28] In recognition of her labours, she had become a member of the family.

In the eighteenth century the Inclusa was not a hospital in the modern sense of the word, and decisions about the health of the infants were left entirely to the matron, who decided when to call in the doctor, or surgeon. A doctor was formally attached to the institution in 1761, and the services of a surgeon were required regularly. The surgeon summoned by the matron was probably not one of the *cirujanos latinos* who had studied at the university for four years. He did not bear the title 'Don,' and Pascual Gonzáles, who served the Inclusa for thirty years, died an apprentice surgeon.[29] Doubtless he had been trained as a barber's assistant, and subsequently passed an exam in blood-letting. Campomanes would have classed him in the rank of hairdressers.[30] From 1700–1760, the allotment for the surgeon was only 235 reales. It went up to 500 reales in 1770 and 800 in 1788. By 1800, the surgeon had become a full-time staff member for 1100 reales per year, or exactly half of the stipend for the medical doctor. At this point his ministrations as surgeon were required less often because the custom of bleeding new-born infants on every and all occasions was beginning to die out.

In prestige and wages the medical doctor was far ahead. Although at the time of the Census of Ensenada in 1754, the doctor was ranked with servants, blacksmiths, woodcutters, and carters,[31] a city doctor might do very well financially. The author and social critic Diego de Torres Villarroel referred to doctors as a group of Frenchified, effeminate charlatans.[32] Not surprisingly, their image improved with their income. A playlet of Ramón de la Cruz satirized a doctor who 'from his bearing, the profound respect showed to him by all, might be mistaken for a fieldmarshal.'[33] This particular member of the profession flaunted a gold-handled walking-stick and a diamond as big as an almond. Such accessories were inconsistent with the traditional costume of the doctor, who usually wore a black undercoat, black waistcoat, three-cornered hat, and frilled white collar (golilla).

The gastos record his rise in fortune. The doctor was first found in the list of wages in 1761 with a gratuity of 450 reales. By 1770 he had become a regular staff member at 1100 reales per year. In 1787 these wages had doubled, an indication of the care required by increasing numbers of sickly infants.[34] Given the demands for his services, the doctor understandably felt a strong sense of injustice when his request for a raise was rejected in 1794, especially since the hospital had not fulfilled its promise of living accommodations. He also pointed out that the book he had written on the care of the foundlings deserved some recognition.[35] As a concession he was given a supplement of 1500 reales in 1798, but with the usual accompanying warning that it was 'for one time.'

He was finally vindicated in 1800 when the Junta de damas, in an attempt to staunch the appalling mortality rate, hired a second doctor to help him. In 1805 this doctor, Antonio Anento, earned a supplement of 1500 reales in consideration of 'the fatigue and distress he had suffered in carrying out his duties' during the appalling conditions of 1804.[36] Unlike other staff members, doctors did receive some recompense in both praise and money as they continued to cope with conditions that can only be described as horrendous. In typical Old Regime fashion, this recognition was often tardy and bestowed in a paternalistic fashion. But because their services were so necessary, the medical profession could successfully demand a wage that became measurably higher as the century went on. Pressures of the times were beginning to bring about certain changes in the traditional ways of the Inclusa, for those in a position to take advantage of the situation. The madre, who had been displaced as medical authority, was not one of those able to profit from the unhealthy condition of most of the foundlings.

Those whose skills were in demand formed a privileged group. Prices were rising much faster than income and the wages of those at the bottom of the scale rose even more slowly than for those who were already better off. For instance, the income of the administrator went up 130 per cent over the century, the accountant 100 per cent, the clerk 60 per cent, and the laundress 40 per cent. Meanwhile, the price of wheat rose 285 per cent.[37] The records of the Inclusa verify the claims of economists that during an inflationary cycle, the poor suffered most; and the case of the unskilled workers makes this fact very clear.

Most unskilled workers were not attached to the Inclusa on a permanent basis and, therefore, were not eligible for the extras, or even the Christmas tips that were one of the benevolent aspects of an institution in the Old Regime. Some of these workers eked out a living doing odd jobs; and it was often the same person or his son doing tasks such as putting down the matting or taking care of the awnings year after year. Their inferior status is evident in the patronizing names these workers were given. The porters who delivered goods from the customs house were called *mozos de aduanas* or 'customs boys'; the coal deliverers were *mozos de carbón*; the mason's assistants, *mozos de albañil*; and street sweepers, *mozos de barrido*. Other *mozos* were called in to prepare the chapel for feast-days and processions and to do maintenance work around the hospital. The term 'boy,' while it lacks the full pejorative implications associated with its application in English, nevertheless reflects, at least etymologically, the inferior status of these workers.

There were actually some cases in the *gastos* of wages that did not change at all from 1700 to 1800. These wage rates are further evidence that there was no shortage of labour and that unskilled workers must have been legion. Jobs were done by the poor who had come to Madrid to find work at wages that only the very poor would accept. Street porters, who delivered bales of remnants for the infants' swaddling cloths, received exactly forty reales every month, every year. The labourers who took up the matting got exactly twelve reales for this task every year until 1800, when they received a raise to sixteen reales.[38] The labourer who put up the awnings was paid between twelve and fourteen reales each time. Men who came in to clean and prepare the chapel and move the statue for the procession were given their first increase from ten to thirteen reales in 1800. But when the same work was done for Holy Week ceremonies, the rate stayed at forty reales for more than a century. This was also true of the coachman who brought the preacher on the feast of St Joseph for eight reales. Granted there were some unskilled labourers whose wages went up. The men who delivered and piled up the coal for three reales a *carro* in 1700 were earning four and one-half in 1789 and seven reales by 1800.[39] But in the overwhelming majority of cases, the increase was either nil or negligible. There were even cases of set-backs: the sweeper who was being given thirteen reales a month in 1770 and fourteen in 1783 had been paid fifteen reales in 1740.[40]

These unskilled and part-time workers were doubly disadvantaged. Not only were their wages kept down, they were not part of the familial structure of the institution that, despite low wages, cared for its own in old age and sickness. There was no set policy regarding age and terms of retirement, but the institution felt some sense of obligation toward its members in their old age. One rector retired on full salary and kept his quarters, whereas the collector preferred to take half-salary and go off to spend his last days with his sister.[41] The clerk, Juan Gonzáles, whose plaintive request for a raise had been brusquely rejected, retired on full salary of seven reales a day.[42] The hospital which exploited them as workers cared for them as family.

This paternalistic sense of family was evident in attitudes toward the female dependants of the administrative staff. Not all took advantage of this policy. As we saw in the case of the treasurer's widow, there were those who continued to work until they died. Lorenza Sarmiento's signature on the account books vouches that she continued to work though almost unable to control a pen. She was taking care of herself, but there were other examples where the institution assumed responsibility for women dependants of their staff. The usual procedure, for instance, was to provide for the widow of the treasurer or accountant from the salary of the new incumbent. This functioned as a kind of insurance policy for women who might otherwise be destitute. But one can only sympathize with the accountant who, in 1799, found himself supporting not only the widow of his predecessor, Josef Závala, but the widow of the one before that, Pedro Závala. This meant he had to forfeit, from his wages of nineteen reales, six for their rations. Moreover, he was assigned the same room as the newly bereaved widow, with a partition constructed to preserve her privacy.[43] One administrator, Don Manuel Muñoz, died leaving all his goods to the hospital but enjoined that his two nieces should be supplied with rations of three and one-half reales a day for as long as they required them. Doña María either married or died in 1783, but Doña Manuela continued collecting her rations till 1799.[44] Without a fixed policy, customs and traditions were honoured.

Overall, the treatment of staff on retirement showed more generosity than when a full day's work was being exacted. This was in keeping with the traditions of the Old Regime, where there was a sense of personal commitment to the old retainer who had given faithful service. But under the pressure of events, the familial structure had begun to break down by the end of the century. Rations disappeared. There was a tendency to rationalize and in a sense standardize the salary scale. Of course, administrators would remain better paid, but they were no longer eligible for a long list of perquisites setting apart their status from that of the rest of the staff. Though occasionally privileges enjoyed by the institution on products such as oil and wine may have worked to the advantage of the employees during an inflationary cycle, the trend toward a straight monetary salary seems to have been welcomed. It was in an attempt to attract employees that rations were replaced by sums of money, even though food supplied through the hospital was probably cheaper than what could be bought on the open market. Obviously employees resented, if only subconsciously, the paternalism of some of the practices of the Old Regime institutions and responded positively to being treated as adults responsible for their own expenses.

The take-over of the Inclusa by the Junta de damas marked an important step toward transforming the hospital into a modern, bureaucratic institution. A large increase in the numbers of staff meant that they could no longer be dealt with in the haphazard, inconsistent, if more personal manner of the past. In 1799 there were ten staff and eighteen wet-nurses. Immediately their numbers went to eighteen staff and twenty-seven nurses. By 1805 the change-over was complete and there were twenty employees (twelve of them Sisters of Charity) and twenty-seven nurses – double the total of those on the wage rolls in 1799.[45]

Such a dramatic change was costly. Of course, expenses had been rising over the whole century. They went from 52,832 reales in 1700 to 95,187 reales in 1790. But in 1800 expenses jumped to 156,059 and in 1805, when the process of revamping the Inclusa was more or less finished, the net cost of operating the hospital annually had reached 264,415 reales.[46]

The salary structure of the Inclusa illustrates the operation of an institution in the Old Regime and the way in which traditional modes of functioning were becoming obsolete at the end of the century. The Inclusa was part of a tightly woven system involving church, state, and society. It also operated in a framework of familial values that we associate with the sense of hierarchy and noblesse oblige of the Old Regime. However, the pressures of inflation pulled at the seams of the whole fabric of the Old Regime. Difficulties were evident in the experience of the hospital and the poor who were dependent upon it in various ways. The Inclusa was one means of helping the poor to cope with their situation and providing social stability, despite the periodic crises of wars and crop failures. Increasing difficulty in carrying out this function can be documented in the salary rolls of the hospital. The wages of everyone in the institution lagged far behind the rate of inflation. The attempt of the institution to provide a familial, paternalistic shelter from the harsh realities of the economic conditions of the time was no longer successful. Meanwhile, by paying wages well below the cost of living, the Inclusa was able to keep its doors open only at the price of exploiting its staff, even though this was done in a familial context.

The Inclusa could no longer operate as surrogate for parents of the foundling, nor could it provide for the expanding staff that the institution required without jeopardizing seriously its financial basis. Wet-nurses' salaries were inadequate to attract any but the most desperately poor and unhealthy women. Even more hopeless was the situation of the group of quasi-dependants who had never been able to take advantage of the privileges of being part of the institution. The most impressive evidence from the *gastos* has to do with the incredible burden borne by the unskilled. These were workers whose wages changed scarcely at all over the century. And this same group had another connection with the Inclusa. It was from the ranks of these victims of inflation that many of the infants who flooded the Inclusa were to come in the critical years of the turn of the century. The incapacity of institutions of the Old Regime to cope with the problems facing Spain's poor at the end of the eighteenth century is made patently clear in the wage rolls of the Inclusa. A few fortunate women had been sheltered by the hospital, but the desperate women who were leaving their infants in increasing numbers were demanding from the institution more than it was able to give. This was one reason for the difficulties of the Inclusa at the end of the century, and it was also a symptom of the difficulties experienced by the poor as revealed in the pages of the *gastos*. In order to learn more about the women of the working poor in eighteenth-century Madrid, we turn now to the records of the *salidas* for an account of the women who came from rural towns to take out the infants as wet-nurses.

PART TWO
THE WET-NURSES

3

Rural Poverty and the Inclusa

The institution of the Inclusa did not exist in isolation. It mirrored the dominant ideas and preconceptions of the period, and it also dealt with everyday, mundane matters of life and death. The admissions records of infants reflect the distress of the poor in Madrid in the eighteenth century and provide a frame of reference for measuring the extent and fluctuation of poverty. The hospital had another point of contact with the poor: the women who came as wet-nurses to take these infants out were part of the same culture of poverty as were their charges. Any description of the Inclusa must take into account these women, who came in from the countryside. As a result, rural poverty is an element brought into focus in the archives of the Inclusa. The records called the *salidas* (those leaving the hospital) fill in the background and setting for the lives of an important sector of the population in the eighteenth century – the rural poor (see fig. 3.1). These records portray the deterioration of the condition of the rural farmer over the century. Independent small farmers were replaced by *jornaleros* or day-labourers in the lists of rural women taking out infants from the Inclusa. This change suggests a proletarianization of the small farmer, a process that accelerated when the rural poor emigrated to Madrid in search of work or charity.

Disaster was a way of life for the small farmer in the Old Regime. The century was ushered in by near famine conditions caused by the crop failures of 1699. The winter of 1709–10 was one of the most frigid in Europe's history. That summer, crops failed again, and this time the situation was aggravated by the War of the Spanish Succession when Madrid changed hands twice and armies ravaged the countryside. In 1723, 1734, and 1747 the harvest returns were below normal, but 1750

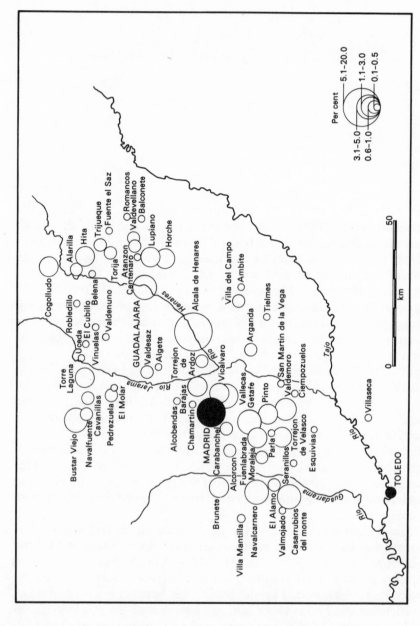

FIGURE 3.1 Towns from which wet-nurses came, 1700–99

was a calamity. Then there was no rain in Castile for a period of nineteen months in 1755–56. The 1760s ushered in another series of bad years, culminating in popular risings in the city and provinces in 1766. In 1780–81 and again in 1785–86 there were crop failures that sent 'the whole of the population from the towns of La Mancha begging to Madrid.' From August 1786 until February 1787, Madrid was ravaged by a severe epidemic.[1] Nor did the notorious years 1788–89 spare Castile. Finally, to end this dismal chronicle, there was a drought in 1793, followed by one of the worst winters of the entire century in 1794–95. The distress of the poor of Madrid and the surrounding countryside was evident in the numbers of foundlings left to the hospital. When one of these disasters, natural or man-made, occurred, the poor who could not afford to feed another mouth sent their infants to the Inclusa (see fig. 1.1).

Poverty was a permanent part of life for most of the rural population. Not that the eighteenth century did not have its share of good years. The period from 1715 to the present has been one of relatively good weather overall, but the agricultural system of the Old Regime was such that often the small farmer barely managed to eke out a living on the edge of subsistence. In a bad year he went into debt; in a good year he recovered enough to keep himself and his family afloat. In a series of bad years he went under. In contrast, the large landowner was able to wait out the bad years and even profit from them by selling his produce at a premium when the price was right. This enabled him to take advantage of the small farmer who needed credit. The nature of the landholding system in the Old Regime worked for the rich at the expense of the poor. In the words of a contemporary economist, Závala y Auñon: 'Those who seed small portions must sell off their product as soon as the harvest is in to pay off the debts which they contracted in the course of the year, and to support themselves ... Others are able to put aside and hoard their crops; they do not sell a single bushel during good years, nor even in average years ... waiting until they can get the best price.'[2]

Even the geography of Spain worked to the advantage of the large landowner. Madrid is set in the heart of an arid plateau where rainfall is never abundant. Spain's mountainous terrain isolated one region from another and the roads between rural villages were often no more than mule tracks. Under such conditions a local crop failure could cause a local famine. When the government embarked on an ambitious program of road building in the 1760s in an attempt to join the capital with Andalusia, Catalonia, Valencia, Extremadura, and Asturias, the expensive highways did little to relieve the isolation of the small farmer in the rural backwater.

The highly centralized government of the Old Regime did not protect the small farmer remote from the seat of power. At the instigation of reformers who had been influenced by liberal economic theory, the government abolished the price ceiling or *tasa* in order to allow free trade in grain in 1765. At the same time, to soften the blow of a consequent price rise, it expanded the network of *pósitos* or public granaries. These were to store surplus grain during good years and ensure the farmer a supply of food and seed grain at reasonable prices. But ultimately this arrangement did little for the small farmer. It meant that sometimes grain was taken out of circulation so that food was scarce for the whole year; or in a period of crisis the provisioner for Madrid scoured the countryside, in some cases leaving towns without enough grain for their own people and interfering with the normal operation of the system. These contradictory policies meant that grain prices remained high even during good years, a factor that again worked to the advantage of those with large supplies on hand.[3]

Agriculture in the eighteenth century was a profitable business for those able to weather the bad years. Grain quotations rose between 150 and 200 per cent in the years 1716–1800.[4] The population expansion that helped to fill the Inclusa with infants was also responsible for creating a demand for food. Land was a lucrative investment for those with capital. Theoretically, the price rise should have meant a profit for all groups engaged in farming. In fact, the gains made by large landowners were much higher than those of the small farmer, and relatively slight for tenants and day-labourers.

Reports from officials in various parts of Castile on the subject of agrarian reform in the years 1766–70 document that the phenomenon of the landless labourer was becoming more widespread; tenants were forced to pay higher rents or were faced with dispossession. Despite an overall increase in the amount of land being worked, the share of the small famer in the earnings from increased production constantly declined. In 1750 there were 6988 small farmers and 5941 day-labourers. That is, slightly more than half the rural workers of Castile were independent *labradores* or *vecinos*.[5] But by 1797 there were only 2379 in this category, which 2965 listed as tenant farmers; an overwhelming 13,004 were day-labourers.[6] In other words, the proportion of landless went from 46 per cent in 1750 to 74 per cent in 1800.

The progressive impoverishment of the group that constituted 71 per cent of the active population of Spain could not but have serious repercussions throughout the whole of society. The purpose of this chapter is to discuss what the records of the *salidas* reveal about the condition of the rural worker, his wife, and the foundling they brought to their isolated hamlet.

The picture of the small farmer that emerges from the pages of the *salidas* confirms the pauperization of the landowner struggling to survive on a small plot of land under adverse conditions. The pattern can be seen in a series of steps. First the independent farmer became the landless day-labourer, and finally he and his family deserted the countryside completely to join the ranks of the urban proletariat in search of a better way of life. In many cases, this hope was doomed to disappointment. The dispossessed rural worker who had moved to Madrid often ended up in the ranks of the unemployed, eking out a living at odd jobs, or living off others. It was a case of the rural poor becoming the urban poor.

The records of the Inclusa trace the transition from rural to urban poverty. At the end of the century the numbers of rural wet-nurses had fallen off considerably. It seems likely that large numbers of the rural poor were moving into Madrid to swell the ranks of the urban poor. The transition occurred gradually as conditions in Castile worsened for the small farmer. The change can be documented by comparing the numbers of wet-nurses whose husbands were independent farmers with those of day-labourers. The distinction between the landless and the landowner is clear. *Labrador* or *vecino* is the name for the independent farmer, and the tenant or sharecropper was included in this designation. The *jornalero* or *peón*, in contrast, was a farm-hand paid wages by the day on someone else's land. There were almost no *jornaleros* listed before 1740 (see fig. 3.2). This is not surprising. The hired hand was probably single. Too poor even to marry, he made his lonely way on wages barely enough to support his own needs. In the secod half of the century, however, there was an interesting development: increasing numbers of wives of day-labourers began to be represented in the list of wet-nurses of the Inclusa. Obviously there were more of this group beginning to marry, and their wives were taking out infants from the Inclusa. There are two possible explanations for this change: it could mean that over the course of the century, day-labourers had become better off (at least for the period 1740–80), or it could mean that during these years increasing numbers of small farmers and tenants had slipped into the ranks of landless day-labourers.

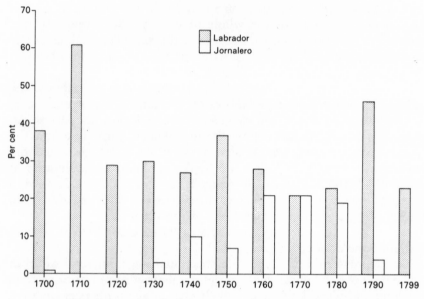

FIGURE 3.2 Rural occupations of husbands of wet-nurses

Most contemporaries opted for the latter explanation. The agricultural commentators of the day would have found in the figures of the
Inclusa further confirmation of their reports on the increasing numbers
of landless labourers. It is certain that after 1740 the proportion of
landless among the wet-nurses began to rise steadily, while the number
of independent farmers declined. By 1760, one-third of the nurses were
married to day-labourers, and the representation of small farmers had
gone down in about the same proportion. The jeremiads of contemporaries who decried the situation of the landless farmer of Castile are
verified in tables 3.1, which shows day-labourers' wives making up a
growing proportion among the wet-nurses of the Inclusa in the towns of
New Castile in the period from 1740 to 1780.

But an argument could also be made that the *jornalero* was becoming
better off, because there were many more day-labourers' wives taking
infants to nurse. Barring coincidence, this could only mean that the
day-labourer was, relatively speaking, more affluent during the period
between 1730 and 1780. He was in a position to marry, to have children,
and, therefore, to have a wife who could supplement the family income
by wet-nursing. This interpretation supports the findings of Pierre Vilar

TABLE 3.1
Rural occupations of husbands of wet-nurses, 1700–99

Year	Labrador	Percentage	Jornalero	Percentage	Other
1700	38	90.47	1	0.3	7.23
1710	61	91.17			
1720	29	96.66			
1730	30	83.33	3	8.33	8.44
1740	27	71.05	10	26.31	2.64
1750	37	69.81	7	13.20	16.99
1760	28	63.54	21	47.73	
1770	21	50.00	21	50.00	
1780	23	41.07	19	33.42	
1790	46	88.46	4	7.69	
1799	23	100.00			

SOURCE: *Salidas*, June, December, 1700–99

about the circumstances of the day-labourer in the province of Madrid. He points out that in 1750 the average income of a day-labourer in the province was four reales compared to 2.56 reales for the average rural *peón* in Spain.[7]

The day-labourer in the provinces was at an advantage in comparison to the day-labourer in Madrid where prices for food were always higher. After 1780 this advantage was wiped out in the overall economic difficulties that assaulted Spain at the end of the century. The records of the Inclusa indicate that by the 1790s the family of the rural day-labourer was no longer using infants from the Inclusa as a means of supplementary income. It seems likely that many rural day-labourers had given up the struggle and were swelling the ranks of the unskilled, the vagrant, and the beggar on the streets of Madrid. The farmer who survived was likely to be one of the *labradores* holding one of the larger tracts of land. But large numbers of his cohorts of the first half of the century had become the *jornaleros* of the second half, and by the 1790s these rural day-labourers had become part of the urban proletariat.

This change could explain why the Inclusa of Madrid was unique in that relatively few of its wet-nurses came from rural towns. In fact, the Inclusa was exceptional in Europe because so many of its nurses were from the city. To understand this circumstance we need to ask why the wives of farmers did not find wet-nursing economically appealing. At the end of the century, inflation may have meant that it was hardly worth her while for a farmer's wife in either category to come to the hospital. Families of the rural poor who were so badly off as to need the

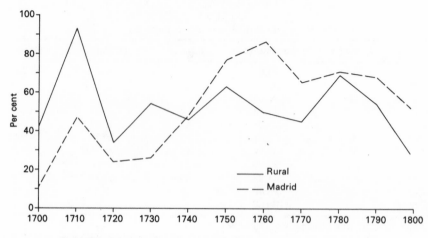

FIGURE 3.3 Rural and urban wet-nurses of Inclusa, 1700–99

pittance the Inclusa paid for nursing had 'given up the struggle and moved into the city in large numbers. The overwhelming disasters of the 1790s had brought the day-labourer, burdened with a family, into the ranks of the urban poor (see fig. 3.3).

It is impossible to know its exact extent, but demographers agree that the growth of Madrid in the eighteenth century was largely dependent on immigration. María Carbajo Isla, in a study of baptismal and death records in Madrid, confirmed that there was no sharp increase in the numbers baptized in the course of the century and nothing to suggest a decline in mortality.[8] Data of Laborde in 1797 led the demographer M. Livi-Bacci to conclude that the birth rate of Madrid was only 75 per cent of the rate in the rest of Spain.[9] Much of the growth of Madrid after 1750 must have come from the rural hinterland.

It had always been true that a tenant or a farmer with a small plot could not keep a family on his earnings from the soil. More than one job was required, and often more than one person's income. Although the pay for wet-nursing from the Inclusa was ridiculously low, it could help a family barely to scrape along until the next harvest. As long as that was the case, nurses continued to come to the Inclusa from the towns of rural Castile. The *jornalero* became part of the urban *populacho* only because he did not have enough land, and his family did not have the opportunity to earn enough to keep them going. The Spanish farmer joined the ranks of the urban poor usually as an unskilled *peón* or –

when even that was denied him – slipped into the indeterminant position of those who worked when they could, and begged or stole when they could find no other means of support. This was the category for increasing numbers of the urban poor. It was from this group that the infants were to come who flooded the hospital in the last years of the century.

The implications for the whole society were important. The small farmer from the rural town left behind a traditional way of life rooted in traditional values, of which the importance of the family was just one. The decision to leave meant a break with more than his physical universe. It could mean a transformation in his psychological make-up. The person too proud to beg in a setting where his honour and that of his family was at stake suffered less trauma in the relative anonymity of Madrid. There the contribution to family income on the part of wife and child could involve begging or worse. The influx of the rural poor into the cities was a phenomenon with cultural and social as well as economic ramifications.

The attraction of the city for the dispossessed tenant or the small farmer was understandable. The farmer trudged sometimes miles to his plot and worked as his ancestors had, either bent double for hours under the hot sun or following an antiquated roman plough pulled by a mule or team of oxen. Half the land was left fallow every year, and grain yielded in most cases a return of no more than three for one. Persuading the small farmers to implement the technological improvements advocated by enlightened reformers would have required money that was not there in the first place. What profits there were went into taxes, seigneurial dues, or *diezmos* to the church. As for the large landowner, it was enough to bring more land under cultivation, and such land accounted for the increase in production that occurred over the century.[10] For the ordinary agricultural worker, conditions remained as they had always been, despite the fortunes to be made by a few from his labour.

Although rural life was hard, it was not necessarily dull. The work calendar of the farm labourer provided for a generous number of holidays. Along with the religious celebrations of Easter and Corpus Christi, spring and summer brought festivities that originated in pagan rites of the soil.[11] The *majas* immortalized in the cartoons of Goya, and the solstices of St John, were the most common expressions of these age-old traditions. August and September had fairs, pilgrimages (*romerías*) to the local shrines, and the important feasts of Santiago and the Virgin. Holidays enlivened the routine for the rural labourers even more often than for the urban worker. Despite the therapeutic effect on the farmer's spirit, the impact on his material welfare was disastrous. Wages for day-labourers in the countryside were based on a 120-day work year, compared with 180 days for the *peón* in the city, which made the pay of the rural day-labourer in Spain ultimately the lowest in the nation.[12] His survival must have depended on having more than one job and one person's contribution to family income.

This variety of occupation was encouraged by the short work year and allowed the farm labourer to make a gradual transition between country and city. Braudel has pointed out that muleteers were often farmers who yoked oxen up to transport goods four months of the year.[13] The unskilled *peón*, the street hawker, or the porter may have come originally to the city for part of the year because he could not support himself on his small plot or because wages were slightly higher, and he gradually acclimatized himself and his family to the urban environment.

Rural towns held few opportunities for the farmer or his wife, and the further away from Madrid the town, the truer this was likely to be. In the towns of the outskirts – towns that are today incorporated into Madrid – were to be found the malodorous industries, the cheap inns, posting houses, stables, and porters' lodges for transients and muleteers. The wine tax of the city encouraged serious drinkers to frequent the *bodegas* of the towns just beyond the *puertas*, and gave many of them a violent atmosphere that only the lowest inns of the city could rival. But at least some of them had work for both artisans and unskilled. Towns more remote from the capital were merely dormitory villages from which farmers went out each morning to work the soil, and to which they returned exhausted at night. In the words of the contemporary social critic and author Diego de Torres Villarroel, rural towns offer 'the ultimate in degradation, where townspeople sweat and strive to support idle courtesans, and so-called politicians.'[14] The hard-working farmer found little that was rewarding in the rural environment. The profits from his work were spent elsewhere by others.

Contemporary observers spoke of the decay of rural Castile, and blamed the vanity and self-interest of nobles who had left for the cities 'where they do not see the miserable condition of their townspeople, and have begun to think of their estates as if they were a foreign country.'[15] Larruga, an economic critic of the day, in an analysis of the problems of Spain at the end of the century, blamed 'the many nobles who have moved out of the Court' for the poverty of rural towns in the province of Guadalajara.[16] Madrid was the court, and it was the pivot of the universe for the nobleman and would-be nobleman. No sooner was one of the wealthier landowners able to provide for himself and his family than he proceeded to fulfil the lifelong ambition of every nouveau-riche and leave his class behind. This meant purchasing a *mayorazgo* to entail his land for his descendants and setting himself up in Madrid. As a result, the towns did not provide the setting for ostentatious buildings built with newly acquired wealth, as they had in the sixteenth century. Floridablanca lowered by half the tax on landowners who resided in their own towns, but there is no evidence that this provision was able to counteract the attraction of the city and court. The farmer continued to drudge in poverty in the rural towns as long as he could make a living that way, while the landowner, as soon as he could get away, basked in the enjoyment of his income in Madrid.

Of course, the basic problem for the farm worker in Castile was that few could make a living off the land. To survive, the farm labourer required a working wife, fair wages, and reasonable grain prices. When one, or any, or all of these were missing, the result was the proletarianization of the small holder. A recent study of poverty in pre-industrial Europe estimates that 40–50 per cent of the population were at the minimal subsistence level. In France it has been estimated that the proportion of day-labourers in the rural population rose from 12 per cent in 1696 to 33 per cent in 1789.[17] When there were opportunities for the wife and children to engage in domestic labour the small tenant or even the day-labourer could survive in the rural setting. Where such opportunities were lacking, there was no alternative but to move to Madrid.

The capital was the one source and market for anything beyond the barest necessities of life for most inhabitants of Castile. Few rural towns had an independent or varied industrial existence of their own apart from the capital.[18] Of the ninety-nine towns sending wet-nurses to the Inclusa, only twenty-five listed an occupation that could be classified as non-agricultural. Aside from wet-nursing, there was no way that the rural woman could find a remunerative income aside from her traditional contribution working the land with her husband, tending the vegetables, etc. Even in those towns that are today part of Madrid and that were close enough to the metropolis to share its market, there were five jobs listed in agriculture for every one in a trade. The bread industry in Vallecas and Barajas, and the presence of masons, stonecutters, and soldiers in Vicalbero and Barajas, show that these towns profited from their proximity to the city, but they were exceptional. A few potters, blacksmiths, shoe-makers, bridle makers, and charcoal dealers, and the presence of textile workers in Vallecas and Canillas, are the only sign of a diversified economy even in the suburbs of Madrid; and many of these workers may have catered to the local trade. In fact, the information from the *salidas* suggests that even Getafe, Carabanchel, Hortaleza, and Melorada (towns today part of urban Madrid) were 100 per cent agricultural.

In most towns of Castile there was only farming and grazing. These were towns where the physiognomy of the men had taken on the character of the craggy terrain and russet soil of the Castilian landscape. These were towns where the women, bent over double from long hours in the fields and garbed prematurely in black dresses and headscarves, were old at thirty-five. In these towns the old ways did not change, only the generations following them. Lethargy and stagnation had become the way of life as the ambitious and vigorous moved out. The few artisans listed as husbands of wet-nurses – blacksmiths, bridle makers, and shoe-makers – were likely to be farmers as well, at least part of the year, or part of the day. The baker, schoolteacher, and surgeon – when the town was large enough to support them – and the priest were the only exceptions.

The *salidas* give some indication as to which of these rural towns possessed an economy of any sophistication. Álcala and Guadalajara, qualified as settings of some vitality. In Guadalajara, though 60 per cent of the occupations of husbands listed by wet-nurses were in farming, there were also two textile workers, two masons, a mat maker, a muleteer, and a potter. Álcala had many more opportunities for its inhabitants. Listed are one sacristan, one schoolteacher, two bakers, one potter, one paper dealer, three tailors and masons, and eleven leather workers – as well as that sign of a well-rounded economy, one *peón* or unskilled worker. There were textile workers in Orche, Bustar Viejo, Fuenlabrada, Trifuegos, and Casarrubios. Fuenlabrada, Trifuegos, and Alcorcón had glass and pottery works. Occasionally a small town at some distance from Madrid, such as Pozuela de los Picos Ardos, had an industry of some importance. Though it lived up to its name for stony, uncultivable land, there was a leather industry, and three tanners, one harness maker, and one *peón*'s wife came from the town. However, even in these cases, the nominal blacksmiths, bridle makers, or potters often farmed a plot of land too small to support a family, or one requiring attention only part of the year. Then they harnessed up an animal and worked as muleteers or took up some other semi-skilled job. According to the census of 1797, 650,000 of the 1,677,172 workers in the agricultural sector of New Castile and Extremadura had subsidiary occupations as local tax collectors or officials of some sort, or as fishermen, sailors, vendors, artisans, or mechanics.[19] If the census had any interest in women's occupations as well as those of the nominal 'breadwinner,' it would have had to add 'wet-nurse of the Inclusa' to the inventory of occupations in these rural towns.

With the records of the *salidas* as a guide, it is possible to outline a pattern of poverty for these towns. Overall, nurses were usually recruited from towns along the main routes to Madrid. The road to Álcala and from there to Guadalajara and the northeast was responsible for 26.6 per cent of wet-nurses. Another 10.2 per cent came from the main thoroughfare to France to the north; 9.3 per cent from the road to Toledo to the south, and 14.5 per cent from the main road to Extremadura in the southwest. In cases such as the suburbs and Álcala there was very little modification in their ties to the capital over the century. The differences occurred in the distribution of nurses from the south and west whose proportions rose, while those from the north and east fell off. Though geographical differences are minimal, there was slightly more rainfall in the northeast, and the presence of the fertile river valleys of the Jarama and Henares meant that the area was more productive. Meanwhile, to the south and west the *meseta* stretched out into the dry plains of La Mancha and Extremadura. The exception was the fertile plain where the Tagus and Henares came together at Aranjuez. Perhaps the fertility of this area may explain why there were no wet-nurses from Aranjuez over the century. But the differences between north and south were so minimal that in themselves they cannot account for the decline in wet-nurses from the area northeast of Madrid.

There were also seasonal differences in numbers of rural wet-nurses. For instance, the administrator of the Inclusa explained in the *Computo necroloïco* (modern sp., *necrológico*) prepared for the archbishops for the period 1764–1812 that at the beginning of summer there were fewer women available because they began collecting thistles and vegetables.[20]

Another reason for the decline in numbers of wet-nurses from the northeast could be that there were more opportunities available for them to do something else. The records of the Inclusa indirectly reveal the opportunities for women to work in something other than nursing, because whenever there was a choice, it seems that women preferred alternatives such as working in the textile industry. This held true everywhere. For instance, in the hospitals of Lyons, Limoges, and Paris, wet-nurses came almost exclusively from rural areas because city women had other choices open to them; witness the case of Guadalajara. In 1757 the Five Major Guilds took over the operation of the textile factory and expanded it by setting up facilities for the production of silks, hats, and jewellery.[21] Of the twenty-six nurses listed in the *salidas* from Guadalajara, only six were recruited after 1750 and one after 1770. But except for the royal workshops, the eighteenth-century factory in Spain was no more than the co-ordination of different aspects of production carried out by workers of the town or of neighbouring towns. The marked decline in the number of wet-nurses from the whole area reflected the opportunities for women to spin and weave in their own homes to supply the factories at Guadalajara. This was verified by the economist Larruga, who stated that the spinning schools of the royal factory had provided opportunities for employment 'especially for women ... Here industries have been established and people work in them with pleasure.'[22] But there were few such opportunities for women in most towns of rural Castile.

Nevertheless, many of these towns were better off in the eighteenth century than they had been in the seventeenth and better off than they were likely to be again in the nineteenth. Accounts written by Pascual Madoz in 1845 and Sebastian de Miñano in 1825 leave the impression that by then the region was in a state of decline after a more prosperous period. Álcala is one outstanding example. The closing of the royal factories in 1808 left agriculture as almost the only occupation for its inhabitants, whose numbers had dwindled from 4000 *vecinos* in 1768 to only 1231 in 1835. 'From a distance,' writes Pascual Madoz, 'the town appears much larger.' But once the visitor entered the gates it became clear that many of its houses, its grand buildings, were empty; its wide streets and ornate plazas deserted.[23] In Alcorcón, the glass industry had been three times as large before the War of Independence had ravaged the towns and caused much of the population to abandon it – a set-back from which it never recovered.[24] In Esquivias, by 1845, the wine industry that had employed many townspeople was no more,[25] and similarly the excellent bread from Vallecas had disappeared along with its almond trees and olive groves.[26]

A study based on the censuses of 1754 and 1827 confirms the

impression of decadence.[27] It shows that the larger rural towns did not evolve into more prosperous communities. Instead, the proportion of the rural population living in towns of fewer than 500 *vecinos* actually increased. Rural towns subsisting entirely on agriculture remained the norm, while towns such as Álcala, Guadalajara, and Bustar Viejo did not go on to develop as independent units with a variety of opportunities for employment for their townspeople.

Further evidence of the deterioration of everyday living conditions for the inhabitants in these towns over the century comes from the death rates of the *expósitos*. Occasionally, the sample taken for the months of June and December happened to list nurses only during the last fifty years, which allows for comparisons with living conditions during the early part of the century in some of these towns. In such cases, the mortality rate in the second half was much higher than the overall average for infants nursed in the rural towns. In Buitrago, of all those infants taken out after 1780, none lived more than six months. In Getafe after 1750, the mortality rate was 84 per cent for those under six months and none lived past a third birthday. Similarly Fuenlabrada had nine-tenths of its nurses recruited after 1780 and their infants were all dead by the age of three years.[28] It was a commonplace that the infant sent out to the country lived longer. More than 10 per cent of those taken by rural nurses lived to come back to the Inclusa at age seven, whereas only 6 per cent of those in urban homes did so. Nevertheless, the infants coming out to these towns at the end of the century were much less likely to survive than those in the first half. Worsening conditions in rural Castile must have been a major factor in the mortality rate of the *expósitos* of the Inclusa.

Finally, one of the most surprising conclusions to be extracted from the *salidas* is that so few rural nurses were coming to the Inclusa by 1799. There were almost twice as many women from the city as from the rural towns. We know that working wives were essential to the support of a family on the poverty line. How could there be growing numbers of destitute in the rural towns and at the same time fewer wives willing to take out an *expósito*?

I have already suggested the answer to this question in discussing the problem of the small landowner and the day-labourer or *jornalero*. As was true for their male counterparts, it was likely that the distinction between urban and rural nurses had become an artificial one. We are talking about the same women who had previously been living in rural towns and then moved in increasing numbers into the city. A study of

TABLE 3.2
Population of the city and province of Madrid, 1717–23 to 1797

Year	City	Province
1717–23	121,720 to 129,473 (Martorell)	38,000 (Ustariz)
	150,000 (Domínguez-Ortiz)	
1750	136,000 (Martorell)	58,195 (Ensenada)
1787	156,672 (Martorell)	58,943 (Floridablanca)
	180,000 (Domínguez-Ortiz)	
1797	167,607 (Martorell, Madoz)	60,193 (Godoy)
	187,607 (Domínguez-Ortiz)	
	200,000 (Ringrose)	

immigration patterns claims that there were relatively few women of child-bearing years in the countryside.[29] At the same time, demographic charts for the eighteenth century show a distinct bulge for women between ages sixteen and forty in the city. Though many of these women were domestic servants and probably celibate, still a certain proportion must have been married and able to nurse. A comparison of the census figures for 1787 and 1797 reveals that the numbers of both men and women between the ages of sixteen and forty were 45 per cent higher in Madrid than in the population of Spain in general. In other words, it is conceivable that 45 per cent of the population at this productive age were immigrants in the city. Soubeyroux, in a study of poverty in Madrid, has inquired into the origins of the vagrants and beggars collected from the streets in 1804 and enclosed in the hospice of San Fernando. He found that half of them came from nearby towns and 81 per cent from the two Castiles and Leon.[30] The urban wet-nurse of the Inclusa was often the rural wet-nurse absorbed into the *populacho* of Madrid.

It is impossible to know the exact extent of immigration into the city. Nevertheless, figures suggest that the population increased from around 115,000 or 150,000 at the beginning of the century to around 200,000 at the end. There was, however, no dramatic increase in numbers baptized in Madrid in the course of the century and nothing to suggest a decline in mortality. The Old Regime city was parasitical, depending for its expansion on immigration. Much of Madrid's growth in population must have come from the rural hinterland.

An examination of the figures on which demographers are forced to rely illustrates what can be known about the relationship between the city of Madrid and its surrounding countryside.[31]

If one accepts the growth rate of 0.43 per cent that has been put forward by Bustelo and Livi-Bacci,[32] then the figures in table 3.2 mean that the population increase of the province of Madrid at 0.56 per cent was above the national average. But most of that growth occurred in the first half of the century, and the increase in the last half was only 0.03 per cent per year. Figures vary widely but there is unanimous assent that the growth rate of the city was much faster after 1750, in direct contrast to the pattern for the province. The more conservative set of figures estimates that the annual growth rate was 0.11 per cent. Revisions suggested by Domínguez Ortiz and David Ringrose would put the rate at 0.25 per cent. Much of the population increase of the city of Madrid must have come from the rural towns of the neighbouring countryside. The expansion in the first half of the century had produced a population that the province could not support. This surplus then came to the city.

After this venture into the uncharted and murky waters of eighteenth-century demographic currents, it is a relief to turn to wading in the shallow but safe figures supplied by the *salidas*. Here we find that in the city in the second half of the century there were rapidly increasing numbers of unskilled *peones* (the urban counterparts of the *jornaleros* or rural day-labourers). These workers in both city and countryside were victims of the same phenomenon: the progressive proletarianization of the rural farmer – a process that agricultural conditions after 1750 served to accelerate. Immigration to the city was an important outlet for the dispossessed farmer of the countryside needing work, or for the day-labourer. There was a steady influx of unskilled workers, even though the cycle of inflation meant that they might be no better off than they had been on the farm. Records of the Inclusa verify that the pre-industrial city often failed to fulfil its promise of a better life for rural immigrants.

Taking the wet-nurse as an index of poverty, women married to urban workers were becoming poorer than their sisters in the countryside over the century. Taking the immigration patterns into account, we are dealing with the same women, but in a new urban setting, which failed to solve the problem of poverty in the Old Regime.

The *salidas* has provided a convincing account of rural deprivation. What happened to the rural poor was for the most part a function of Spain's economic problems. We have seen that wives of independent farmers were replaced as a source of wet-nurses by wives of rural day-labourers, who in turn gave way to wives of urban workers. Taking the wet-nurse as a criterion for poverty, it is obvious that the rural poor were either becoming better off, or moving into the city in desperation. What we cannot document directly is the impact that these changes were likely to have on the individual worker, his wife, and his family. Could the family keep intact in Madrid the traditional religious, moral, and social values that were associated with the small village? How many of these small farmers left the town of their birth because they could not cope with the social pressures of poverty? Contemporaries, both Spanish and foreign travellers, were appalled by the hordes of beggars to be found on the streets of Madrid. The concept of honour that animated the poorest Spaniard may have prevented the ultimate degradation of begging in a setting where the good name of his family was at stake. Poverty drove families to the city where, for a number of complex reasons, begging and opportunities for begging were available that did not exist in his village. Could the townsman who could not find work keep his self-respect when forced to beg himself or to send his wife and children into the streets to beg? How long before the contrast between the very rich and the very poor in Madrid eroded respect for political authority? How long could the charity dispensed by the church mitigate resentment at the wealth flaunted before the poor in the name of Christ's glory? How long before institutions like the Inclusa, and even the foundlings themselves, were to be seen as no more than part of a system to be taken advantage of by the poor as long as it was to their advantage?

The rural woman who came to Madrid from one of the small towns of Castile found herself and her family in a setting where the old ways and the old values were no longer able to provide support, and where the ability to adapt to new ways might provide the only route to survival for herself and her family.

We find that many *expósitos* came from families of the poor who could not find work at wages that could enable them to support another child. These foundlings were increasingly likely to be illegitimate as well. The poverty of an increasing number of *madrileños* could explain a change in the numbers of foundlings, both legitimate and illegitimate. It would be highly unrealistic to suppose that the same kind of social control that made a high standard of sexual behaviour the norm in rural towns could continue to operate in Madrid. How much control could the local parish exercise over young people that the curate was unable to identify let alone supervise? Moreover, marriage had an economic as well as a cultural and social function. If there was no economic advantage to marriage, then one of its supports vanished. How many unions among the poor were simply common-law arrangements between the rootless and derelict – unions that reflected the instability of

TABLE 3.3
Rural and urban addresses of
wet-nurses of the Inclusa, 1700–99

Year	Rural towns	Madrid
1700	43	11
1710	93	47
1720	34	24
1730	54	26
1740	46	48
1750	63	77
1760	50	86
1770	45	65
1780	69	71
1790	54	68
1799	28	52

SOURCE: *Salidas*, June, December,
1700–99

the situation of many of the poor? There was no place for their issue but the Inclusa.

Certainly, at the end of the century the Inclusa was providing a shelter for more and more infants of the poor. These infants had always come in much greater proportions from the urban poor. The rural family and rural society had provided an atmosphere where abandonment was rare for a number of reasons. The farmer who immigrated to Madrid to keep his family together may have found that the most the city offered was an institution where he could leave his infants. It had become an institution where it was probable that the infant left there would die there. Not only was there a shortage of rural women to take out foundlings, there were fewer nurses at all coming to the hospital. Wages had fallen behind inflation at the end of the century to the point where only the most deprived were attracted to the work, and even they were in short supply. Table 3.3 shows that urban wet-nurses began to play a larger role in the care of foundlings after 1740 and that at the end of the century the Inclusa was having difficulty in recruiting women from either sector.

The problem of the foundling hospital was part and parcel of a larger scene – the rural poverty of the eighteenth and early years of the nineteenth century. Rural wet-nurses, their foundlings, and their families can be seen from this same perspective. The Old Regime no longer provided a set of values and standards that enabled the rural poor to function in a traditional setting and in a traditional way. The problems of the rural wet-nurses of the Inclusa illustrate the social and cultural aspects of a collapse that has been described in economic terms in all the major studies of eighteenth-century Spain. But the problems of the rural poor are inseparable from problems in the city, and this brings us to the subject of urban poverty.

4

Urban Poverty and the Inclusa

Madrid was a magnet not only for poor from the surrounding country-side. It also attracted the needy and the adventuresome from as far away as France, Italy, and Ireland, but it could not provide jobs for all of them. Despite its importance as the capital of Spain, Madrid was never able to provide full employment for its population. Even though the eighteenth century was a period of economic expansion and relative prosperity, the economy of the pre-industrial city was not built on a solid base. The presence of the court attracted the nobility, those catering to them, and hordes of office seekers. There was a demand for luxury items, but these were usually imported from France. The government tried to establish textile industries without much success, and the bulk of the population, working at menial jobs in the tertiary sector, did not provide a market for consumer goods.[1] Nor was there a market in the rural hinterland. Nevertheless, the poor continued to come.

Madrid devoured people. Like most political centres, it was an artificial, almost theatrical construct where much of the population lived on hope, and the rest off the government and each other. Along with the courtiers, office seekers, and bureaucrats directly attached to the seat of power came an army of servants, cooks, dancing masters, tailors, shoe-makers, wig makers, coachmen, musicians, and actors. In the background, sponging off these relatively productive groups, were the more colourful element: criminals, beggars, and gipsies. Finally, this population was augmented by the poor unable to eke out a living from the countryside and hoping for better things from the city and court of Madrid. Prominent among these were widows, and deserted wives whose husbands had given up the struggle of trying to provide for a family, and their unfortunate children.[2]

On the streets of the capital of the Catholic king slouched, hobbled, and squatted Spaniards who were a constant reminder to the pious and upright that the progress and promise of a 'New Spain' was still far from a reality. They were a living reproof to intellectuals and reformers and a challenge to their faith in the potential of Spain. No wonder the government periodically attempted to round up these ragtaggle ends of society and hide them away in institutions. Illustrations of the period show how the poor dominated the scene in public places: lying in wait for the faithful after mass, importuning shoppers as they left with their parcels, wheedling the servant girl or housewife at the market, and trailing the conspicuous foreign visitor.[3]

The poor seen begging on the streets of Madrid were only the most flagrant examples of the problem of urban poverty. According to Hamilton, 'repeated complaints by shrewd observers in the second half of the century show that workers were utterly unable to live on their money incomes.'[4] During the period 1751–1800 there was a rise of almost 100 per cent in commodity prices and more than double that for food prices, while wages rose only 20 per cent. This meant a loss of four-tenths of real income for the Madrid worker. And we saw from the *gastos* that there were others even worse off than that. These workers were not the most dramatic and conspicuous element of the populace of Madrid. They did not usually go begging. Though they may have lived in an environment of petty thievery, they were not criminals. As long as good health, good luck, and good weather favoured them, they remained solvent. But so close were they to the edge that any accident of fortune – an extra mouth to feed, a prolonged illness, old age, the loss of one of the partners in a household that depended on two incomes – in short, any one of a thousand factors, could push them over that fine line that separated honest poverty from outright indigence. This was the company from which the wet-nurses of the Inclusa were recruited.

In this chapter we see the wet-nurse of the Inclusa – a woman of the urban working poor – using all the resources at her disposal, including the institution, to keep her family intact despite the adverse economic conditions at the end of the century.

The *salidas* provide a record of who these women were, based on where they lived and what their husbands did for a living. We can even hazard a guess as to the relative degree of their deprivation from the information on how long the *expósito* was likely to live. These details give a picture of the life and work of a wife of the urban poor in eighteenth-century Madrid.

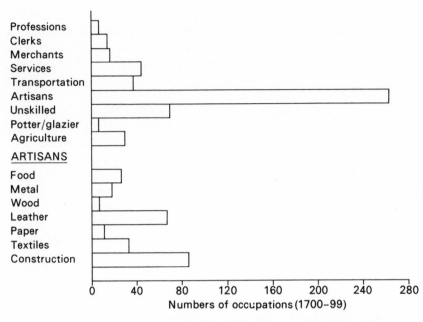

FIGURE 4.1 Occupations of husbands of urban wet-nurses, 1700–99

We can go further to form some impression of the personality of the woman who became a wet-nurse of the Inclusa. From the experience of the hospital administrators there is evidence that this group of women had become increasingly volatile at the end of the century. The fiery, passionate temperament we associate with the *maja* was a characteristic shared by the more pedestrian wives and mothers taking out infants from the Inclusa as a means of supporting their families. Because the wet-nurses of the Inclusa were in many ways typical of the working women of the lower classes of Madrid, a case can be made for the progressive radicalization of this segment of the population under the pressure of events. Although it would be an anachronism to use the term 'feminists' to describe the wet-nurses of the Inclusa, they evidently were, nevertheless, women who called forth respect tinged with fear from the male-dominated power structure.

The *salidas* list ninety-nine occupations for the husbands of the wet-nurses (see fig. 4.1 for a selection). The elite among them, usually working and therefore able to make ends meet, were the skilled craftsmen or artisans. Carpenters, tailors, harness makers, blacksmiths, bakers, tanners, shoe-makers, and masons were guild members and had a settled locale of work. However, the presence of masons and shoe-makers in the *salidas* in growing numbers indicates that even they found times difficult. Their apprentices and journeymen, though a rung lower in status, pay, and security, were privileged to live with the master, eat at the same table, and may even have slept in the same room. But the largest proportion were simply labourers in these various crafts – the workers who hauled the bricks and did the menial tasks associated with the various skills of the craftsmen. A second set found work as servants, lackeys, coachmen, or stewards in the household of the king or some noble or well-off bourgeois. Though poorly paid, they had the security of knowing that as long as the master was eating, so were they. Another group was in the enviable position of being able to supplement its low salaries with tips and bribes: an army of clerks and minor officials (such as mailmen and tax-collectors) of various types who found work in the bureaucracy of the court. Lacking these advantages were the pedlars of all sorts: water sellers; oil vendors; hawkers of fruits, vegetables, and drinks; chocolate grinders; mat makers; and those marketing combs, ribbons, and birds. The *salidas* list twelve different kinds of street vendor. At the bottom of this category came the rag-pickers and old-clothes dealers, who were often no more than fences for stolen goods. Then there were those who depended completely on their physical strength: these were street porters who waited at the customs-house for bales to deliver on their backs, or were employed as coalmen, or tile and bricklayers, to transport heavy loads into houses or up stairs where a donkey could not manoeuvre. Finally, at the lowest end of the scale by any standards, came the unskilled *peón* or odd-job man. He did what he could when he could. Often he was listed as a *peón de albañil*, or helper in the building trades, or as a *peón de la villa*, which meant a garbage collector or street sweeper. In any case, he was just one step above the mule with all of the prestige that went with that position. The urban unskilled were usually listed in the *salidas* as either *mozo* or *peón* and made up 8.9 per cent of husbands' occupations listed by wet-nurses. Another 9.3 per cent were masons who were often merely unskilled hod-carriers.

We know little about the working poor and women of the working poor in particular; therefore, the information provided by the *salidas* sheds light on this dark corner where these women and their children eked out an existence. The occupations of husbands most commonly listed by the wet-nurses of the city of Madrid are shown in table 4.1.

TABLE 4.1
Principal occupations of husbands of
wet-nurses in Madrid, 1700–99

Occupation	Percentage
Mason	16.8
Unskilled	13.1
Halter/shoe-maker	12.2
Coachman-muleteer	7.2
Baker	4.8
Soldier	3.9
Textile worker	3.5
Blacksmith	3.1
Tailor	2.8
Barber/wigmaker	2.2
Bookbinder/seller	2.0
Agricultural day-labourer	1.8
Other	25.0

SOURCE: *Salidas*, June, December, 1700–99

Other occupations included some not ordinarily associated with the poorest strata of society, such as clerks, customs officials, teachers, surgeons, and even a few shopkeepers and innkeepers. Others one might expect to find are rarely listed. Servants, who made up the single largest group of workers in Madrid, represented fewer than 1 per cent of the wet-nurses' husbands. Domestics were, however, notoriously celibate, if sexually active. Eighteenth-century literature is replete with examples of the buxom servant being pursued by her amorous employer, while carrying on her own intrigues with the menservants. They were more likely to be sending infants to the Inclusa than taking them out.[5] Another occupation rarely listed in the *salidas* is that of street porter. They were usually immigrants from Galicia or the Auvergne who came for short periods and then returned home with their savings.[6] Beggars are mentioned only indirectly. The blind musicians were closest to the classification, but many of the widows who took out infants may also have had to beg for a livelihood. Since only one nurse formally listed her husband's occupation as *pobre y manco*, it is impossible to know how many supplemented the family income with begging as well as wet-nursing.

Baker, street vendor, blacksmith, and servant were all occupations whose numbers varied very little over the century. Soldier had an eccentric pattern that reflected the political rather than the economic

TABLE 4.2

Patterns of occupations of husbands listed by urban wet-nurses

Occupation	Urban totals	1700–49	1750–99
Masons	99	32	67
Shoe-makers	90	31	59
Coachmen	45	9	36
Unskilled	78	5	73

SOURCE: *Salidas,* June, December, 1700–99

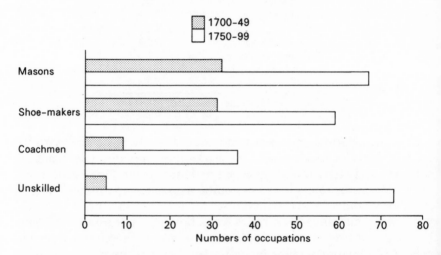

FIGURE 4.2 Changes in proportions of occupations, 1700–49 and 1750–99

situation; 37.5 per cent of all the soldiers listed could be found in 1740, the year of the War of the Austrian Succession. The last decade of the century also saw their numbers increase. Some occupations, such as teacher, surgeon, and sacristan, were listed only rarely after 1750, while textile workers, clerks, constables, and customs officials can all be found in much greater numbers after that date. Barbers and wig makers were not listed at all in the first fifty years of the sample. Numbers of bookbinders and stone cutters peaked in the year 1780. But the most remarkable expansion occurred among the four groups sending the largest number of wet-nurses to the Inclusa: masons, shoe-maker/ halter makers, coachmen, and unskilled (see fig. 4.2). True, there were increasing numbers of infants involved. Yet, even though the numbers of infants almost doubled, the increase of numbers in these four occupations was even more striking. Moreover, the pattern of the increase that took place after 1750 was similar. In the second half of the century, masons and shoe-makers doubled, coachmen quadrupled, but the most dramatic rise was in the ranks of the unskilled. The sample listed only five between 1700 and 1740 and seventy-three between 1750 and 1799 (see table 4.2).

The presence of large numbers of unskilled in the work-force of Madrid can be explained by the attraction of the city for the poor of the rural hinterland. Their predominance among the husbands of the wet-nurses of the Inclusa was a symptom of the rising cost of living. Inflation was hardest on the wage-earning class of the working poor and the poorest of that group suffered most: the unskilled. The *gastos* record that there were some categories of odd-job men, such as porters and the labourers called in to put down the matting and awnings in the fall and take them up in the spring, whose wages did not change at all in the course of the century. Poverty in Madrid and poverty in the rural areas were closely connected, as the records of the Inclusa make abundantly clear.

Wives played an important role in the economy of the working poor. It is unlikely that such women suffered from the sense of inferiority that may have afflicted their pampered sisters in other sectors of Spanish society. Their wages were lower than anything their husbands could bring in, but in families that depended on the salaries of two people, women did not lack a sense of self-worth. If the characters in the *sainetes* of Ramón de la Cruz can be taken as prototypes, women of this lower classes were more than a match for their aggressive and colourful male counterparts. *Sainetes* were popular entre-act short pieces set on the very streets of Madrid on which lived many of the wet-nurses of the Inclusa. Though the women in his cast usually had more glamorous occupations than that of a wet-nurse (often flower sellers, lime vendors, or hawkers of drinks or trinkets), details of everyday life in the *barrio* of Lavapies of Rastro or the Puerta del Sol depicted in these skits help fill in the background on the neighbourhood of the wet-nurses. Women of the same class may have lived in this way before marriage and infants turned them into more prosaic and more representative residents of Lavapies, Mayor, or Maravillas.[7]

The occupation of wet-nurse was typical of the kind of work done by wives of the working poor. It could be done at the same time and in addition to caring for a family, and probably in conjunction with a series of other part-time jobs that served as a means of keeping the family together. It was just one of many tasks the woman performed in what Louise Tilly has referred to as 'the strategy of the family.'[8] She took care of the goat or chicken or vegetable patch on which even urban families depended. Along with sewing and knitting, she wove her own cloth. Textiles were still a domestic effort except for the royal factories. If her husband was an artisan or vendor, she helped him. All this could be done while nursing an infant from the Inclusa.

Unmarried women had fewer alternatives, aside from domestic service; but the most disadvantaged of all were the widows, especially those with small children. There were large numbers of them and their resources were few. In the province of Madrid they outnumbered widowers by five to three.[9] Almost 7 per cent of the wet-nurses of the Inclusa were widows and there seem to have been cases where they were given charge of even new-born infants.

These widows had already crossed the barrier between poverty and destitution. So had the woman who listed her husband's occupational status as 'poor and one-armed,' for this meant he qualified as *pobre de solemnidad*, one who was obviously unable to work and therefore could beg with impunity.[10] It is possible that some of these occupations listed by the nurses were merely nominal because the husband was unemployed or able to find work only part of the year or part of the time. Obviously, for some of these families, the pittance paid by the Inclusa, and any other income the wife could scrounge, enabled them barely to survive.

The wife in a family of the poor might find much variety but little choice; similarly the administrators had few options open in their choice of nurses. The women who offered their services as wet-nurses were from the very poor. The pay was low and women not already suffering from the physical, moral, and temperamental difficulties sometimes accompanying poverty could have found better-paying situations working for individuals rather than for the institution. At the wages offered, the administration could not be selective, and as a result the wet-nurses only too often justified the low opinion in which the profession was held. The curate acted as a formal liaison and the nurse left with a printed statement and a layette for the infant, but the form was merely part of the accounting system to keep track of her pay. The Inclusa could have profited from a *bureau de recommandresses* such as the one that screened wet-nurses in Paris after 1715.[11] When the Junta de damas took over the Inclusa in 1799, attempts were made to tighten up procedures. Certificates were required from the *alcalde de barrio* or from the justice of the town, and one of the nuns was responsible for examining the nurses' milk, but even these measures failed to protect the infants from bad nurses. These were mothers who were either desperate, or at the very least willing to deprive their own infants of milk for money. This meant taking the chance of passing on to their families syphilis or any number of infections that the *inclusero* was subject to. Not that the risk of infection was one-sided. The doctor of the Inclusa hinted darkly that the reason many infants left the hospital in a healthy state and were brought back close to death was because 'they were taken out not to care for them, but to relieve breasts they fear giving to their infants, or to bring back milk again, or for other sinister reasons.'[12] The latter probably refers to the practice, supposedly common among beggars, of renting out one or two of the more weak and crippled infants to pass off as their own in order to play on the sympathies of donors.

The institution was vulnerable and wet-nurses had a store of tricks at their disposal. In a number of cases the clerk refused to pay a nurse who was unable to return the child's clothing after its death. Presumably it had been sold for what little value it had. But there were many instances where the hospital had either no way to prove its suspicions or no recourse. It was generally believed that there were wet-nurses who dropped off their own child or paid the midwife to bring it to the Inclusa, and then arrived to claim it themselves and collect a salary for nursing their own infant. A variation of this routine was to make a private arrangement with the wet-nurse who took out the child, and then claim it again after it had been nursed at the Inclusa's expense. Some nursing mothers, more forthright in their approach, offered to nurse infants in the hospital, but brought along their own and sometimes older children as well, depending upon how desperate the hospital was for their services.[13]

The most common means of defrauding the institution was the simplest. Some of these women were in fact incapable of nursing an *expósito*. Undernourished, either they had no milk at all, or the most that they could do was to keep their own baby fed, let alone take on another. Then there were cases of the same woman taking out as many as three. Those infants were given animal milk or gruel, sometimes too strong for the digestion of a new-born, often in containers that had been carelessly cleaned out, with a grotty residue left at the bottom. Not surprisingly, one of the principal causes of death was diarrhoetic complaints.[14] Even with the best of nurses, when the *expósito* shared the breast with the nurse's own child there was sure to be some discrimination.[15] Which was the worse decision – to deprive her own infant or to deprive the foundling? The wet-nurse was charged on both counts.

Another form of rivalry threatening the well-being of the *expósito* was the number of time-consuming tasks that occupied the attention of the wife of the working poor. The country woman who left the child swaddled to a board and suspended from a hook on the wall while she attended to these was notorious. The high death rate for infants in August and September could be attributed in part to accidents occurring while the woman neglected the infant for the harvest. Tenon, the French surgeon, spoke with authority about the risks for the child left alone in a cradle on the floor of a country cottage:

While the women attend to the vineyards, the infant remains alone, crying and hungry in putrid diapers. Often the child cries so hard it ends up with a hernia. I have found many cases of this in very tiny infants ... Sometimes the doors are left open, and geese and chickens wander in and out ... If turkeys get at a crib they can peck out the eyes of a child, or injure other organs ... Children have been known to fall into a fire, or to drown in pails or washbuckets left carelessly on doorsteps. Still others have gone too close to pigs and had their hands and fists chewed.[16]

How many deaths were due to neglect by the wet-nurse will never be established. Even when a death certificate was required, it did not necessarily specify the cause of death. But careless and overworked nurses were certainly at fault in many instances.

Nor was it only the country woman who failed in this respect. In 1804 a criminal procedure initiated against Barbara Olivera, laundress, a widow of thirty years 'more or less,' illustrates the way the Inclusa failed to protect the infants from unfit nurses.[17] The washerwoman was accused of having left three children, aged two, three, and four years, tied up in an attic garret or the *guardillas* of 29 calle de Magdalena while she took clothes down to the river to wash. The testimony brought by neighbours indicated that her treatment of the children was both inhumane and cruel. Kept 'ragged and bare, sickly and starved,' they lived in terror of their nurse, who handed out blows and vituperation freely when they wandered off or dirtied themselves 'as children tend to do.'[18]

Martina Domínguez, the wife of a mason's apprentice who lived in the basement of the same dwelling, had taken to giving the children a few crusts of bread when she saw them. Indignant at their treatment, she tried to bring their plight to the attention of the countess of Llerena, one of the administrators of the Inclusa, but was put off by the lady's maidservants. She next took her concern to the *alcalde* or constable. When he refused to do anything, she returned to the charge with five neighbours. Shamed into action, the *alcalde* summoned a locksmith who broke down the door. There they found two of the children tied up by the shoulders and wrists with ragged ends of sheets; one of them face down on the floor, the other on his side, and the two-year-old sitting on a pile of straw in the middle of the room. Immediately a cry went out for the nurse, who was hauled back from the river and subsequently taken off for trial.

At the hearing a doctor testified that although the actual tying up had not injured them, the children were close to 'dropsy' from the effects of malnutrition, and that weaknesses in the shoulders and other parts of the children's bodies could be attributed to the squalid conditions in which they lived. In her defence, the laundress claimed that she had tied them up only to protect them from injuring themselves while she was away for a short period. But even this argument shows how desperately hungry those children must have been. They were tied up because on a previous occasion 'they had tried to eat some silk stockings that had been left in a pan of soapy water.' Admitting that the children were weak and frail, she insisted that this had been their condition when they left the Inclusa. And in all fairness it must be granted that *incluseros* were bad risks even before nurses like Barbara Olivera took them.

What emerges from this testimony is that despite the fact that the condition of the infants was a local scandal, it was only the most extraordinary perseverance on the part of a neighbourhood 'busybody' that caused the authorities to intervene at all. One wonders how many similar cases are recorded only in the mortality figures of the Inclusa.

While there is some reason to sympathize with a poor widow earning a living as a laundress and taking care of three children at the same time, there is no doubt that she was guilty of criminal negligence. She was sentenced to four years, subsequently reduced by ten months when she voluntarily returned to jail after having been 'liberated' by the mob during the rising of St Joseph in March 1808.[19]

The countess of Montijo, reviewing the incident, admitted that such episodes occurred only too frequently. She hoped a stern warning from the government that certification was a matter of serious responsibility, not to be granted casually in return for a tip, and that the publicity given to the case of Barbara Olivera might help to remedy the abuses. Obviously it was possible to get a character reference by bribing officials. However, the real source of the problem remained what it had been throughout the eighteenth century: 'The growing numbers of infants has meant a shortage of women to take them out, and the pay is so low that only nurses who are poor and incredibly ignorant are willing to do so.'[20]

The wet-nurse was certainly poor, probably unhealthy, and usually overburdened with the extra tasks required to keep a poor household operative in eighteenth-century Spain. Probably she had more than one infant to take care of and was likely to suffer the character deformation associated with living on the edge of indigence, that is a willingness to cheat the Inclusa and a lack of sensitivity toward her charge. Although there were occasions when the wet-nurse grew to love the child, and asked to be able to keep it and raise it as part of her own family 'for devotion,' in the vast majority of cases the child was returned with alacrity once she was no longer paid for its support. Around 2 per cent were adopted by their nurse; the rest were either exchanged once weaned for a new nursling because the pay was higher, or brought back after seven or eight years when the term was up. Unfortunately, only too often the wet-nurse lived up to a reputation for carelessness, callousness, and cupidity.

Generalizations about the character, personality, and morals of the wet-nurse can only be impressionistic. Except for the case of Barbara Olivera, most of our information on these highly subjective matters comes from the doctors and administrators of the hospital. The doctor had an extremely idealistic version of what a wet-nurse should be. The classic set of qualities – 'brunette, good teeth, good disposition, firm breasts, age slightly younger than that of the mother etc.' – were taken word for word from the medical treatises of the period and guaranteed that the doctor would be disappointed in any real woman who came to the hospital.[21] Nor were administrators, who saw the wet-nurse as a problem in staffing, in a position to be objective. They may well have labelled all their nurses with the characteristics of the most memorable examples. For less-biased data, we can turn to the records of the *salidas*, which give (as part of the accounts of their pay) the addresses of the wet-nurses, and enable us to look at the urban poor from another perspective – the neighbourhoods in which they lived.

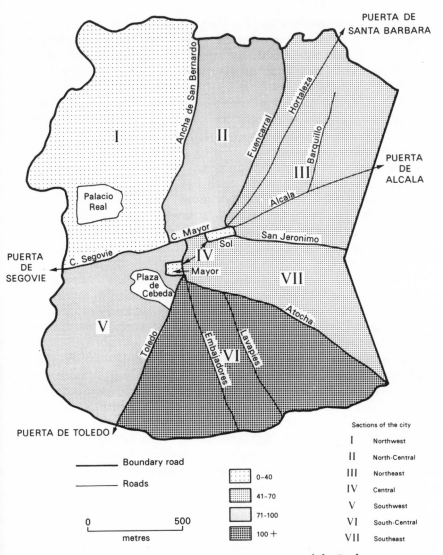

FIGURE 4.3 Addresses of urban wet-nurses of the Inclusa

Some of these streets housed their inhabitants in such wretched conditions that the *expósito* had almost no hope for surviving the environment. Moreover, as a further proof that the situation of the poor was deteriorating, before 1750 most nurses were concentrated in streets

to the south and centre; after 1750 they could be found in any area of the
city. The streets where the wet-nurses lived were the streets of the very
poor, and the records enable us to see who lived in some of these
neighbourhoods, and to draw up a veritable 'poverty map' of Madrid (see
fig. 4.3).

The *salidas* list addresses from 210 streets in Madrid (see table 4.3).
Madrid in the eighteenth century consisted of about 650 narrow,
twisting, and badly paved streets that could sometimes be steep and
even precipitous. In many cases, stairways of stone steps led from one
narrow alley to another so that many streets had a double appellation of
alto and *bajo* to distinguish the parts. In the crowded areas of the older
section, streets suddenly twisted to merge into miniscule squares and
plazas. This feature of the *morería* or Jewish quarter had enabled its
inhabitants to fend off periodic assaults by their persecutors in preced-
ing centuries. In this bewildering quarter, street names changed from
one turn to another, and the popularity of saints such as Joseph (four),
Michael, Mary Magdalen, and Catherine (three each), as well as the
various forms and embellishments of the name of Jesus, Mary, and the
Cross, make for a degree of confusion that could never be tolerated in a
modern city. Despite this difficulty, it is possible to delineate in broad
terms those areas that sent large numbers of wet-nurses to the Inclusa.

For administrative purposes, the city was divided into eight quarters
and these were subdivided into eight *barrios*, each with a unique flavour
and personality. For the most part, the districts were identified with one
of the thirteen parishes. These differed radically in size, from the tiny,
crowded jurisdictions of Santiago, San Salvador, San Nicolás, and San
Pedro in the area around the Plaza Mayor, to the sprawling parishes of
San Ginés and San Martín, which took up almost half of the city to the
north and northeast. For this discussion, the city has been divided
roughly in half, with three sectors to the north, three to the south, and
one small area in the centre around the Puerta del Sol and Plaza Mayor
(fig. 4.3).

Listed below are the parishes situated in each sector, and noted in
parentheses is the administrative designation given in 1768 to the eight
quarters of the city that roughly approximate the geographic divisions as
outlined.[22]

1 Northwest: City limits to Ancha de Convalescientes de San Bernardo; parishes
of San Martín, San Juan y San Gil, Santiago (Afligidos)

II North-centre: Calle de Convalescientes de San Bernardo to calle de Fuencarral; parishes of San Martín, San Ginés (Maravillas)
III Northeast: North of San Jerónimo, east of Fuencarral to city limits; parish of San Ginés (Barquillo)
IV Central: Area of Puerta del Sol and Plaza Mayor; parishes of San Ginés, San Miguel, Santa Cruz (Plaza Mayor)
V Southwest: South of calle de Segovia and Plaza Mayor to calle de Toledo; parishes of San Andrés, El Salvador, San Nicolás, Santa María Almudena (Palacio and San Francisco). The ancient section of blind alleys and one-way streets known popularly as the *morería* is in the section of San Francisco.
VI South-centre: Calle de Toledo to calle de Atocha; parishes: Santa Cruz, San Justo y Pastor, San Sebastian, San Pedro (Lavapies)
VII Southeast: Calle de Atocha to San Jerónimo; parish San Sebastian (San Jerónimo)

Streets that gave the *expósito* the least chance for survival were Jacometrezo (IV), Pelegrinos (IV), and Norte (I). No infant assigned to a nurse living on those streets lived longer than six months. Other streets with a high mortality were Rodas (VI), la Paloma (V), San Bernabe (V) Embajadores (VI), Calatrava (VI), Cruz (VII), Maravillas (II), and San Pedro Maravillas (II), where no child survived as long as two years. Three-quarters of these streets of high mortality were in the south and southwest.

Looking over the addresses listed by wet-nurses, one is struck by the ubiquitous nature of the poor. Nevertheless, there are some areas of higher concentration than others. A line drawn along the calle Mayor to the Puerta del Sol and then continuing east along Álcala divides the city almost exactly in half. To the south of this lived approximately 60 per cent of the wet-nurses of the Inclusa and almost one-third of this group came from the sector around the Ancha de Lavapies (section VI in fig. 4.3). This part of Madrid is familiar to the modern tourist as the location of the Rastro, or Sunday-morning flea market. It is the setting of many of the *sainetes* or entre-act skits of Ramón de la Cruz. The life on these streets was colourful to say the least. It was very well known to the justice officials of the period because the street names occur regularly in many depositions of the time, usually in connection with squabbles between neighbours, or tavern brawls.[23] In this *barrio* could be found the largest number of streets named for the occupation of their householders. There were streets belonging to tanners, halter makers,

TABLE 4.3
Addresses of nurses taking out infants of the Inclusa

Streets	Absolute frequency	Per cent	Streets	Absolute frequency	Per cent
Section I			La Ballesta	1	0.2
north and west			Barca	4	0.8
Ancha de Conv. de			Turco	1	0.2
San Bernardo	8	1.5			
Almirante	2	0.4	Total	89	17.1
Beatas	1	0.2	*Section III*		
Leganitos	3	0.6	*north and east*		
Limón (alta)	1	0.2	Agostinos Recoletos	1	0.2
Norte	4	0.8	Barquillo	3	0.6
Palma	4	0.8	Bélen	2	0.4
San Dismas	1	0.2	Clavel	1	0.2
Santo Domingo	4	0.8	Cabellero de Gracia	2	0.4
San Marco	2	0.4	D. de Alba	1	0.2
San Vicente	7	1.3	Florida	3	0.6
			Hortaleza	4	0.8
Total	38	7.2	Infantas	1	0.2
			Jardines	1	0.2
Section II			Plaza de Armas	2	0.4
north and central (Maravillas)			Requeros	5	1.0
Buenavista	6	1.1	Reynas	1	0.2
Conchas	1	0.2	San Antón	17	3.3
Cruz Verde	8	1.5	San Joseph	1	0.2
Desengaño	1	0.2	Santa Maria del Arco	2	0.4
Escorial	1	0.2	San Juan	1	0.2
Estrella	2	0.4			
Espíritu Sancto	1	0.2	Total	52	10.3
Fuencarral	3	0.6			
Jesus del Valle	7	1.3	*Section IV*		
Minas Altas	1	0.2	*central*		
Panaderos	5	1.0	Capellanes	1	0.2
Pez	4	0.8	Carmen	1	0.2
Posas	2	0.4	Conchas	1	0.2
Maravillas	8	1.5	Espejo	2	0.4
Rubios	3	0.6	Fuente	2	0.4
Tudescos	5	1.0	Herradores	1	0.2
Santa Barbara	1	0.2	Negras	2	0.4
San Damaso	1	0.2	Pelegrinos	4	0.8
San Ildefonso	3	0.6	Plaza Mayor	2	0.4
San Gregorio	3	0.6	Santiago	3	0.6
San Miguel	2	0.4	San Ginés	1	0.2
San Pablo	1	0.2	San Luis	4	0.8
Santa Veronica	1	0.2	San Martín	1	0.2
Tesoro	8	1.5	Jacometrezo	6	1.1
Silva	1	0.2	Zarza	1	0.2
Valverde	1	0.2			
Leones	1	0.4	Total	32	6.3

TABLE 4.3 (Concluded)

Streets	Absolute frequency	Per cent	Streets	Absolute frequency	Per cent
Section v *southwest (Moreria)*			Cobos	3	0.6
			Comadre	25	4.8
Aguas	1	0.2	Curtidores	1	0.2
Aguila	5	1.0	Cayetano	2	0.4
Almendro	1	0.2	Compañía	3	0.6
Calatrava	5	1.0	Carnero	2	0.4
Cava Baja	2	0.4	Embajadores	8	1.5
Cuchilleros	1	0.2	Espino	1	0.2
Conde de Barajas	1	0.2	Dos Hermanas	1	0.2
Estudios	2	0.4	Fé	1	0.2
Escalerita de Piedra	1	0.2	Imperial	1	0.2
Moreria	11	2.1	Jesus y María	12	2.3
Orna de Amato	1	0.2	Juanello	1	0.2
Paloma	17	3.3	Magdalena	4	0.8
San Bernarbe	3	0.6	Mesón de Paredes	6	1.1
Santa Isidra	3	0.6	Ministrales	2	0.4
San Francisco	3	0.6	Olivar	9	1.7
Toledo	7	1.3	Olmo	1	0.2
			Osso	3	0.6
Total	64	12.5	San Cosme y Damian	3	0.6
			San Lorenzo	4	0.8
Section vi *south-central (Lavapies)*			San Pedro	10	1.9
			Santa Ana	1	0.2
Abades	3	0.6	Santa Isabel	7	1.3
Arganzuela	9	1.7	Rodas	6	1.1
Ave Maria	5	1.0	Tenerias	2	0.4
Ancha de Lavapies	11	2.1	Torecilla Leal	2	0.4
Barrio Nueva	1	0.2	Zurita	4	0.8
Bastara del Rey	4	0.8	Rastro	4	0.8
Buenavista	6	1.1			
Cabestreros	6	1.1	Total	174	33.9

sail makers, and hat makers, as well as one named after the patron of surgeons, San Cosme y Damian. Here as well was the single street with the largest contingent of wet-nurses in the city – the calle de Comadre, or the street of the midwife. We can take this street as representative of the neighbourhood of the wet-nurse of the Inclusa.

The calle de Comadre provides a cross-section of the working poor and makes it possible to reconstruct some details of the life of the time. On the calle de Comadre lived wet-nurses whose husbands represented thirteen different occupations in the pages of the *salidas*. There was one surgeon, one constable, one royal servant, one textile worker, one tailor, and one porter. The tone of the street was set by eleven leather workers: six of them halter makers, four shoe-makers, and one tanner. Representing the least prestigious group of workers were three masons and two unskilled *peones*, and a blind musician – a euphemism for a beggar. Finally, it was the address of one goatherd and one field hand. It would be interesting to know if these men travelled to the country to work, or if they actually tended goats in the vacant lots and backyards of the calle de Comadre.

The calle de Comadre illustrates the close ties that the Inclusa had with the poor of Madrid. The area of Lavapies was one of the poorest sectors of the city. Children who attended the *escuelas pías*, or free schools, of the *barrio* sometimes had to be provided with clothing and shoes to come to classes.[24] But the families who lived on these streets were by and large artisans; only a few were day-labourers and beggars. They were the prototype of the poor we have been describing – families just managing to scrape along with the help of every means at their disposal, one of these being an *expósito* from the Inclusa.

Women of the *barrio* of Lavapies have projected an image that has lived on not only in the literature of the period and its folklore, but also in its political history. In March 1766, it was women and children leading the procession of Palm Sunday who deflected the route to the royal palace where thirty to forty demonstrators, many of them women, were shot by the Walloons. In other words, it was women who were responsible for turning the religious occasion into the political one that has become known as the Rising of Esquilache. The unrest that had simmered during a series of years of high grain prices erupted when the Italian minister of the king, Squillache, instituted measures forbidding the long black cape and slouch-brimmed, three-cornered hat that had been the traditional garb of the Madrid male, but that effectively disguised malefactors. In the wake of the ensuing disorder, the king and his family fled the capital, and during the following weeks women sang their defiance to the *tambour de basque* in the working quarters of the city, sometimes carrying their voices to the seat of power. On one occasion, a shaken count de Aranda could count fifty *majas* under his windows.[25] The *majas* that figured in the *sainetes* of Ramón de la Cruz as colourful exemplars of the lower classes – the flamboyant and temperamental orange sellers, flower or chestnut vendors, or women engaged in some similar occupation where their attractiveness was an asset – could also provide a serious threat to the stability of the Old Regime.

Moreover, these women were taken seriously. One condition made by the chastened king before conceding to return to Madrid after the events of Easter 1766 was to enjoin on the *Consejo* a plan to cool down anger in neighbourhoods with a high concentration of the poor. As part of urban renewal, the plan was projected to dilute the choleric temperament associated with the lower classes by an injection of some of the phlegmatic humour of the bourgeois citizen who was more likely to have a stake in the status quo. Lavapies, Barquillo, and the Rastro were the principal areas of attention for the authorities, though the project never passed the planning stage.[26] Obviously women of the areas with a high proportion of wet-nurses were a volatile force in a potentially explosive situation. To confirm the suspicion that the authorities were in some trepidation over the women of this *barrio*, we find that in July 1771 there was a report from Benito Barreda, *alcalde de casa y corte* and member of the royal council, ordering no more than four women at a time to congregate together at the fountains, streets, and doorways of houses in the *barrio* of Lavapies.[27]

Are we justified in reading into this that the wet-nurses of the Inclusa were women of fire and passion? After all, these women were not 'Carmen,' but married and burdened with responsibilities. Even the *sainete* of de la Cruz set on the calle de Comadre featured as protagonists more engaging occupations than that of wet-nurse. In answer, we do have some further testimony to the spirit and personality of the wet-nurse, and to the respect that the establishment held for her. The *alcalde* was on the salary roll of the hospital, and was present on all the ceremonial occasions such as the Feast Day, Holy Week processions, and the pay-days of Pentecost and Nativity. His function was to see that the streets were cleared for the processions and to lend official approval to any public gathering. Does it not seem extraordinary to call in a constable for the days that women came in with their infants in their arms to collect their pay as wet-nurses? The administrators did not seem to think so. Nor were they above exploiting this potentially volatile situation to extract funds from a reluctant government.

I have discussed elsewhere the financial problems of the hospital. By the end of the eighteenth century there was a bienniel crisis as the institution struggled to provide enough funds for the growing numbers of infants in its charge. In 1797 the treasury held 25,000 reales and the nurses were expecting wages coming to 130,000 reales on the Feast of Pentecost. The administrator, treasurer, and chaplain joined forces to impress on Joaquín de Murcia of the royal council the seriousness of the situation. If the wet-nurses from the towns are not paid, they wrote, 'there will be the greatest uproar this hospital has ever witnessed, and just the thought of what this could mean is enough to alarm us greatly.'[28] In 1801 the situation was no better. The countess de Trullás solicited aid, claiming that 'daily, forty to fifty women will be coming, accompanied by their husbands and nurslings, looking for their pay for the previous four months ... If this cannot be provided, two serious incidents will follow: first, there will be a public disturbance made by these disappointed women, and secondly, they will go off and leave the infants with us.'[29]

Obviously, the wet-nurses of the Inclusa did not acquiesce quietly to disappointment. These women possessed one characteristic that set them aside from the indigent and those whom poverty had completely devastated. Unhealthy, ill fed, immoral in the sense that they were willing to use all the means at their disposal (including the foundling and the hospital) to float themselves and their families on the waves of inflation that constantly threatened to cast them up on the shores of destitution, these wives of the working poor were women of spirit. They were women whose wits had been sharpened by the challenges involved in keeping a family of the poor together. Both the hospital and the government were wary of the anger these women could sometimes vent on the heads of the powerful.

The state in the Old Regime was a complex set of institutions aimed at keeping order. There were prisons for the dangerous and criminal, hospices for the beggars and vagrants, the Inclusa for unwanted infants. For instance, a woman who had been unfaithful to her husband could be committed to a special prison for as long as he deemed fit.[30] In the pursuit of an ideal of absolute control, the government provided places for those who could not or would not provide for themselves in a manner acceptable to the community. The Inclusa of Madrid was just one of a number of welfare organizations whose purposes were charitable in origin but who incidentally worked to shore up the stability of the Old Regime.

But not only did the Inclusa provide a form of temporary relief for the poor by taking children off their hands, it also provided a form of income for the wife in a working family. The wet-nurse of the Inclusa was a woman who knew only too well the fear that she might have to abandon her infant, but at least for the moment, she was working to keep her own family together, sometimes at the expense of the Inclusa, sometimes at the expense of the foundling.

As the century went on, it became more difficult for the government of the Old Regime to subdue individuals who were protesting against the difficulties of providing a living wage for themselves and their families. The events of the 1760s were political, but they were also an expression of the frustration and anger of the families of the poor in Madrid. At the end of the century these problems worsened. The *salidas* show growing numbers of poor having more difficulty supporting themselves and they prove that these difficulties went back to as early as the 1750s, when the numbers of unskilled (probably many of them immigrants from the rural hinterland) began to play a significant part in the occupation rolls of the Inclusa. These difficulties were not taken with forbearance by at least one sector of the working poor – the wet-nurses of the Inclusa.

The Old Regime was no longer functioning viably. The Inclusa, the foundlings, and the wet-nurses provide clear evidence that the stability of the structure was under serious strain. With the recession at the end of the century and the political turmoil that followed, the discontent of the poor became evident. The incidents of 1808 acted as a catalyst for the poverty-stricken masses in the same way as had those of 1789 in France. The events of that tumultuous period were presaged and prepared in the growing distress of the urban and rural poor that can be documented in the pages of the *salidas* of the hospital of the Inclusa. We turn now to the place of the foundling in this series of events.

PART THREE

THE INFANTS OF THE INCLUSA

5

The *Expósito* as Bastard: Illegitimacy and the Enlightenment

The poor are the redundant members of a society. The economy has neither place nor need for them, and they are unable to provide for themselves. In the Old Regime where unemployment, vagrancy, and begging were facts of everyday life, unwanted infants were an unhappy but inherent concomitant. While the wet-nurses of the Inclusa illustrate the problems of the poor, the *expósitos* witness their numbers. Like the poor in general, the *expósito* in particular offered to the eighteenth century the ultimate paradox. In an age where a belief in progress underlined the attitudes of reformers in government and society, the abandoned infant provided a dilemma and a challenge. The dilemma was the inescapable evidence that this group of the poor was increasing in unprecedented proportions; the challenge was how to deal with this problem in a context of enlightened optimism. If the poor can be defined as those for whom there is no place, then the *expósito* was the pre-eminent example of the outcast. This chapter contrasts the traditional attitudes toward the foundling with the new views of the Enlightenment; subsequent chapters show the way these new ideas were to affect the role and function of the foundling hospital.

In the traditional view, the *expósito* was assumed to be illegitimate, but increasingly it was recognized tht the foundling was likely as often to be a product of poverty as of indiscretion. How many of the foundlings who were flooding the Inclusa at the end of the eighteenth century were actually illegitimate infants? If indeed there was a dramatic increase in illegitimacy, what does this tell us about the poor in Madrid at the end of the eighteenth century? In order to understand the management of poverty in the eighteenth century, the relationship of the foundling to the poor in the society of the time must be examined.

Abandoned and illegitimate children did not constitute a new problem. But society at different times and in different countries has treated these infants in different ways – ways that reflected attitudes toward women, children, and the family. In classical times it was taken for granted that any deformed, weakly, or female new-born could be exposed with impunity. A text written by a Roman physician was entitled 'How to recognize a new-born that is worth saving.' Less advanced tribes, like the Vikings, threw their new-borns into the sea to save the expense of bringing them up. From the time of the Theodosian code in 396 AD, the care of such infants became a matter of public concern. Throughout the Middle Ages there were sanctions against those who did the abandoning, though there were no positive measures in either royal or religious law to provide for the child. It was taken for granted that the abandoned infant was illegitimate, and the church was torn between concern for the human life at stake and a regard for the family unit. Some hospices discriminated by admitting only the orphan, and other institutions made separate provisions for legitimate infants and bastards, including in the latter those abandoned without any information as to their status.[1]

But all ages were similar in that the official reaction to the abandoned infant was rejection and dislike, at least on the part of the respectable, whose position and power depended upon the stability of basic institutions like the family. As Montesquieu put it: 'If one must chastise concubinage, then one must repudiate the issue of such unlawful arrangements.'[2] Attitudes toward the foundling and attitudes toward the family were inextricably connected. The Old Regime, with its emphasis on the patriarchal family and the authority of the father, saw the illegitimate infant as a threat.

While they paid lip-service to the ideal that the *expósito* was a human being eligible to be part of the brotherhood of man and the body of Christ, in practice neither state nor church could overcome an inherent distrust of the outsider to the point of acknowledging rights to full membership in the community. A study of bastardy edited by Peter Laslett has found that there have been communities that accepted premarital sexuality and a high degree of illegitimacy as neither immoral nor unusual, but they tended to be subgroups within a society.[3] Certainly Spain in the Old Regime did not permit leniency. In Madrid women accused of infidelity could be sent away by their husbands to a special prison.[4] Society punished both the sinner and the innocent victim of the sin. Rejected by even the womb that had borne it, the *expósito* was the prototype of the outcast.

Seen in this context, the illegitimate infant was burdened with complicated psychic connotations. In Spain the concept of honour has played a basic role in the psychology of the 'national temperament' (assuming that such an intangible quality exists). This role has been traced back to the medieval knight, who often possessed little more than his horse and sword and a highly developed sense of his own self-worth. The character of Don Quijote best epitomizes the devotion to an idealized picture of the self and a willingness to defend the escutcheon sheltering this fragile ego from anything that could be interpreted as derogatory or defamatory. Expressed as an ideal in the novels of chivalry, it inspired characters as diverse as Columbus and Pizzaro and Santa Teresa of Avila. In the collective mind of the Spanish male of the eighteenth century, it found its expression in the figures of the toreador and Don Juan. Honour and a sense of importance depended very much on one's good name and the public recognition of it. For the male, honour and importance seem to have become identified with sexual prowess. *Machismo* was a word coined in Spain to describe the characteristic personality of the lower-class Spanish male whose pride and reputation were associated with a picture of himself as an irresistible sex object.

In a society where the masculine concept of honour was synonymous with *machismo*, it was a matter of pride to seduce as many women as possible. Both the Don Juan and the duenna are Spanish institutions that take for granted that any woman left alone would automatically succumb to the spell of the Spanish male. In contrast, the good name of the whole family was dependent upon the woman's success in resisting this fatal attraction. The typical theme of Spanish drama and opera deals with attempts upon the honour of the heroine and struggles to foil the Don Juan's plans; if it was too late (usually by the second act), the family's good name was avenged in duels and sword-play even to the death. Ironically, the honour of the male depended not only upon his own *macho* qualities, but also on the virtue of the women to whom he was tied: his wife, his sister, his daughter, or his mother could bring disgrace upon the whole family.

This traditional form of honour survived much longer in the *pueblo* where neighbours could know everything about the individual, and among the uneducated attached to the basic values of the past. The city allowed a degree of anonymity for dalliance, and certain levels of society in eighteenth-century Spain accommodated infidelity as long as affairs were carried out with discretion. But the popular classes had nothing but scorn for what they deemed the Frenchified manners and lax morals adopted by the nobility and by their imitators from the new bourgeois class. The ruling classes, who had taken up French styles and customs with so much enthusiasm, were seen as a threat to the essence of Spain and the Spanish spirit. The partisans of these new fads, the eighteenth-century *petimetra* and her *cortejo*, were ridiculed as being effeminate and effete when they were not dissolute and degenerate. Disdainful of their compatriots, despite their common love of finery, the *majo* and *maja* of the working classes saw themselves upholding the honour of the Old Spain in their dress, music, manners, and morals.

An increase of illegitimacy among the lower classes who had always subscribed to a strict code of sexual morality, at least for women, could be taken as evidence that this ethos was undergoing a transformation under pressure of economic difficulties of the end of the century. Consequently, an increase in the numbers of *expósitos* could be taken as evidence that there was a radical change occurring within Spanish society. Attitudes toward illegitimacy were inextricably connected to the concept of honour in the beliefs of the ordinary person. If there was, in fact, an increase in the number of bastards, then something very interesting was happening to the Spanish psyche as well as the Spanish economy at the end of the eighteenth century.

In popular parlance, the terms abandoned and illegitimate were taken to be synonymous. But as their numbers increased after 1750, it became evident that not all of these foundlings were bastards. Notes attached to the ragged blankets attested that at least some of the children were the legitimate offspring of poor but honourable parents who had fallen on hard times and would return to reclaim them once the situation improved. Ribbons, amulets, and tokens bore mute witness to a resolve that was seldom carried out. It was clear to administrators of the Inclusa at the end of the eighteenth century that a significant proportion of the clientele of the Inclusa, though abandoned, were not necessarily illegitimate infants.

There have been various and contradictory estimates as to how many of these infants flooding the foundling hospitals everywhere in Europe in the last decades of the century were actually illegitimate. A study of the hospital in Lille by Evelyne Buriez-Henaux concluded that 40 per cent were not bastards.[5] Jean Claude Peyronnet put the number of legitimate infants among the abandoned at Limoges as high as 80 per cent.[6] But an assessment by Léon Lallemand of the *procés-verbaux* for the Paris foundling hospital found only 14.6 per cent to be legitimate.[7] A recent study of the same hospital by Delasselle led him to opt for a legitimacy figure of between 20 and 30 per cent.[8] An administrator of the Inclusa of Madrid at the end of the century estimated that more than half of the abandoned were of legitimate parentage. Pedro de la Vega, rector of the Inclusa for twenty years, pointed out in response to the royal inquiry of 1790 that the Inclusa did not serve as simply a shelter for *expósitos* or infants of unknown parents as had been commonly believed. 'In fact,' he asserted, 'more are legitimate than not.' He went on to explain that

Many of these belong to poor mothers who have been delivered in the Pasión [hospital for poor women] ... others are the infants of poor widows who leave them so that they can find work as servants or earn their living in some other way. Another large group belongs to poor married women who, only seven or eight months after having had one child, find themselves pregnant again and so expose the nursling in this Inclusa. These infants are the worse for having been weaned at such an early age on soups of milk and wine and they have become so weak that it is impossible to save them. In such cases, it is commonly asserted that these people bring their infants to the house of God and of the King because they cannot bear to see them suffer and die in their own homes. The same reason is given for abandoning infants sick with smallpox, syphilis, skin ailments, and ulcers – they have even brought us dead infants.[9]

Apparently, the *expósito* was likely to be a victim of the poverty of his parents almost as often as of their shame.

In 1794 even the king reacted to the fact that the status of foundlings could be ambiguous. He proclaimed that they must be considered legitimate and eligible for all civil privileges, and he instituted punishments for persons referring to them as bastards or in other defamatory terms.[10] This was a formal affirmation that the bastard was an outcast, beyond the pale of honour, and for this very reason the legitimate *expósito* had to be ensured his rights as citizen, even if that meant some overlapping to include genuine bastards. In fact, Pedro de la Vega used the king's statement as an argument for providing better health care for the *expósito* – or at least for the legitimate ones. In one of the most forthright expressions of this kind of prejudice imaginable, he stated, 'It is for this reason a distinction has to be made between the classes of infants who are received and their state of health, so that mortality [i.e., of some] can be limited.'[11] Because it was almost impossible to make this kind of distinction, the foundling in Spain was to be given the benefit of the doubt and become the recipient of rights denied to the abandoned elsewhere in Europe.

In France, the noble sentiments of the Enlightenment and its egalitarian principles were never extended to include bastards. Those famous defenders of human rights who legislated *enfants-trouvés* into *enfants de la patrie* during the French Revolution found they were *pères de famille* when it came to a conflict between their ideals and their family feeling. The Law of 12 brumaire in 1793, while it outlawed bastardy as a distinction among citizens, was followed almost immediately by measures destined to ensure that this law should pose no threat whatsoever to the bourgeois family. Illegitimate children were to be given civil rights only if the father wished to acknowledge them. In addition, the *récherche de paternité* was forbidden and no married man was permitted to acknowledge illegitimate progeny. The property-owning class has always supported the legitimacy principle because any questioning of succession rights poses a threat to their claim to power and privilege. For this reason the same legislation went on to make a specific distinction between those born of parents free to marry and those born of adulterous unions. In the case of the latter, such infants were eligible for only one-third of the portion they could expect if they had been born in wedlock.[12] The treatment of the foundling made explicit some of the contradictions between principles and practice as the Old Regime struggled to accommodate new principles in a framework of traditional paternalism.

The new theory that came to dominate the practice of welfare in the eighteenth century was utilitarianism. Welfare in general was directly connected to a number of important issues during the last days of the Old Regime. Attitudes toward beneficence delineated and defined the individual's political and religious position. On the one hand, there were those who identified with the traditional and conservative past, and on the other, those who looked to the future and propounded the progressive and humanitarian ideals we associate with the Enlightenment.[13] Both groups shared a strong sense of duty and dedication to the principles of charity, but attitudes toward the *expósito* brought into focus and highlighted the differences between the two. For the traditionalist, the connection between family patriarchalism and state paternalism was obvious. The function of the foundling hospital was to provide for the honour of the mother and the soul of the child. The hospice was not a hospital, but a way station where an unwanted infant could be brought, baptized, and sent out to a nurse. If the child died, and it was taken for granted that many would, at least it died a Christian, and did not leave behind a legacy of guilt for a crime of infanticide. This time-honoured interpretation of the function of the foundling hospital was being challenged by thinkers inspired by a more utilitarian view of welfare. For them the foundling was to be an instrument of progress, an agent to be set to work for the good of the state. They wanted to see the foundling, like the rest of the poor, carry out God's will here and now rather than in some hereafter outside history. This meant addressing the welfare of the foundling primarily as a temporal (not a spiritual) problem, and it called into play a new set of preconceptions about what the foundling should do for the state, not just what the state should do for the foundling. The foundling was to be incorporated into the larger picture of the economic and social progress of the state.[14] Furthermore, for some of these men of the Enlightenment, the *expósito* was to become a prime object to illustrate the superiority of these new theories.

From this aspect, traditional paternalism that viewed the foundling as a threat to the honour of the family played a secondary role to a new form of paternalism that could be termed economic paternalism. This form envisaged the foundling as a component of the state and separate from the family – a unit to be utilized for the public good. Large numbers, instead of being a scandal, were to become a useful source for Spain's armies, her industries, and her fields. The impact of this new approach to social welfare on attitudes of the powerful was of critical importance in eighteenth-century Spain. These men proposed bringing the welfare system increasingly under the aegis of the state in order to use it as an instrument to put into effect a new, enlightened policy of utility and humanitarianism for the good of the state. Their influence could be seen in the élite group of Spanish reformers called the *amigos del pais* who worked through their clubs or economic societies to encourage the government to provide for the poor in a practical, positive sense – ultimately for the good of the state. Examples of the influence of this kind of thinking can be seen in the records of the Royal Economic Society of Madrid. There, the influence of important theorists of this philosophy such as Bernardo Ward, Pedro Rodríguez Campomanes, and Gaspar de Jovellanos on the discussions of the bureaucrats and church- men who made up its membership is very clear.[15] The Madrid society was to become directly concerned with the Inclusa through its auxiliary, the Junta de damas. In a surprising twist of perspective, utilitarianism was to transform the foundling from a source of shame for the family to a positive advantage for the general community.

Though these groups never went so far as to suggest that increased numbers were a positive good, there was, nevertheless, a sense that foundlings could be turned to good account and could provide soldiers for the king, farmers for the soil, and artisans for an economic expansion that would bring Spain apace with her rivals France and Britain. A utilitarian approach was required to the problem of poverty in general; then the foundling would become an asset instead of a drain and would bring Spain into the modern world. However, on a local level, authorities faced with the cost of caring for the large numbers of infants flooding into the hospitals found it hard to share the more lofty overview presented by those reformers infected by the optimism of the Enlightenment.

Spain, of course, was not alone at the end of the eighteenth century in experiencing a remarkable increase in the numbers of abandoned infants. The causes of this expansion are still debated. Some modern historians agree with the contemporary accounts of moralists who attributed this phenomenon to a change in the moral standards of the population. They suggest that a kind of sexual revolution took place in most of western Europe in the second half of the eighteenth century and that the overcrowded foundling hospitals were a witness and proof of this radical transformation in mores.[16] And although there may be some dispute about the proportion who were illegitimate, there is no question about an increase in the absolute numbers of abandoned infants in all the cities of western Europe. In hospitals in Paris, London, Dublin, Lyon, even in small cities such as Limoges, Lille, Pamplona, Valladolid, Ceuta – wherever records have been consulted – the same phenomenon has been observed.

Whether this influx was seen as a sign of the moral collapse of society or as a challenge to be put to good effect, there is no question but that growing numbers of foundlings exposed and aggravated the financial problems facing welfare systems everywhere. It is not surprising that the reaction on the local level was usually concern over the charge on the community, and authorities did all they could to discourage the abandonments that were depleting the public purse. In Galicia, the midwife was enjoined to demand the name of the father at the moment of delivery on the grounds that at that point the woman would be too preoccupied to prevaricate, and thus the man could be traced and made to support his own progeny.[17] But Spain never resorted to the extreme measures taken in England where some municipalities paraded the child through the streets in the hope that someone would be able to recognize it, and where parishes hounded parturient women from one boundary to another and even paid carters to haul women in no condition to protest over the county line to the neighbouring parish.[18] Nevertheless, administrators of foundling hospitals everywhere developed s siege mentality: concern for finances gradually absorbed all their attention to the exclusion of the human, philosophical, or charitable issues involved. Even such a noted philanthropist as the Duc de la Rochefoucauld-Liancourt conceded with some bitterness that 'the number of infants has grown with the facilities to care for them.'[19] The constant struggle with finances led to a degree of cynicism and callousness on the part of those directly responsible for caring for the overwhelming numbers of infants coming into the foundling hospitals.

Though often discouraged and sometimes panic-stricken, the administrators of the Inclusa never placed restrictions on the numbers admitted, or turned anyone away. The government of Spain explicitly forbade anyone to question or interfere with someone making a trip to one of the foundling hospitals with an infant.[20] There was one brief attempt by the Inclusa to deter parents of legitimate infants from abusing the system. In 1796 they ordered that parents must relinquish any claims on a deserted infant, but this order only served to add to expenses because it discouraged parents from reclaiming their child, and it was repealed at the request of the Junta de damas in 1801.[21] The ony reference to tracking down parents referred to a sum of twelve quartillos in the *gastos* of June 1700, given to someone who 'informed' on the parents. This generosity of spirit seems to have been more in keeping with the traditional attitude toward the foundling based on its right to baptism. Obviously, the Spanish response to the problems that the foundling explosion presented to the theory and practice of welfare differed in important ways from that of its neighbours.

Given the sensitivity of traditional Spanish attitudes to the illegitimate infant, it is with particular interest that we examine the *entradas* for further information about what proportion of abandonments were actually bastards. The admissions records supply data on individual infants as well as statistical summaries that make it possible to trace the growth in numbers and to illustrate some of its characteristics. Sex, age, origin, address, and occasionally parentage are given, as well as the length of time the nurse kept the child, and the date of its death or adoption or return to the hospital at the end of a term of seven years for boys and eight for girls. There are 949 cases based on the admissions of the months of June and December at ten-year intervals from 1700 to 1799. These data allow an estimation of how many of the abandoned infants of the Inclusa were also illegitimate, and the information given on these cases helps to determine whether there was indeed a radical change in the sexual mores of the poor in Madrid at the end of the century.

At the top of the page was the name. Infants almost always came with a name attested to by the bearer, or fastened somewhere in the wrappings, even when it was only a first name. In the left-hand margin the age is noted, perhaps only a rough estimation because it is difficult to guess the age of a new-born, and sometimes left blank for the same reason. In the right-hand margin were recorded any sums, however inadequate, that had been submitted toward paying the wet-nurse. The body of the page summarized details that might make later identification possible. Apparently the Junta de damas ordered these details recorded separately in a book called *reconocimientos*, but these are not extant in the archives of the Inclusa.[22] References to ribbons, amulets, or distinguishing marks are rare, as are descriptions of how the child was dressed. The only exceptions are those wrapped only in bloody rags or those decked out in laces and fine ribbons. But in most cases the résumés are brief. The following excerpts from the year 1701 are a representative sample:

24 May, a girl brought by Gabriel Sanchez, surgeon of the parish of Santiago. The mother has a reputation as a *doncella* (virgin), and the child has been brought with the consent of the father.

26 May, sent by the monks of San Gerónimo of the Escorial, after having been exposed in the doorway of the monastery. The porter, Manuel Martínez, brought this girl with a certificate from the curate.

26 May, a boy, brought by Josefa Perez (who then became) a wet-nurse of the Inclusa.

1 June, a boy brought by Vicente de Almandrez, bookseller, found on the steps of San Felipe el Real, at eleven o'clock at night.

22 December, a girl brought by mother, both parents named (but precise names not given), living in calle de Beatas.

24 December, a boy brought from Álcala by porter Juan Diaz, with a baptismal certificate from the parish priest of San Justo y Pastor.

The most consistent feature of the record is the baptismal data given at the end of the page. In cases where the certificate has been supplied by the parish priest, it was noted; when the child had not been christened, the phrase was '*no tener agua.*' In doubtful circumstances, the child was taken to the font of San Ginés and baptized *sub conditione*. Finally, a note was made of the name of the nurse responsible for its care within the hospital, and a postscript stated the place where the infant went with his outside nurse. But often only the brief epitaph '*muerto en sala*' closed the books for the infant.

The statistical summaries that supplement these individual details give totals for almost every month of every year from 1700 to 1802 concerning *entradas* (admissions), *despechados* (placements), *entregadas* (taken back by parents or adopted), and *muertos en sala* (deaths within the hospital itself). For the second half of the century these records can be compared to similar data for the whole city. María Carbajo Isla has compiled the figures on deaths and baptisms for the hostels and parishes of Madrid from 1742 to 1836.[23] With the aid of these quantitative and sociological data, we are able to assess in general terms the origin, status, and parentage of these infants. Though the poor were nameless, nevertheless we can learn something from these records about how and when they abandoned their offspring.

Perhaps the most useful data in the *entradas* deal with where the infants came from. There were six official or royal hospitals in Madrid. Additional care was given by several independent institutions, some run by religious, some devoted to foreigners in the city. The Irish, French, Portuguese, and Italians each had their own hospital. Finally, the welfare network was supplemented by a number of charitable societies of pious laymen called confraternities or brotherhoods. Some of these had their own facilities, others worked in conjunction with the royal hospitals. Because each of these institutions catered to the needs of a particular group of the poor of Madrid, the infants from each tended to have their own, unique identity. For instance, the hospital, La Sagrada Pasión, was responsible for poor women, while the Beatario of San José and the Congregation of the Esperanza were concerned with reforming prostitutes.[24] Other infants came from the women's prison, and about 20 per cent from the various parishes, convents, and monasteries of Madrid and the surrounding towns. Knowing where the infant came from makes it possible to sketch a profile for some of these nameless numbers.

It is more difficult to do this for the infants who were brought directly to the doors of the Inclusa by individuals. These were infants who had been found in corners, or on doorsteps, or at the portal of a wealthy noble who was then expected to support the wet-nurse from his own largesse – a literal application of noblesse oblige. And as the century went on, it was becoming more common to bring the child directly to the hospital. Midwives, surgeons, relatives, even the parents themselves deposited their burden with the clerk. The notation *en casa* beside the child's record indicates a growing preponderance of infants in this category. In the first part of the century, under 25 per cent of arrivals came without some official intermediary. Around 1740 this procedure began to change. By 1790, 62.3 per cent of infants were admitted directly; in 1800 it was 75 per cent.[25]

This change had serious repercussions on the finances of the Inclusa, for it was difficult for the administration to exact pay for the service provided in the case of individuals, often poor. When the foundling was merely dropped off at the *pozo del zaguan* or fountain in the entry way, it was impossible. The modification in pattern also had interesting sociological implications. These infants were from the rootless; occasionally, some among those who deposited an infant with the office were without an address to supply, and the clerk had to note *sin domicilio*. They were without ties to a parish or a curate. They were anonymous but they were conspicuous, and becoming more so.

The infants for whom we have the most information were from La Sagrada Pasión, the women's section of the General Hospital of Madrid. These were admitted because the mother was sick, or was recovering from a difficult delivery, or was even deranged. The women in the *sala de locos* were attended by members of their own family or by convalescents from other parts of the hospital.[26] Infants from the Pasión were special in the sense that the names of both parents were invariably given along with the address. This information was usually supplied only when the child's legitimate parents wanted to be sure to be able to reclaim their infant. They were exceptional in many ways. First of all, though 93 per cent were under one year of age, still only one-third were just born. Second, the chances were that for most of them the stay would be brief; almost half of them (43.2 per cent) were reclaimed by their parents. As a corollary, the mortality rate was only 49 per cent – considerably lower than for any other group. Unfortunately, the infants from the Pasión were not typical. They made up 11.2 per cent of all the admissions to the Inclusa in the years 1700–99, but the proportion tended to decline in the period after 1770. Perhaps the Pasión also was having difficulty with its finances, and balked at subsidizing the care of infants except in desperate cases. Moreover, parentage information is available for all these cases, and only 3 per cent were illegitimate. For members of this privileged company, all circumstances worked to their advantage. More likely to be legitimate, more likely to be reclaimed, and more likely to live, the infant from the Pasión was not a genuine *expósito* at all but more a boarder in the charge of the administration of the General Hospital.

Infants admitted from the Hospital of Nuestra Señora del Carmen, or the Desamparados (helpless) as it was familiarly known from its function as a shelter for orphans, were more representative. This hospital supplied 12.7 per cent of admissions over the century. It had been founded by a group of religious in 1592 and was situated at a corner of the calle de Atocha near what is today a train station. In 1676 it consisted of twelve administrators, plus a staff of ten including a surgeon, a doctor, and a group of artisans teaching carpentry, barbering, weaving, shoemaking, locksmithing, and tailoring, as well as the more academic skills of reading, writing, religion, and music. One brother was in charge of arrangements for children to attend funerals and burials.[27] The custom of renting out orphans as professional mourners will be familiar to readers of Dickens. In 1676 Desamparados had in its charge 330 children whose numbers had increased to 3614 by 1845. These details are of interest because the infants of the Inclusa who lived out their term with the wet-nurse went on for the most part to the orphanage of the Desamparados.

As well as sheltering children, the hospital at the end of the seventeenth century had forty beds for paralytic women. These were the dregs of society, rejected by the Pasión as incurable, and referred to as *carracas* or 'old boats.'[28] There were also a number of beds set aside for *paridas clandestinas*, unmarried girls who came there secretly to deliver illegitimate babies.

Because this is one of the few groups where we can be almost certain of the status of the infants as illegitimate, it is interesting to see just what is distictive about the admissions from the Desamparados. First, they were invariably new-born, and second, they had a disproportionately high number of deaths – 81.9 per cent. The two are not unconnected. The older the infant, the better the chances of surviving the hostile environment of the Inclusa. Even today, the unmarried mother in New York is more likely to have a premature delivery or a stillborn child, and the new-born runs double the risk of dying in the first year of life.[29] Unmarried girls take pains to hide their condition, or hurt themselves attempting to terminate a pregnancy. In Spain the shame attached to producing an illegitimate infant must have brought many unmarried women to take desperate steps, injuring the foetus when they did not succeed in aborting it. Pedro de la Vega pointed out that 'many infants arrive in a deplorable state because of the mishaps they have undergone while still in the womb from abortificants, compressions and other means that their mothers have used in an attempt to hide their dishonour.'[30] Of the infants who did not die, 7.8 per cent were adopted, and the rest returned to the Desamparados as orphans. The institution was the closest to a permanent home some of them would ever know.

Other infants, almost certainly bastards, were brought by the Confraternity of Nuestra Señora de la Esperanza y santo zelo de la salvación de almas, or as it was commonly called, the Brotherhood of Mortal Sin. This organization devoted itself to reclaiming single girls from a life of prostitution. Founded in 1744, it was associated with the Church of Santa María Magdalena de mujeres arrepentidas, or Las Recogidas (the Saved). The group made the rounds of the streets in the seamier districts of Madrid chanting, 'Souls in sin, if you should die tonight consider where you will find yourself,' and collecting alms tossed from the windows by those whose guilt had been activated.[31] The sample involved is small – only 1.5 per cent of admissions – but the picture of the illegitimate infant from this group is clear and uncomplicated: 100 per cent were new-born and 100 per cent died.

Numbers admitted from the Desamparados and the Brotherhood of Esperanza increased over the century, but not disproportionately to the total admissions to the Inclusa. Distress among the poor must have had some impact on illegitimacy rates, but evidence based on numbers from these groups would not verify that it was a factor of major importance.

The most representative, in a sense the 'classic,' expósito was admitted under the patronage of the Royal and Holy Brotherhood of Refuge and Mercy, or the Refugio. Even the mortality rate of 72 per cent was the same as the overall average. This was a confraternity founded in 1651 by a Jesuit and a group of aristocratic laymen in order to involve their members directly in the care of the poor. The ronda of noble stretcher-bearers went through the back streets and public squares collecting the dregs of humanity, the sick, and the destitute, providing them with a night's shelter, 'bed and breakfast,' or delivering them to the local hospital.[32] The infants they brought to the Inclusa had been abandoned in the fullest sense of the word. They were likely to have been left by unmarried girls or by parents who were vagabonds and homeless by either choice or necessity – people with no shelter except what they could find in the streets. Infants were admitted to the Inclusa at a special rate of eighteen reales per month for nursing expenses, although strictly speaking the Refugio preferred to limit itself to charity on a short-term basis. During the first half of the century, admissions from the Refugio averaged around 85 per year, though occasionally, as in 1761, they were as high as 116. Overall, the brotherhood was responsible for 10.7 per cent of admissions, but by the end of the century its role in the charitable system of Madrid was becoming less important as was reflected in its ties with the Inclusa. Perhaps a symptom of its decline was the fact that the *entradas* indicate that the actual stretcher-bearing was being done by the servants of the nobles, not by the aristocrats themselves.

Though infants coming from the brotherhood's rounds were wretched, it might be presumed that the group from the women's prison would be even worse off. A quick survey of the numbers admitted from La Galera after 1797 would suggest that there must have been a crime wave undertaken by a group of pregnant women. Prior to this date entries were sporadic – one here and there, perhaps half a dozen a year. Then there was a sudden jump from a total of 15 for the year 1796 to 129 in 1797. In fact, what happened was that a small group of noblewomen had begun to take an interest in the deplorable conditions prevailing in the prison for women. They found that one reason few infants came from the prison in the past was the widespread use of the alternatives of infanticide and abortion in these hell-holes. In 1793 they arranged for a special room called *reservadas* where the inmate could deliver her child in clean and quiet surroundings. Then this service was expanded to provide two more rooms for young girls of the upper classes and women *honradas* whose reputations were in jeopardy. Queen María Luisa financed the furnishings in all three sections of the institution. Although advertised in the *Gaceta de Madrid* of 9 June 1797, arrangements were carried out in strictest secrecy to the point that the women wore thick, black veils during the delivery itself. They received free medical attention, a good diet, and a week later returned to their place in cell or society and their babies went to the Inclusa.[33] That this process can be taken as a sign of moral decadence among the aristocracy is doubtful. The nobility has always had less stringent norms for sexual behaviour than the rest of society. Even so, such admissions could scarcely make a significant difference because the proportion of nobility in the population was so small.

To find out if there was indeed an important rise in illegitimacy, we have to return to the poor. Usually, the abandoned and illegitimate infant was left with the parish or the local convent or monastery. It was taken for granted that the church would provide for the care of the helpless. About 20 per cent of abandonments in the century came through the mediation of the parish priest or the local monastery. But there was a significant falling off in the importance of this group as the century went on. Although in 1700 almost 50 per cent of admissions were directed by this route, at the end of the century it was little more than 5 per cent. The poor, for whatever reasons, were bypassing the local clergy in order to abandon their infants. The age and mortality rate of this group was average, and only 7.8 per cent were taken back by their families. But about half the ones who lived were adopted, which is exceptionally high. This could be taken as confirmation of the suspicions of the administration that there were cases of poor mothers presenting themselves as wet-nurses in order to take out their own infants and subsequently adopting them after collecting pay for nursing them. It was a venial offence that allowed the poor woman to keep her own child while acting out the charade of abandonment.

The poor in increasing numbers were bringing infants directly to the office of the Inclusa or leaving them clandestinely at the *pozo del zaguan*, the fountain in the patio, instead of bringing the infants to the parish priest or leaving one at the door of the monastery or convent. This group, designated *en casa*, is the most difficult to categorize. These were the infants about whom we know least, and it is the group we would like to know most about because it is this company that was flooding the Inclusa at the end of the century. They made up 20 per cent of admissions in 1700, but 62.3 per cent in 1790 and 75 per cent in 1800. This was the kind of foundling that was responsible for the crisis facing the Inclusa at the end of the eighteenth century. If there was a startling increase in illegitimacy in the last half of the century, then these infants were its product. In an attempt to define the status of this group, we must try to reconstruct a picture of the infant whose identity was concealed under the designation *en casa*.

Names were the first clue; those with names were more likely to be legitimate, of course. Parents who left names vouched for their hope of reuniting their families. But there were subcategories even within the nameless. Some infants were designated *padres conocidos*: their

TABLE 5.1
Percentage of legitimate and illegitimate admissions of infants
to the Inclusa

Year	Assumed legitimate	Assumed illegitimate
1700	13.04	86.96
1710	35.39	64.60
1720	15.38	84.61
1730	34.88	65.12
1740	44.74	55.26
1750	49.00	51.00
1760	50.40	49.60
1770	56.14	43.86
1780	50.00	50.00
1790	39.51	60.48
1795	37.80	62.20
1800	32.41	67.59
1805	42.00	58.00

SOURCE: *Entradas*, 1700–1805

parents were *honrados*, people whose good name would not bear being stated, but who were known to the administration, and presumably listed elsewhere in some private record. Claude Larquié suggests that this group were the poor who qualified as such because of illness or infirmity (the infant equivalent of *pobres de solemnidad*), and that many were in the care of the hospitals in the city.[34] However, my information makes a clear distinction between those admitted through mediation of some hospital and the *padres conocidos*. There were, in contrast, *padres non conocidos*, and we do not know enough about this group even to speculate, although they seem to be a category of their own distinct from the ordinary nameless *expósitos*. There were other infants with the name of one parent – usually the mother, occasionally the father. These could probably be lumped with the *solteros* whose parents' status was unquestionably not regularized by either church or state. Finally, there are the nameless who had been definitively abandoned without any clues at all to their identity, and who were most likely illegitimate as well.

Using names garnered from the names or lack thereof, together with information on their origin, it is possible to estimate roughly the status of these infants (see table 5.1). In broad terms, it can be assumed thta *padres conocidos*, infants from the Pasión, and infants with both parents named are probably legitimate, whereas infants from Desamparados, Esperanza, La Galera, *solteros*, and infants with the name of only one parent are more likely to be illegitimate. The lack of any hard data on the status of these infants is the excuse for presenting a table based on what little information is available.

What conclusions can we draw from these figures? The Inclusa had been set up to deal with the abandoned infant, and in most cases (more than 80 per cent in the early part of the century) the *expósito* was a product of some illegitimate alliance. However, in periods of distress such as 1710, the proportion of legitimate infants was often very high as well. Then, as conditions for the married poor improved, legitimate's numbers tended to fall off. But as early as 1730 there was a gradual change in this pattern. More and more legitimate infants were found in the ranks of the *expósito*, so that by 1750–80 they made up about one-half of the abandoned.

Sometime around 1790, there began to be a dramatic change in this pattern of admissions, reflecting a change in the pattern of behaviour of a growing sector of the population. Infants started coming in increasing numbers, and the proportion of illegitimate infants grew as well. These did not replace the number of legitimate infants who were also being left in increasing numbers, but more bastards were listed among the admissions of the Inclusa. Our first tentative conclusion is that the figures of the Inclusa support the assertion that there was a change in the pattern of sexual behaviour at the end of the century. Those who speak about a 'sexual revolution' seem to have some justification for their argument on the basis of actual numbers from the *entradas*.

While it may be an exaggeration to describe this as a sexual revolution, there was evidently a transformation of some kind going on in the mores of the poor of Madrid in the period 1795–1805. There was almost no change in the numbers of abandoned who were illegitimate before 1790 (see table 5.2). The numbers of legitimate infants increased after 1720 and then remained fairly steady from 1750 to 1800 at under 400 annually. About one-half the infants of the Inclusa were clearly of legitimate birth. If anything, this is likely to be a conservative estimate because it is not inconceivable that many of the married poor left infants nameless. For instance, the two children aged two and four who were left at the *pozo del zaguan* in 1804 were almost certainly legitimate even though the parents did not grace them with names.[35] However, after 1790 and certainly by 1795 there was a change in the pattern of admissions. Growing numbers of these infants were obviously illegitimate. It would seem that the disastrous period 1790–1805 had affected

113 The *Expósito* as Bastard

TABLE 5.2
Numbers of *incluseros* assumed legitimate/illegitimate
(1700–1805)

Year	Admissions	Legitimate	Illegitimate
1700	443	58	385
1710	804	284	519
1720	426	65	360
1730	526	183	342
1740	617	276	340
1750	809	396	412
1760	693	349	343
1770	685	384	300
1780	748	374	374
1790	811	320	490
1795	1022	386	635
1800	1202	385	811
1803	1364	710	653
1804	1784	915	868
1805	1250	525	725

SOURCE: *Entradas*, 1700–1805

not only the economy of Spain but also its social and cultural values. There were more and more illegitimate infants being brought to the Inclusa. Changes were occurring in the sexual behaviour of an important part of the population of Madrid at the turn of the century.

However, dramatic changes in behaviour such as increased sexual activity or a breakdown in traditional moral standards cannot be isolated from what was happening in the society in general. Changes were occurring but could they be called a 'sexual revolution'? There are three possible explanations: (1) the distress of the poor of Madrid and its surrounding countryside that led families to abandon infants they could not afford to keep, and thus contributed to an increase in the number of abandonments; (2) the general rise in urban population that could account for expanding numbers of exposed infants both legitimate and illegitimate; and (3) a change in age patterns so that there were more older infants as well as new-born. The hospitals had originally been intended to shelter new-born infants. The increase in numbers might merely reflect a transformation in the *expósito* population if at the end of the century there were also significant numbers of older infants and children.

Distress of the poor can be verified easily. The statistical summaries show that admissions doubled from under 500 a year in 1700 to over

1000 a year by 1795 and reached 1728 before levelling off. The year 1780 marks the beginning of the incremental influx. Not that admissions were consistently low in the early decades of the century: 1710, 1738, 1750–51, and 1754 were all years when numbers peaked at over 800. These totals were not reached consistently again before 1783. But in the early 1700s, such numbers were clearly short-term reactions to the periodic grain crises that plagued the economies of the Old Regime. Crop failures and high prices for food caused distress and sometimes desperation among the poor, and the infants they could not feed were left to the Inclusa. The quantitative data available on admissions can be compared with grain prices and the correspondence is striking. On both a short-term and a long-term basis, the relationship can be graphically demonstrated (see fig. 1.1).

In mathematical terms, the correspondence between the two is expressed by the correlation coefficient 0.77. When the price of wheat went up, so did the number of infants coming into the hospital. The same relationship can be demonstrated for the second year as well, at a correlation coefficient of 0.73, confirming that a price rise affected admissions during the following year at almost the same rate. Then as food supplies again became available, numbers declined and the pressure on the institution fell off. More serious was the gradual and cumulative increase that battered the Inclusa at the end of the century. It was wave after wave of increasing numbers of admissions that gradually succeeded in undermining the foundations of the hospital.

If distress on the part of the poor was responsible for the short-term influx of infants, could it also explain the gradual and long-term increment of *illegitimate* infants whose percentage has been estimated to have gone from around 50 per cent to around 67 per cent? Again we must go back to the figures of the Inclusa. Here the proportion of legitimate to illegitimate throws an interesting light on the question. For the years 1803, 1804, and 1805, the proportion of those assumed to be legitimate was back at around 50 per cent – the same as for the pre-1790s. Although there was, in fact, an absolute increase in the numbers of illegitimate infants, the proportion of bastards in the admissions was under 50 per cent until 1805 when something like a 'normal' pattern asserted itself again, and the majority of the infants were illegitimate (see table 5.3).

The illegitimacy that was a feature of the population of Madrid in the period 1794–1804 could hardly be described as a change in the pattern of behaviour of the poor as much as a temporary breakdown in the normal

TABLE 5.3
Percentage of admissions to the Inclusa
presumed legitimate/illegitimate

Year	Legitimate	Illegitimate
1803	52.12	47.88
1804	51.33	48.66
1805	42.05	57.94

SOURCE: *Entradas*, 1803–05

life of the city. As E.A. Wrigley has pointed out in his study of marriage and fertility in eighteenth-century England, in periods of hardship the number of marriages declined drastically. Marriage was often, in pre-industrial times, just the formal recognition of a relationship already consummated. The pregnancy of the woman marked the point of transition, or the last stage of courtship.[36] In periods of economic distress, people who would normally do so were reluctant or unable to marry, even though the woman had become pregnant. The period 1794–1804 was not normal in any sense of the word except that disaster followed disaster. Armies, both French and Spanish, took over Madrid. Shortages of food, epidemics, even extremes of weather harassed the suffering populace. Unrest to a degree unlike anything since the early years of the eighteenth century ensured that the experience of the populace of Madrid was typical of only the worst periods of crisis that plagued the Old Regime. As confirmation of this interpretation, we can look at the figures for 1710 – the only year of the century that combined in the same way the presence of foreign troops, crop failures, a harsh winter, and epidemics among the populace of the city. Conditions of 1709–10 can be taken as a preview of what was in store for Madrid on a long-term basis after 1794, and here again there was the same pattern of illegitimacy. Infants of the married poor and infants of the unmarried poor were admitted in numbers not equalled again until tht 1790s. But in 1711, as conditions improved, the situation within the Inclusa stabilized as well, and the proportion of legitimate infants among the *expósito* population declined.

The admissions of the Inclusa mirrored the distress of the populace of Madrid during a short-term as well as a long-term crisis. The rootless, restless elements of the city were reinforced by starving peasants from the countryside in search of food and work. As the years went on, with no relief that would make it possible for families of the poor to lead a normal life, admissions figures of the Inclusa for the decade 1794–95 to

1804–05 reflected this misery. Unfortunately, it was a pattern that was not to improve for many years. The critical situation of the end of the eighteenth century became the norm for the nineteenth. Again, this circumstance was evident in the records of the Inclusa. In the year of famine, 1813–14, infants flooded the institution and every infant admitted to the Inclusa died.[37]

But the overall population of Madrid increased as well in the course of the century. Is it possible that the increase in abandoned infants merely reflected this increase in population, and not any real change in the pattern of behaviour of the people of Madrid at the end of the century? To turn to the second hypothesis: instead of the poor getting poorer, were there simply more of them to send infants to the Inclusa?

A comparison of the population growth of Madrid with the *expósito* population of the Inclusa shows that along with certain similarities there were important differences. Some have estimated that the city grew from 115,000 in 1717 to around 180,000 or 200,000 by 1800.[38] In fact, there are many similarities between the demographic pattern of the city and the *expósito* population of the Inclusa. The records of baptisms and deaths in the parishes of Madrid indicate that births were only slightly ahead of deaths, probably because epidemics of yellow fever, smallpox, and cholera were still common. Moreover, there was a levelling off in the birth rate after 1768 in Spain and admissions to the Inclusa also reflected this situation.[39] But in the 1790s, a discrepancy between the numbers of infants born in Madrid and the numbers abandoned became striking. Baptismal records demonstrate that the birth rate of Madrid climbed again in the mid 1780s, took a sharp dip in 1794, and remained low until well into the nineteenth century. This pattern was in direct contrast to the admissions to the Inclusa, which continued in increasing numbers throughout the last years of the eighteenth century and the first years of the nineteenth. In other words, while there was a rough correspondence between the baptisms of the city and admissions to the Inclusa for much of the century, the increase in abandonments at the end of the century was an independent phenomenon that cannot be explained as part of the normal birth pattern within the city as a whole.

Another way that comparisons can be made between the pattern of births within the overall population of Madrid and the pattern of abandonments is to look at the series of monthly admissions to the hospital for the eighteenth century. Monthly averages show the way in which absolute numbers increased over the century (see fig. 5.1).

Monthly ratios above and below the mean illustrate the variations within these absolute numbers (fig. 5.2). The ratios set out clearly the two phases within the patterns of monthly admissions. In the first period, before 1770, the majority of *expósitos* were admitted in the first three months of the year with a second peak in the months of early autumn, usually October. This pattern was normal for the Old Regime, reflecting spring conceptions and pre-Lenten marriages. However, in the last decades of the century, a second pattern asserted itself. Admissions spread out to take up three months at the beginning of the year, and extended in a similar fashion to take in the four months from September to December. In other words, from September to March, and sometimes April, there was no decline in the numbers of infants. The only exception to these patterns occurred in the decade of the 1720s. Barring a high in October and a low in December, there was little deviation from the mean. This decade was one of the few periods of relative stability (grain prices were high in 1723–24, but the admissions total is missing). Because the 1720s was one of the more prosperous decades, it provides a useful basis on which to evaluate conditions during the adverse periods.

Though the *expósito* was not necessarily new-born, the pattern showing admissions above and below the mean for the period 1700–70 resembles closely the normal distribution of births among a population in the Old Regime: the largest number were born during the months of January to March as a result of spring conceptions; a second high occurred in October because of pre-Lenten marriages. In the eighteenth century February, and to a lesser extent November, were favoured for weddings because of the church's proscription of Lent and Advent. Religious practices were also responsible for the few births in December because the church counselled abstinence from sexual relations during Lent. In fact, the admissions for December were consistently below the norm before 1770. From 1700 to 1770 the admissions to the Inclusa conformed remarkably to the standard pattern of births during the Old Regime.

But after 1770, the pattern of admissions no longer conformed to the rhythm of births within the population as a whole. What was in operation in the *entradas* was a 'hardship pattern.' Admissions numbers were an index of the months as well as the years of greatest hardship for the poor – and these months were those of winter, particularly the months just before a new crop of grain or vegetables appeared to bring down the price of food, at least temporarily. Of course, the first trimester

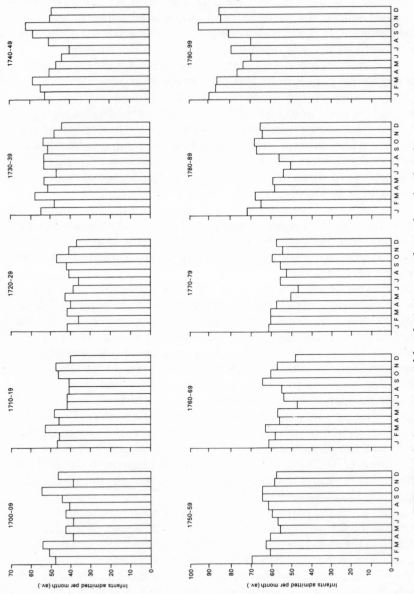

FIGURE 5.1 Average monthly admissions to the Inclusa by decades, 1700–99

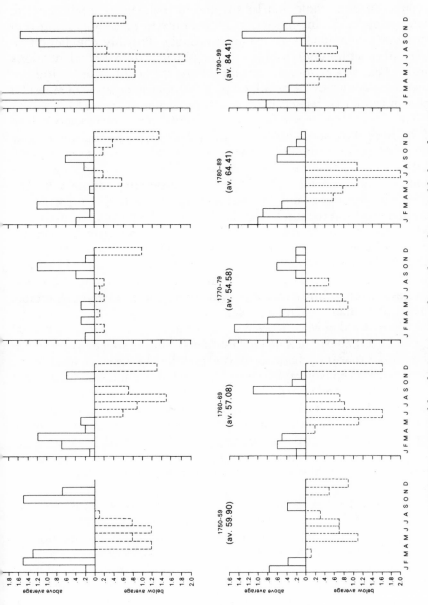

FIGURE 5.2 Monthly admissions to the Inclusa above and below the mean, 1700–99

was also the season with the largest number of births within the population as a whole, but by the end of the century a falling off in admissions to the Inclusa was confined only to those brief months of summer when food was readily available. Possibly the fall-off in December admissions meant that abstinence from sexual relations during Lent was no longer common among the populace of Madrid and that there was a growing secularism in the urban population of Madrid, a phenomenon that had occurred ten years earlier in France.[40]

There is another reason that the pattern of abandonment was likely to differ from the normal birth pattern of the general population. During the Old Regime, cities did not depend upon their birth rate for growth. Cities were accused of being parasites – huge sinks sucking in the young, strong, and able-bodied from the surrounding countryside. The poor, the destitute, and the needy made up a large proportion of immigrants from the rural hinterland. In periods of crisis, the rural poor were attracted to Madrid by a cheaper and comparatively plentiful supply of bread. As proof of Madrid's pampered situation, the government had to forbid the exportation of bread to nearby towns in 1788.[41] But if subsidized bread could not be taken out, there was nothing to stop the poor from coming in for it. Moreover, the numerous charitable institutions made Madrid a Mecca for the destitute. In February 1789, the Hermandad of Misericordia set up soup kitchens that fed 800–900 persons a day above their normal numbers.[42] I have already shown from the *salidas* that the proportion of the unskilled in the work-force of the city increased considerably after 1750 (see figs 4.1 and 4.2). Madrid did not have to depend on its birth rate: the rural hinterland could supply people, and incidentally infants for the Inclusa. The poor, both adult and infant, were increasing in numbers, but this increase was not a factor of the normal fertility pattern. An examination of the birth patterns in the normal population supports the original proposition, i.e., that misery was a factor of major importance in the expansion of the *expósito* population of the Inclusa.

The third proposition that might offer an alternative to this explanation concerns the age of the foundling. Is it conceivable that the increase in abandonments reflected an increase in the numbers of older infants? In other words, was the *expósito* explosion the reflection of a change in the behaviour patterns of parents who had decided to abandon an older child, whereas in the past they had left mostly new-born infants? The criterion of age is one that has interesting connotations. Research on foundlings in the hospitals of Paris and Limoges during the eighteenth century has shown that illegitimate infants were abandoned immediately after birth, and their numbers afterwards were insignificant.[43] The decision to abandon an illegitimate infant was usually made before its birth, whereas a legitimate infant had been kept longer, and abandoned only when parents found it absolutely impossible to care for it. That is, the new-born infant was more likely to be a bastard; the one over a month old more likely to be legitimate. Could the increase in admissions be a result of increasing numbers of older infants being left to the hospital?

Though the figures for the ages of the infants left to the Inclusa are only approximate, there is reliable information on the numbers who received the sacrament of baptism after their admission, and this would confirm that there were more older infants among the *expósito* population. When there was no proof of baptism, or when there was any doubt involved, the infants were taken to the sacristy of San Ginés, sometimes half a dozen at a time, given the name of the saint of the day, and baptized. Those infants who had not been baptized before their admissions had often been brought directly after birth by the midwife or surgeon or come from the Desamparados; others whose baptism was questionable had been found in some doorway or corner or left at the courtyard of the hospital. Such an infant – new-born, nameless, and unacknowledged – was more likely to be illegitimate, whereas older infants who had been baptized and then brought to the hospital were more likely to be legitimate. The unbaptized infant was in all probability illegitimate.

Figure 5.3 shows the proportion of new-borns to admissions for the period 1744–99 and indicates that the proportion of new-borns (i.e., unbaptized) declined drastically after 1768. Before 1759 new-borns formed approximately 90 per cent of admissions; then in 1761–66 there was a period of instability not unusual in demographic patterns, until a trend established itself definitively. Finally, after 1768 and for the rest of the century, a large proportion of older infants became a permanent characteristic of admissions to the Inclusa.

The third possible explanation for the increase in the numbers of abandoned infants, like the second, has not proved to be an alternative to the distress of the poor, but a further ramification and substantiation of the original proposition. All the evidence leads to the conclusion that the misery of the poor was the principal reason for the increase of abandonments to the Inclusa of Madrid at the end of the century. Poverty – not simply changing sexual behaviour – was at the root of the foundling explosion in Madrid at the end of the eighteenth century.

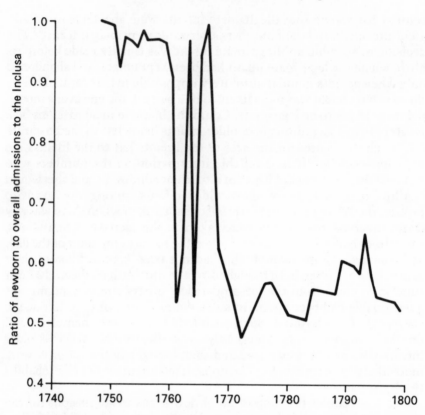

FIGURE 5.3 Ratio of new-borns to overall admissions, 1744–1880

Changes in sexual behaviour accompanied, coexisted with, and resulted from the hardship suffered by the poor.

I have examined the three factors that could conceivably account for an increase in the numbers of abandoned infants: distress of the poor, an increase in the 'normal' population of Madrid, and an increase in the 'illegitimate' population (i.e., a sexual revolution). All the evidence gleaned from the *entradas* leads to the inescapable conclusion that the misery of the poor was responsible for the increase in abandonment at the Inclusa of Madrid of infants both legitimate and illegitimate.

The hospital of the Inclusa showed in microcosm what was happening to the society as a whole, as well as to the poor in Spain at the end of the century. Under the pressure of a population that had outstripped the resources available for its support, the government (like the hospital and the city) could not respond adequately to the demands being placed upon its resources. Spain, involved in costly wars, saw its treasury becoming depleted. Trade with the Indies, disrupted during the War of American Independence, was cut off again by the British blockade of 1793. Economic recession made it more difficult for the poor to find jobs. Those on salaries had their income consumed by high prices and depreciated by inflation. The influx of rural poor during the periodic crises and harsh winters of the decade 1794–1804 and the presence of troops (both French and Spanish) in Madrid made for increasing numbers of rootless and restless citizens whose mores were reflected in increasing numbers of illegitimate infants. Unfortunately, it was not a situation that was likely to improve; in fact, if anything, conditions for the poor of Madrid would deteriorate before they got better.

There was indeed a change in the behaviour of the populace of Madrid under the stress and duress of events of the turn of the century, though the term 'sexual revolution' is misleading. More difficult to assess was the likelihood of some change in the psychology of the Spanish populace under this strain. It is possible that the father who was too proud to beg in his *pueblo* had been forced to leave for psychological as well as physical reasons. It is possible that the family that could depend upon the local curate, neighbours, or relatives for physical and emotional support now found itself isolated and alienated in an urban setting that promised more than it could fulfil, even in a material sense. It is possible that poor women who could not find work for themselves, or their daughters, saw prostitution as the only available occupation. It is possible that the concept of honour – dearly held by the Spanish populace at all times and closely tied to the sexual purity of the woman – was under severe strain during the decade 1794–1804, and that this stress was reflected in the growing numbers of illegitimate infants admitted to the Inclusa. It is possible that the unrest of the period affected even the institution of marriage, especially for the rootless who had no stake in preserving traditional patterns of behaviour. If the *expósito* was a synonym for the outsider with no stake in the community, then it could only be expected that these numbers would be on the increase. The ranks of outsiders were also swelled by infants of legitimate birth who in more favourable circumstances would have remained part of a family – perhaps suffering want, but never rejected by their own.

The poor, the government, and the hospital were caught in the same web of circumstances. Spain was in serious trouble and one symptom of it was the abandonment by the poor of their offspring. The economy was no longer able to provide for its people, and the first to bear witness to this deprivation were the infants brought to the hospital of the Inclusa, where many would die under official auspices.

The challenge that the *expósito* offered to the optimism of the enlightened Old Regime was to meet its most stringent trial in the mortality rate in the foundling hospitals. Reformers of the day saw the horrific loss of life in these hospitals as a waste of Spain's potential, and as undercutting any chance that she might have of taking her rightful place in the modern world. This view of the foundling implied a revision in the traditional attitude toward the foundling as a product of a mother's and family's shame. Instead of preserving the pride of the traditional family or tiding it over an economic crisis, the foundling hospital was to provide a model of utilitarian service to the state. One of the first steps facing reformers was to see to the survival of the foundlings, and the next to use them productively. Finally, measures designed to save the lives of foundlings were expressed in terms of a new philosophy that called for a re-examination of the functioning, as well as the function, of the foundling hospital. The foundling hospital was to be a means of attacking poverty at its roots. It was to be the model of the new progressive approach to the poor – a means of turning the weakest and least likely of subjects, the foundlings (even illegitimate foundlings), into productive citizens. We turn now to examine the mortality figures of the Inclusa that thwarted the designs of the most progressive thinkers of the time.

6

The *Expósito* as Victim:
The Mortality in the Inclusa

'They die of hunger one after another like waves on the ocean. They die of neglect, treated like a corpse while still alive ... I call out to God and I call upon men to bear witness to it.'[1] The highly charged words of Bilbao y Durán were not an exaggeration. Admission to the Inclusa was the first step on a road that led to death for three-quarters of the *expósitos*. As the century went on, the length of time the infant lived became painfully short. The *entradas* document how factors such as the age of the infant, conditions within the hospital, the nurse who took care of the new-born in the hospital, or the one who took it out, the town or street she lived on, and even the occupation of the wet-nurse's husband could affect chances of living out a term of seven years as an *inclusero*. More important than any of these was the growing crowd of cohorts. Records have faithfully preserved in numbers the increasing hopeless-ness of the situation. As more infants were admitted more were likely to die (see fig. 6.1). From an average of around 58 per cent in 1700, the mortality rate of the infants abandoned to the Inclusa approached 87 per cent at the end of the century.[2]

Central to a history of the Inclusa lies the issue of death, the incredible waste of life that went on in these institutions. During a period when the child, even the abandoned child, was beginning to be seen as a valuable member of society, more women were leaving their infants in settings that cut off almost any hope for survival. These mortality figures reflected the deteriorating situation within the hospital, the quality of the women hired as wet-nurses, and finally the economic problems of the hospital, all of which directly affected the chances of the infant's survival. This chapter examines the conditions that resulted in the deaths of so many of the progeny of the poor. What were the various

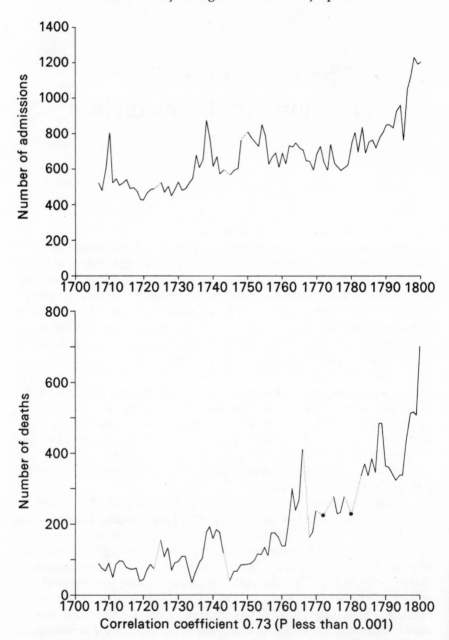

FIGURE 6.1 Admissions and mortality of infants of the Inclusa, 1700–99

factors within the society of the time and within the hospital itself that contributed to, and allowed for, the deaths of so many of the infants abandoned to the Inclusa?

When the chance for survival to age seven of the average child was only fifty-fifty, it is questionable whether the death of an infant was taken with the same degree of seriousness as it might be today. There is some evidence from the medical treatises of the time that the new-born was seen as not yet fully human. Hippocrates had designated a pre-human state of seven days, but in the course of time this had stretched to forty. During this probationary period the creature could neither see nor hear. Eighteenth-century doctors pointed out that the humours of the eye of the infant were thick in order to protect it from the sun's rays. 'One can make all sorts of noise without waking it ... it does not laugh or cry; it cries but they are not cries of pain.'[3] Only later can the infant express the happiness, love, sadness, and anger that distinguish it from the animals. In the theory of humours, which had been the mainstay of all physiology and pathology from the time of Hippocrates, the human body was composed of four humours corresponding to the four natural elements of earth (black bile), air (blood), fire (yellow bile), and water (phlegm). The new-born was a creature whose humours had not yet completely coagulated so that it was not a solid substance at all. Its bones were soft, almost cartilaginous; its muscular tissue lax and flabby; its head a ball of paste or soft wax susceptible to all impressions. In general appearance, it was an amoeba-like creature of gelatinous consistency, constantly secreting moisture from all its pores. For instance, the flaky, dry skin sometimes found on the skulls of new-borns and usually referred to as 'milk crust' was said to be simply the nerve tissue of the brain drying out as it made contact with the air.[4] As the new-born aged, its muscles and bones would harden and tighten up and its humours coalesce to form an adult human being. In an intereting sidelight to this theory, women never completely developed into mature adults. Their bodies remained flaccid and weak, their skin did not harden and produce beards (at least not until they were very old and no longer functioning as women), their voices did not deepen, and they remained perhaps more sensitive and finely tuned, but never became completely full human beings.[5]

In the seventeenth century the iatrochemical school associated with the name of Jean Baptiste Von Helmont (1577–1644) developed a theory of ferments and gases as a theoretical framework for understanding the workings of the human body. In this adaptation of the theory of humours, water was the most important substance. Eighteenth-century physicians combined iatrochemical theory with the mechanistic ideas of Descartes to analyse the physiology of the infant and explain its illnesses. In the words of the most famous professor of medicine of the century, Hermann Boerhaave, 'The laws of hydraulics can be applied to the human body which is composed of canals, of reservoirs, of fine tubes through which liquids circulate.'[6] In other words the child was not so much a product of primeval slime as a complex of pipes conducting its humours – pipes that in the new-born were only loosely held together, but through which liquids coursed in perpetual motion.

Despite these efforts to assimilate the infant into the prevailing explanations of human nature, the new-born was considered by doctors as practically a subspecies. If doctors reflected the mentality of the general public, then it helps to explain a certain degree of callousness on the part of parents and administrators. For instance, the practice of the Inclusa of Santiago de Compostela of paying the surgeon to 'mark' the arm of the infant – the equivalent of branding it as an *expósito* – could be explained in this context.[7] The term used for the new-born in the records of the Inclusa was *criatura*, which can be taken as a term of endearment and is used as such today in Spain; it also has overtones that connote a being as much animal as human. The new-born, 'possessing neither mental activities nor a recognizable bodily shape with which to make itself lovable,'[8] was a vulnerable, pitiable, even a repulsive object. The archdeacon of Saragossa wrote: 'Only a mother could be capable of the kind of care that the imbecility of the new-born requires.[9]

The crowded *sala* of the Inclusa at the end of the century is evidence that, for many of the poor, the maternal instinct may not have been highly developed. The very existence of foundling hospitals was an attempt to limit infanticide and abortion. Mothers had become conditioned to expect the loss of a high proportion of their progeny. Energy in the family of the poor had to be expended on those who remained, rather than in mourning for an infant whose existence could only be an added burden. Many of these infants would have died within the normal course of events. For the poor, the death of a new-born was unfortunate but not unexpected. Mourning was a luxury the poor could not afford. Indifference to the new-born may well have been a defence mechanism, given the harsh realities of the situation. Parents who abandoned an infant to the Inclusa often did so with a certain degree of stoicism if not cynicism.

Many of these infants were in poor condition before they were ever admitted. They had picked poor parents to start with, or had only one responsible for their care. Born into a cycle of deprivation, the illegitimate among them were more likely to die in any case. Lallemand described the plight of these infants: 'They arrive after having gone through a pregnancy where it was in the interest of the mother to disguise her condition, and where she often continued to work or to engage in debauchery despite her condition.'[10] There was a desperately high mortality among infants coming from organizations caring for unmarried mothers. Surviving the trauma of childbirth was no small feat even for legitimate infants. Unless the delivery was a normal one, there was almost nothing the midwife or surgeon could do, and the best of them recognized that harsh reality. The worst of them delivered monstrous and imbecilic creatures whose twistd limbs and malformed heads were living evidence of their clumsiness. Midwives' mistakes were responsible for the many idiots with distorted heads among the populace. Even those who survived pregnancy and delivery still had to undergo a post-natal regime that was the equivalent of a barbaric initiation rite. Commonly, attempts were made to form the child's skull or nose, perhaps to conform to some aesthetic ideal of the midwife, perhaps to remedy the signs of a difficult delivery. Purges were administered to clean out its system; routinely the cord of the tongue was cut to enable it to swallow more easily. Evidence from the medical treatises of the time indicate that the welcome to the world outside the womb was a cruel one and it is not surprising that many infants decided within a few hours to have no part of it.

Sometimes the trip itself was a major factor in its death. Children admitted to the Inclusa were usually from Madrid, its suburbs, or one of the nearby towns such as Álcala (33 kilometres). Madrid did not have the same problems as, for example, Paris had, where the foundling hospital became the focal point for children from as far away as Strasbourg.[11] Nevertheless, for new-born infants coming even the short distances over bad roads, the trip was often fatal. The porter was some local fellow whom the curate sent off without arrangements for nursing the infant or seeing to changes in its wrappings. 'Borne on the porter's shoulders in a straw basket, the infant arrives soaked in dirty linen and his own tears.'[12] The surgeon of the hospital in Pamplona, Lorenzo de Mariategui, reported that in one week two infants were admitted after such a trip, one crippled and the other badly injured. They both died shortly after. In another case, the infant was taken out at the end of the journey bruised from head to foot. The porter had stopped for a snack and then carelessly tossed a porcelain jar of honey into the basket with the baby.[13]

Throughout the eighteenth century the system of admissions to the Inclusa were much less dramatic than the stereotypical abandonment we have described, where the child was left in a turnstile to protect the anonymity of the bearer and the honour of the family. Though there is evidence the turn existed in other cities in Spain, it was not installed in the Inclusa before 1801. (Sister Iréne, the archivist in the modern children's hospital whose records trace its history back to the Inclusa, stated that the turn was removed in 1917, the year before her arrival, after a child was accidentally decapitated). In most cases the procedure was more formal. In a small office, information given by the bearer was transcribed; the child was then taken into a room called *collares* and placed in a numbered cradle. Here a cord of silk was put around the neck to fasten a lead disc. On one side of this medal was stamped 'Inclusa of Madrid,' on the other a page number that would be the infant's identification during its term as a charge of the Inclusa, and indeed as long as the child lived.[14]

Abandoned by their own mothers, *expósitos* had to depend on a series of substitute mothers. For the wet-nurses, the infant was a source of income, so a degree of insensitivity was only to be expected. The first surrogate was the *madre de la sala* who passed the infant on to a resident nurse but continued to oversee its care and feeding. The *madre* was just that, a housemother in a household that might number fifty or sixty infants and a few older children. In addition, she had the supervision of the health, work, and deportment of as many as twenty wet-nurses, who could be more trouble than the infants. When there was a choice, she decided who would be hired and when they were to be dismissed, and saw to their behaviour in between. The latter involved supervising diets to see that they did not sell off part of their ration, or supplement it with spices and strong drink. She also had to make sure that the wet-nurses used the soap ration to keep themselves and the infants clean, and that they did not dose colicky babies with soporifics. In all, her position called into play the talents of headmistress, accountant, director, and sergeant-major.

While the *madre* embodied many and diverse skills, the nurses needed only one: the ability to produce enough milk to feed two infants. There may even have been cases where that faculty was lacking. The nurses had notoriously bad reputations. They were accused of being mercenary to the extreme because they were willing to deprive their

own infants of milk in order to sell their services. Some, it was
suggested, became pregnant for just that purpose. As a matter of fact, it
was not unusual to see the notation in the *entradas* that the mother of a
particular infant was *ama de la sala*. These were women, probably
unmarried, who sent their own infants out to nurse while they took up
residence in the Inclusa. Then there were nurses who did not relinquish
family responsibilities but brought them with them to be fed at the
hospital's expense. When nurses were in short supply, no questions
were asked; it is possible that some of these women were prostitutes.
The administrator of the foundling hospital in Pamplona states that
they were bad types, better suited to kill than to care for infants,
referring to the fact that 'some of them already have venereal disease
which they pass on to the infants.'[15]
Whatever their deficiencies in health and character, their behaviour
left much to be desired. They evaded the strict vigilance of the *madre* to
escape to the streets where they wasted time shopping, chatting, and
worse – all of which affected the quality of care they gave their charges.
Careless and irresponsible nurses were a decisive factor in the deaths of
many of these infants who were sick and weakly to begin with and
whose only hope was constant and painstaking mothering. However
wet-nurses of the Inclusa were hardly ideal surrogate mothers.

Women who nurse in this house behave disreputably, and try to get away with as
much as they can, because they know how essential their services are in these
times when the house is overwhelmed with *expósitos*. No one can reprimand
them because they will troop off in a group and abandon the infants. In any
conflict all the administrator can do is be patient and give in to whatever they
wish, pretending he does not notice the insults, the lack of respect and the
insubordination, not to mention certain acts of insolence that I blush to repeat
and which you could scarcely imagine.[16]

In the view of the harassed administrators, wet-nurses of the Inclusa
could be blamed for causing infants' deaths as often as saving their lives.
But from the standpoint of the nurse, the woman who may have given
up her own infant so that she could register as a wet-nurse received very
little in return. The environment of a hospital full of sickly infants, with
space to dry linens at a premium, must have been depressing. With sick
and well in the same room, perhaps with the same nurse, diseases spread
rapidly. A justified fear for her own health and that of her family may
have had some bearing on the way she treated the nursling. Though the

optimum number of infants was supposed to be two and at most three, there were actually cases of one nurse assigned seven infants in the hospital of Pamplona.[17] There were many reasons why the inclusas of Spain found nurses in short supply.

Under such conditions the wet-nurse often carried out her duties with reluctance, distaste, or at the very least a cold reserve. Emotional deprivation was another burden that the abandoned child had to bear. Never played with or cuddled, handed from one woman to another routinely, 'For such infants it is a holiday when they are taken for a walk around the room by the nurses, or when they get a little attention at the time of getting dressed or fed.'[18] The results of neglect can take many forms and the deaths of some of these infants may have had emotional as well as physical causes.

It is a safe generalization that the poor quality of wet-nurses in the hospital itself was a further reason for finding infants their own nurse and foster home, preferably outside of Madrid, as quickly as possible. But as the century went on, inflation cut back on the real value of their small stipend and fewer country women were willing to make the trip from neighbouring towns for a foundling. More urban women were recruited, to the detriment of survival chances for the infant. When numbers of infants did not abate, it was evident that steps had to be taken to make up the growing shortfall between nurses and infants. It became clear that the crisis was approaching emergency proportions. In 1790 salaries went up from twenty to thirty reales per month for wet-nursing a new-born, and rose from twelve to twenty for caring for an older child.[19] But even this was only a stopgap. Infants continued to come in greater numbers and to sicken and die before someone rescued them from the crowded, unhealthy environment.

The picture of degradation in the *sala de niños* may have depressed nurses and administrators but it horrified an outsider coming upon it unprepared. To judge from the words of Doña Josefa Diaz de Cortina, secretary of the Junta de damas in 1799, it made a lasting impression:

It is a veritable pit, a *canoa* [hold], where infants are thrown in without any distinction between sick and well, male and female, or even social class. Many of them have been brought back because the wet-nurse had not been paid and the institution can do nothing about its lack of funds. In this horrible receptacle they are left without help, without someone to change them, bereft of the breasts to which they are accustomed, suffering the hunger that in time will kill them. It is a room of filth, filled with ceaseless crying, where their lack of decent covering, their misery and consequent infirmities combine to bring about their death within a few days.[20]

As the century went on and numbers increased and soon outstripped the supply of nurses, foundlings were sentenced to longer terms in the 'hold.' The Inclusa, because of the shortage of nurses, was turning into an institution full of sick infants. It was becoming a hospital in the modern sense of the word. But hospitals before the twentieth century were commonly considered, with justice, to be health hazards. They were places where the suffering contracted diseases they did not have before and where slight illnesses became serious and serious ones mortal. Leaving an infant to the Inclusa was becoming the equivalent of leaving it to die.

The spread of infection from one infant to another was a serious problem in the overcrowded *sala de niños*, with sick and well bundled indiscriminately into the same crib. Neglect was a major factor. Numbers sapped the strength, sympathy, and attentiveness of the staff. The administrator of a foundling hospital in Pamplona described the way in which slight indispositions tended to deteriorate in the atmosphere of the hospital: 'When treated sensibly, indigestion, constipation, sluggishness, surface blemishes and skin eruptions do not pose a serious problem. But sensible treatment is not always given. Instead, the infant is subjected to a heavy gruel when his system should be given a rest ... or treatment arrives too late because staff and doctors are overworked.'[21]

The child's best hope for survival was to leave as quickly as possible, but not only were nurses becoming harder to get, they were becoming harder to keep. From the viewpoint of both child and hospital, the ideal was one nurse who would take the infant, wean it, and maintain it for a full term of seven years. However, women were increasingly turning to the hospital for emergency relief to tide them over a short-term crisis and then returning the infant. The hospital gave out salary advances before the usual pay dates of December and Pentecost to keep women on the books, but the turnover remained high. For instance, in 1700, 71.1 per cent of infants had one nurse and the mortality rate was only 56.8 per cent. In the course of the century the percentage with one nurse declined to the point that in 1780 one-third of the infants had three or more nurses. Shuttling the infant back and forth could only have disastrous consequences for the *inclusero*. It is probably not a coincidence that as the number of nurses increased so did the number of deaths. In 1790

TABLE 6.1
Mortality of infants and number of nurses

Year	Per cent with 1 nurse	Per cent with 3 or more nurses	Mortality
1700	71.1	7.9	56.8
1710	79.6	3.4	56.4
1720	88.0	4.0	58.3
1730	78.8	4.5	67.2
1740	77.5	9.8	87.3
1750	64.9	12.8	75.6
1760	62.5	16.9	73.6
1770	68.1	23.2	69.6
1780	54.9	33.2	66.2
1790	73.4	11.5	72.1
1799			86.1

SOURCE: *Entradas*, June, December 1700–99

those with only one nurse became the norm again, but for a different reason. Now they had only one nurse because they did not live long enough to be subjected to more than one. In the first half of the century the rate of deaths was around 58 per cent and the numbers with one nurse around 70 per cent. In 1780 only 55 per cent had one nurse; in 1799, 86.1 per cent of those leaving the hospital with a wet-nurse died (see table 6.1).[22]

But even though the odds weighed more heavily against them as the century went on, most infants left the institution with a nurse. Usually the child who was taken by a country woman had a better chance of survival. However, location, even distance, could still cut back on life expectancy. Many frail new-borns did not survive the trip in the arms of the nurse as she walked or rode in a clumsy, open cart over poor roads in bad weather. The towns the women came from tell a great deal about the infant's chances of survival. If the destination was one of the wind-swept isolated villages of the southwest, the chances of living out the weaning period of eighteen months were slight, the hopes of surviving a full term of seven or eight years almost nil. Assignments to Alamo, Baldassar, Getafe, Fuentelabrada, Pinto, and Torija, all to the south or southwest, were the equivalent of a death sentence.

Nor could the vaunted fresh air always be depended upon. Some rural towns were prey to what we would call today industrial diseases. The townspeople of Alcorcón to the west of Madrid were subject to *cólicos saturnicos*,[23] a chronic chest inflammation found among workers in glass or metal works and attributed to alcohol fumes from the local factory. Glaziers, painters, and potters were liable to mercury, copper, and lead poisoning. This early version of minimata disease was characterized by coughing, trembling, and eventually paralysis. Workers in the tanning trade contracted anthrax in their work, and here, too, strong fumes could be harmful to infants. Neither Alcorcón with its gas works, nor Pezuela with its leather industry, had a single infant from the Inclusa survive as long as six months.

Geographical dictionaries written by Pascual Madoz (1845–60) and Sebastian de Miñano (1825–29)[24] describe in detail the conditions in these towns and the problems of health and climate that were likely to affect the chances of survival of a new-born. The Guadarrama mountains sent down cold winds over the whole area which left the inhabitants of the plateau with a propensity to pulmonary and rheumatic complaints and subject to chest pains that may have been tuberculosis. The cold could be especially hard on the poor. In towns like Alcobendas, ten miles north of Madrid, 'the inhabitants are so poor that they cannot cover themselves adequately.'[25]

Almost all the sites were subject to quatrains or tertians, sometimes called 'intermittents.' These were complaints characterized by periodic bouts of high fever. Even towns given a clean bill of health were prey to *estacionales* – a version of spring and fall flu that accompanied the change of seasons. Although information given in these dictionaries is often quite precise, there does not seem to be a consistent pattern associating certain areas with certain illnesses. For instance, Parla to the southwest was 'very cold with resulting feverish inflammations, intermittent typhoids, and chest colds,'[26] but Getafe only three miles away was termed healthy. Esquivias in the same general area was described as having a 'peaceful climate,' although its inhabitants were prone to rheumatism and tertians.[27] In Carabanchel, favoured as a summer retreat for wealthy Madrileños, the locals were subject to 'nervous and cerebral attacks' that may have had a bearing on the fact that all the infants brought by nurses to the town died within six months. Occasionally, the diagnosis of symptoms and causes is quite precise. Madoz pointed out that in Brunete the limestone soil, which did not allow adequate drainage but permitted stagnant pools of water to form, was responsible for the malaria-like infections common in the town.[28]

Not all the hamlets and towns of the province of Madrid were unhealthy. El Molar and Navalfuente in the valley of the Jarama attracted invalids from Madrid to their mineral springs, and Álcala, which accounted for 17.7 per cent of the wet-nurses, provided that exceptional conjunction of a favourable physical environment, a healthy economy, and a large number of infants from the Inclusa. However, in most cases, the foundlings went to homes of women who were poor and unhealthy in towns that were poor and unhealthy.

Even so, the infant sent to the country stood a better chance of survival to the age of seven. If he or she was fortunate enough to be taken out by a small independent farmer, it could be 15 per cent, whereas in the cities only 6.7 per cent could expect to return to the Inclusa at the end of their term. Streets, air, and houses were foul in a way that can scarcely be imagined today. Because sewers were non-existent before 1760, streets had been graded to slope toward the centre to facilitate the languid drift of sludge that accumulated from the householder's custom of dumping refuse and sewage into the streets – often by way of an open window. This *marea* or tide, as it was euphemistically termed, made the streets little better than open cesspools.[29] To prevent the filth from periodically engulfing the curbs, a force of street cleaners, accompanied by a cart, stirred up the current, while sweeping along the residue as best they could.[30] Fortunately, the admirable climate of Madrid with its high quota of dry, sunny days and fresh, clean air from the surrounding mountains may have prevented the situation from becoming absolutely intolerable. However, there were days when the wind blew dust and effluvia about in such a way as to make the air too thick to see through in the broader thoroughfares of the city.

Nor was human excrement the only problem. Because the streets were so unappetizing for the pedestrian, anyone who could afford to had a coach, and others rented them. This use, of course, only complicated the problem by stirring up more dust and adding to the pollution. Horses and mules were everywhere, delivering goods, hauling bricks and boards, and turning wheels for power in the various mills and construction sites.[31] There is no way of estimating the feathered and four-footed population of Madrid, but husbands of wet-nurses living in the heart of the city were often goatherds, poultry raisers, and bird sellers. In addition, the notorious pigs of the Order of San Antón were privileged to use the 'pastures' of Madrid to the point of constituting a traffic hazard. Such was the contamination of Madrid air that, according to one observer, it blackened the silver and was responsible for the pale, unhealthy complexion of Madrid women that had become fashionable.[32]

Pollution offended the ear as well as the nose in eighteenth-century Madrid. Nothing could be done about noise, soot, and fumes from masons, brick makers, butchers, blacksmiths, tinsmiths, cutlers, tanners, potters, glaziers, and various metalworkers. However, an attempt was made to control the noise from heavy wooden-wheeled coaches and wagons. A Benedictine, P. Sarmiento (1695–1771), found some comfort in the provision that closed off to traffic for a few hours or days the street on which someone was dying, allowing a modicum of peace in his or her last hours. Laws repeatedly tried to limit the numbers of those who drove private coaches and the number of mules allowed to pull them. In an attempt to curb the mettlesome spirit of coachmen who raced through the streets and blocked traffic to indulge in insult and argument over the right of way, heavy fines and penalties as stern as six months at hard labour were imposed. There was even a surtax when the driver was under seventeen years of age.[33]

Madrid earned the title of the dirtiest capital in Europe, but under Charles III a heroic attempt was made to slough off that dubious honour. Citizens were ordered to sweep their house entrances daily, to keep garbage in a receptacle for the purpose, and to sweep refuse into a central gutter ready for removal by street cleaners. But according to the *Diario de Madrid* of 1791, certain sectors remained unaffected. 'Inhabitants of the lower quarters ... neither have garbage cans, nor do they need carts to carry away refuse from their streets, for they have never been swept or sprinkled, or for that matter even paved.'[34] These, of course, were the streets on which the wet-nurse and the infant from the Inclusa lived. Madrid was not a healthy place for an infant either inside the hospital or in the home of the wet-nurse.

The child taken to a farm was indeed fortunate. Even when the wet-nurse was the wife of a humble day-labourer, there were no more than four city occupations that offered an equal chance for survival. Only 57 of the 523 infants with city addresses in our sample were fortunate enough to be taken by wives of sacristans, bakers, potters, or mat makers. In contrast, more than half went to the homes of masons, leather workers, coachmen, or unskilled *peones* (see table 4.1). There, approximately one-third survived past six months and only 6 per cent lived to return to the hospital at age seven. Conditions were most deplorable in the homes of the unskilled, masons, servants, and leather workers, where anywhere from two-thirds to 90 per cent died by six months. But other occupations where fumes were involved also levied a heavy toll. No child taken by blacksmiths, silversmiths, painters,

TABLE 6.2
Occupations and mortality rates: urban/rural

Occupation	Per cent dead by 6 months	Per cent living 7 years
Urban occupations with best survival rate		
Potter	50.0	30.0
Sacristan	57.1	28.6
Mat maker, seller	66.7	16.7
Baker	71.3	17.6
Urban occupations with worst survival rate		
Coachman	68.3	6.8
Leatherworker	68.7	3.6
Mason	65.7	6.5
Unskilled	76.0	5.3
Servant	87.5	12.5
Rural occupations		
Independent farmer	56.8	15.7
Townsman (vecino)	65.6	9.0
Day labourer	71.7	7.1

SOURCE: *Salidas*, June, December, 1700–99

TABLE 6.3
Percentage of admissions by sex
to the Inclusa, 1700–99

Year	Male	Female
1700	32.4	67.6
1710	49.5	50.5
1720	43.8	56.3
1730	54.0	46.0
1740	46.4	53.6
1750	54.9	45.1
1760	52.6	47.4
1770	50.0	50.0
1780	45.7	54.3
1790	56.2	43.8
1799	54.3	45.7

SOURCE: *Entradas*, June, December, 1700–99

coppersmiths, or charcoal makers survived as long as three years. The *expósito* taken out by a small independent farmer had the best chance to survive to age seven, with the exception of the relatively few infants taken into homes of bakers, esparto workers and sellers, potters, and sacristans in Madrid. Finally, in any case, just 11.3 per cent of the infants lived out their term with the wet-nurse. Table 6.2 shows the city occupations with the most survivors, those with the least, and the comparative death rates among infants taken out by nurses listing rural occupations.

Though death was increasingly indiscriminate, it did have its favourites. The young were the first to go. Perhaps it was because they were the most frail and the most in need of a mother's care or perhaps because they were more likely to be illegitimate and thus doubly disadvantaged. The older child was more resilient, for by a process of elimination the weakest had already disappeared. Among the group analysed for 1700–99, the mortality rate was 88.4 per cent for those under one month, 70.4 per cent for those from one to six months of age, 56.9 per cent for those from seven to twelve months, and 50 per cent for those from one to two years of age. Of course, 96.5 per cent of admissions were less than a year old. In this game of 'Catch 22,' the youngest were most likely to die and the majority admitted were new-born. In summary, 72 per cent of infants admitted to the Inclusa died before age seven.[35]

The sex of the *expósito* had little bearing on its chances for survival. Abandoned in almost equal numbers (50.7 per cent boys to 49.3 per cent girls), they remained equal in death: 50.3 per cent of the boys died compared to 49.7 per cent of the girls. In the first half of the century, girls tended to be left more often than boys, but after 1750 this distinction disappeared (see table 6.3). It could be inferred that as the situation became more hopeless for the poor, boys were being abandoned as well as girls. However, since the sample on which these data were based included the years 1700 and 1740, which were both years of serious distress for the poor, it is likely that these infants of both sexes were desperate cases to begin with, and therefore whether they were boys or girls was more or less irrelevant. Where the numbers do show some interesting variations is in those taken back by parents. Here the males had a better record: 53.2 per cent were reclaimed compared to only 46.4 per cent of females. However, girls had a better chance of making a permanent attachment to the wet-nurse. Though the overall numbers were small, still 56.3 per cent of those adopted by nurses were female. Similarly, a much larger group of girls were adopted by others: 73.3 per

TABLE 6.4
Deaths within the hospital, 1764–87

Year	Admissions	Deaths sin salida	Mortality in hospital (per cent)
1764	747	238	
1765	708	266	
1766	710	342	
1767	658	255	
1768	656	203	
1769	573	178	
1770	680	237	36.52 (1764–70)
1771	728	263	
1772	667	242	
1773	666	200	
1774	724	312	
1775	675	220	35.75 (1771–75)
1776	599	235	
1777	614	210	
1778	606	247	
1779	663	224	
1780	760	225	35.21 (1776–80)
1781	843	244	
1782	711	300	
1783	713	290	
1784	725	320	
1785	788	337	39.44 (1781–85)
1786	764	383	
1787	723	345	49.64 (1786–87)

SOURCE: *Entradas*, monthly summaries, 1764–87

TABLE 6.5
Deaths within the hospital, 1791–1801

Year	Admissions	Deaths sin salida	Mortality in hospital (per cent)
1791	849	363	
1792	835	360	
1793	928	321	
1794	962	355	
1795	954	343	39 (1791–95)
1796	1044	455	
1797	1123	570	
1798	1333	523	
1799	1110	579	
1800	1205	720	50 (1795–1800)
1801	1140	629	

SOURCE: *Entradas*, Totals, 1791–1801

TABLE 6.6
Deaths within the hospital, 1800–05

Year	Admissions	Deaths sin salida	Surviving (with nurse or parents)
1800	948 (1205)	660 (720)	288 (193)
1801	896 (1140)	560 (629)	336 (176)
1802	869 (1202)	402 (1010)	467 (192)
1803	937	471	466
1804	1036	727	309
1805	915	631	284

SOURCE: *Entradas*, Totals, 1800–02 and Ruiz de Luzuriaga, 'Estadística político-médica,' I: 44, 45

cent compared to 26.7 per cent boys. Perhaps some families felt that a girl could make a contribution to helping around the house and doing small chores better than a boy. That is, boys had a better chance of returning to their own families; girls had a better chance of being taken into another family.

We come to the end of this depressing account with a final set of figures that gives the overall mortality picture within the hospital. Tables 6.4–6.6 are of two types: those based on annual totals (tables 6.5, 6.6) and those based on monthly aggregations (table 6.4). These can be compared with the overall mortality rates for the infants who left with nurses, but whose respite was only temporary (tables 6.7, 6.8). The figures come from the *entradas*, but are supplemented by an account of the mortality rates in the various foundling hospitals of Spain put together in 1815–17 by a doctor of the Academy of Medicine in Madrid, with membership in medical societies of Edinburgh, London, Marseilles, Montpellier, and Barcelona and a particular interest in child care – Ignacio María Ruiz de Luzuriaga. His numbers for the Inclusa were collated under the administration of the Junta de damas, and there is some discrepancy between his and those of the *entradas* (see table 6.6). Nevertheless, Luzuriaga's figures are useful because they supply numbers for infants dying outside the hospital in some years when the distinction is not always explicit in the *entradas*. Taken together, the data show that the mortality rate of infants in the hospital before they were taken out by nurses (*sin salida*) rose gradually after 1730. It stayed around 35 per cent until the 1780s, then rose to around 40 per cent in the period 1785–95, and after this began a precipitate increase than in some years reached 87 per cent, but which averaged around 70 per cent in 1800–04. Tables 6.4–6.6 deal with mortality within the hospital itself.

These infants were victims of the crowded conditions within the institution and of the shortage of nurses to take them out.

Further information about the pattern of mortality within the hospital comes from monthly summaries. These monthly totals, faithfully recorded in the *entradas*, demonstrate how deaths fluctuated seasonally as well over a long term. They suggest that the situation of the infants of the poor worsened after 1760. By averaging the monthly figures and comparing them with the mean by decades, certain patterns emerge. During the period 1700–40, the largest numbers died in mid summer and early fall even though these were also the months with the lowest admissions. This information is not surprising, given that summer months, and especially August, were particularly dangerous for the new-born. Infants being weaned were fed concoctions mixed with animal milk that were open to contamination from summer heat, flies, and insects. After 1740, deaths were increasingly evident in the months of early spring as well, possibly the result of bronchial and pulmonary complaints. But beginning in 1760 the pattern of monthly mortality figures began to bear a remarkable similarity to monthly admission rates (see figures 6.2 and 6.3). The over-average highs of the month of August disappeared, and more deaths occurred in the spring and winter months. Finally, after 1780 infants of the Inclusa were increasingly likely to die regardless of what month of the year they were admitted. Whether they died for different reasons, such as the deteriorating hospital environment, or whether it was because more sickly infants were being admitted is difficult to say. For whatever reason, the pattern of mortality was not marked by seasons; deaths were spread more or less evenly throughout the whole year. The children of the poor could no longer depend on seasonal respite from the inexorability of their fate.

Collating these statistics has made it possible to reconstruct the overall mortality of the *expósito*, that is, the death rate for all infants admitted to the Inclusa, dying within the hospital itself, and once taken out with nurses. One version of this analysis has been done on the basis of the records given in the *entradas* for June and December of the decade years. It is only an approximation. For instance in 1740, the mortality rate was 87 per cent, a figure that held only for the year 1740 itself (a disastrous one for the poor of Madrid), not for the whole decade. However, generally speaking, the decade years provide a general, overall picture, which is supplemented by complete totals for the period after 1787. These are available in the *entradas* for those dying with outside

TABLE 6.7
Total deaths based on
entradas for June and
December of decade years,
1700–90

Year	Per cent dying within hospital and with nurses
1700–09	53.8
1710–19	57.0
1720–29	56.0
1730–39	66.6
1740–49	87.0
1750–59	74.0
1760–69	73.8
1770–79	68.0
1780–89	66.0
1790–99	72.1

SOURCE: *Entradas*, June, December, 1700–99

nurses as well, so that for those critical years a more detailed outline can be clearly seen. It is at this point that the records began to list systematically deaths both inside and outside the institution (see tables 6.7 and 6.8). While most of these deaths would be of infants admitted within the year (because the youngest were the most likely to succumb), the records do not make a distinction based on what month the child was admitted.

The deaths of infants dying within the hospital and in the homes of wet-nurses are a consequence of the economic and social conditions that were making it increasingly difficult for the poor to keep their infants, and for the wet-nurses who were taking them out to provide for them with any degree of success. The mortality rate of the *expósito* reflected not only the financial difficulties of the Inclusa itself, but the problems of the government and society as a whole at the turn of the century. We have seen that the hospital's income from alms declined at a steady rate over the century, but that the rate of inflation accelerated. As a result, the permanent assets of the Inclusa were worth less and less while its expenses increased. This financial problem could only be reflected in the kind of care the infant received. Finally, the deaths

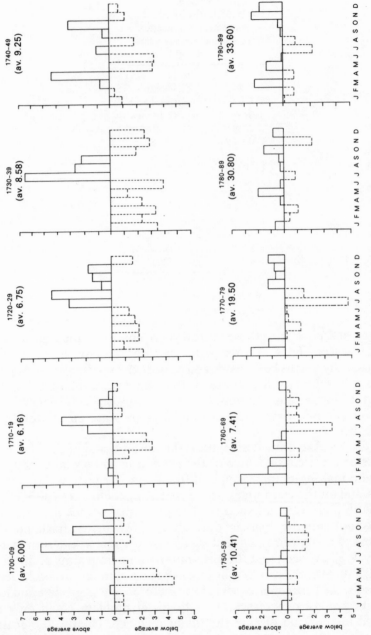

FIGURE 6.2 Monthly deaths of infants above and below the mean, 1700–99

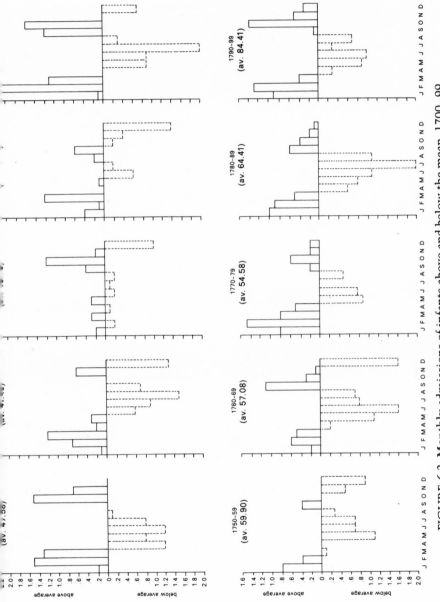

FIGURE 6.3 Monthly admissions of infants above and below the mean, 1700–99

TABLE 6.8
Total deaths based on
annual summaries, *entradas*,
1787–1802

Year	Per cent of deaths to admissions
1787	79.75
1788	81.5
1789	84.0
1790	75.6
1791	79.4
1792	80.0
1793	85.8
1794	78.4
1795	82.8
1796	82.1
1797	87.6
1798	76.4
1799	83.1
1800	83.9
1801	84.5
1802	84.0

SOURCE: *Entradas*, Totals,
1787–1802

described were also a function of the growing difficulties that the ordinary citizen, and especially the wage worker or the unemployed, was experiencing in Madrid. The correlation between grain prices and deaths (fig. 6.4) and between grain prices and admissions (fig. 1.1) is clear evidence of the way in which the cost of living and the consequent distress of the poor found its expression in the mortality records of the Inclusa.

But despite this gloomy résumé, not all infants died (see table 6.9). In the period 1700–99, 11.3 per cent returned to the hospital, 13.2 per cent were reclaimed by their parents, and 3.6 per cent found adoptive parents.

The problem of what to do with these children who had no home but the institution was a universal one. In medieval Milan, wards at age eight had been 'free to live where it pleases them.' In sixteenth-century Lyons, administrators, when they could not find suitable employment at hand for a child of seven, provided him with a placard stating 'orphan leaving the Hôtel Dieu, and asking for alms for the love of God.'[36] A few

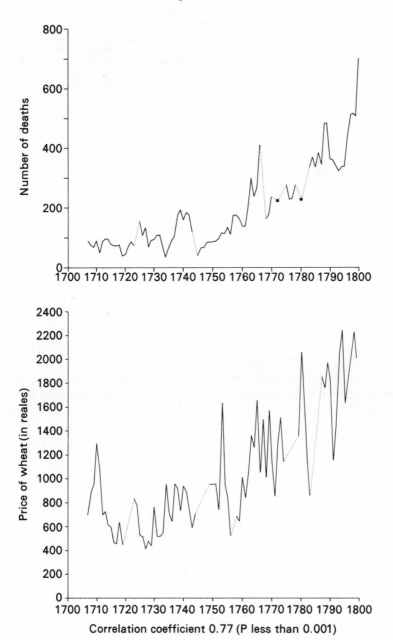

FIGURE 6.4 Mortality of infants of the Inclusa and the price of wheat, 1700–99

TABLE 6.9
Fate of infants abandoned to the Inclusia, 1700–99

Year	Died	Returned	Adopted by parents	Adopted by nurse	Adopted by others
1700	56.8	8.1	0.0	5.4	29.7
1710	56.4	15.5	20.0	7.3	0.9
1720	58.3	22.9	12.5	4.2	2.1
1730	67.2	17.2	10.9	3.1	1.6
1740	87.3	2.8	9.9	0	0
1750	75.6	4.4	16.7	2.2	1.1
1760	73.6	10.3	14.9	0	1.3
1770	69.6	13.0	17.4	0	0
1780	66.2	8.5	25.4	0	0
1790	72.1	16.3	11.6	0	0
1799	86.1	8.9	5.1	0	0

SOURCE: *Entradas*, 1700–99

of the infants of the Inclusa were taken by a group called the Beatas who cared for orphan girls, but most went to the orphanage of the Desamparados. Here they were taught a skill with the hope that someday they might be able to provide for themselves.

However, children raised in such institutions tended to be a pathetic lot. An observer of foundlings in Dublin described them as 'stunted creatures, neither childlike nor human ... At play they sit close-packed against the wall or gathered into knots, dull and stupified on their nursery floors ... Workhouse training makes them in outward appearance very much alike. They have a downcast, frightened look; like little machines they are always falling into line and putting their hands behind their backs as if to put themselves out of the way as much as possible.'[37]

In the words of the Duc de la Rochefoucauld-Liancourt, member of the Council of Hospices and president of the Committee on Mendicity in Paris in 1790: 'Such children raised in hospitals never become men. Their physical and moral faculties remain undeveloped ... The State has spent huge sums to make these children useless, miserable, and as a result, dangerous.'[38] A study of children raised in a present-day institution in Lebanon shows that even in modern circumstances those adopted as early as age two exhibited an absolute mental retardation that was directly related to how much time they had spent in the hospital. Those who remained institutionalized reached, as adults, a mean mental age of eight years, and almost never achieved a grade one level of education. Of the girls only two out of thirty-five married, and six ended up in psychiatric hospitals.[39] Infants who returned to the Inclusa and then were sent to an orphanage were not likely to be very much better off after their terms in such institutions than those who did not survive.

In fact, there is almost no information about these eighteenth-century *incluseros* once they became adults. Considering the numbers admitted and the attention the government paid to their plight at the end of the century, that in itself is remarkable. They seem to have disappeared without a trace. Perhaps it was because the family played such an important part in the society of the time, and they had no family and therefore no place. There was no one to arrange a marriage, to see to a dowry, to find an apprenticeship except the hospital. Probably many found anonymity in the ranks of the poor in the large cities or joined the crowds of beggars who were already outcasts from society, but the fate of the vast majority of foundlings is no mystery.

Joaquín Xavier de Uriz, the administrator of the Inclusa in Pamplona, who devoted so much attention to attempts to save the lives of these children, conducted his own personal survey of the areas sending infants to the foundling hospital: 'I have investigated in different parishes of various congregations and scarcely even one has ever been married. I know of many parts of Navarre, and the towns are very small, one cannot hide the composition of their families. But the fact is that rarely can anyone recall any *expósitos* ... Then where are they all? Have they all left Navarre in the past thirty years? What new towns can you point to where they are living? What regiments have they formed, or what useful workers have they provided for the country?'

The conclusion of his inquiry is both moving and convincing: 'Do not waste time looking for them. They are to be found in the graveyards and nowhere else.'[40]

7

The *Expósito* as Patient:
The Medicalization of the Inclusa

And die they did, by the hundreds in individual hospitals, by the thousands in individual countries. The picture is clear. Abandonment to a foundling hospital was almost the equivalent of a death sentence – one that might be carried out on the way to the hospital, inside the hospital, in the care of the wet-nurse, or after the return to the institution. To survive one of these stages was to become eligible for the next. Few, fortunate, and far between were the foundlings who survived exposure and grew up to become adults. Moreover, the foundling hospital and the wet-nurses in charge of the infants were considered to be the agents of their destruction.

Observers did not equivocate. They described the institutions as 'killing places.' Richard Ford, redolent with the sense of superiority that nineteenth-century Englishmen reserved for the benighted heathen (and the Spaniard), described the foundling hospital of Seville in 1846 as 'a place where the innocent are martyred, to which unnatural parents bring their children to be killed from slow starvation. Death is a blessing for the child and a saving for the institution, for if the life of a man is worth little, that of an abandoned infant is worth still less.'[1] But Spaniards themselves were just as harsh in their condemnations. 'Up to now, exposing these infants has been the same thing as killing them,' wrote Bilbao y Durán. 'Their extermination has been effected with the same means as had been set up to preserve them.'[2] But the English were in no position to take a high moral tone. Buchan, an English doctor, condemned the British system just as forcefully: 'Here under the mask of charity, barbarity immolates infants ... A policy similar to that of China would be an act of charity compared to the guardianship of the parishes.'[3] When the Junta de damas took over the Inclusa in 1799 the secretary wrote: 'The Inclusa of Madrid has become a sepulchre where infants find almost certain death.'[4]

The poverty that resulted in the exposition of so many infants and the appalling mortality rate in these institutions provided a challenge to the medical profession, which had confidence that science could resolve all the problems of the universe. The *expósitos* had always been a popular cause: noble families left them funds, churchmen encouraged charitable works devoted to their care, even enlightened reformers could hardly make their case against the 'undeserving poor' applicable to this group of disadvantaged. Now doctors fired with the nascent optimism of the century joined the worthy company of champions of the *expósito*. They brought to the problem a new focus: the idea that medical science could succeed where all else failed. Part of the solution they envisaged was to replace the nurse and nurse's milk with a substitute that would involve doing away with the human factor and replacing the women with goats, which were easier to control. For men of science the wet-nurses of the poor were seen in scientific terms as one of the causes of the deaths of so many infants, and the hospital as a laboratory where techniques could be evolved to remedy the situation.

The publicity given to the plight of foundlings served to focus attention on their medical problems and to mobilize efforts to do something about them. This chapter looks at the Inclusa and the practice of medicine at the time and the endeavours that were made to deal with the *expósito*, not simply as a social or economic problem, but as a medical one. It also assesses the role played by the wet-nurse in the perception of the medical profession. What were the medical reasons that these women were considered a threat to the welfare of the new-born? Why were these women seen as an obstacle to be eliminated before any improvement could be expected in the lot of the foundlings?

The conditions in the foundling hospitals may have had a galvanizing effect on the process of medicalization that was beginning in the eighteenth century. These institutions – where hundreds of infants, many of them sickly, were collected together – gave doctors a unique opportunity to observe, try out remedies, and develop new techniques. In what may be the ultimate paradox, these institutions, accused with justice of being themselves a factor in the deaths of many infants, may have played a positive role in the long-term development of medical care. By the end of the eighteenth century, the Inclusa had become a hospital for sick children, if only inadvertently. Ironically enough, the conditions that were causing the deaths of so many infants called attention to their plight and turned the *expósitos* into a medical problem, one that doctors and administrators like the Junta de damas believed could be solved. The Inclusa of Madrid is an example of the evolution of a foundling hospital into a paediatric institution.

Medical literature of the period indicates that at the end of the eighteenth century paediatrics was at the point of taking off as a separate discipline with a rationale and system of its own. A plethora of medical treatises, inspired by the eighteenth-century belief in progress, focused on the infant as the logical place to start the process of improving the human race. Locke (himself a physician), Rousseau, and Pestalozzi are credited with inventing the doctrine of the child as the agent of human perfectibility. But the apostles who preached the message and dispensed the means of salvation were doctors. The writings of the doctors such as Santiago García and Agustín Ginesta reveal that medical theory and practice in Spain shared fully in the preconceptions, prejudices, and attitudes of the Enlightenment, which were particularly evident in the treatment of the child, sick and well.

Doctors in eighteenth-century Spain imported their theories from France in a long series of medical treatises dealing with the care of the new-born. These medical treatises were by and large an exposition of the doctrines of a professor of medicine in Leyden, Hermann Boerhaave, the most influential teacher in Europe. One of his pupils, La Mettrie, took his master's principles to their logical conclusions in the notorious work *L'Homme Machine*. The author was hounded out of both France and Holland, ultimately to find security in that haven for iconoclasts, the court of Frederick of Prussia. Meanwhile his master remained highly respected, and his ideas permeated the medical thought of the period. When the Royal Academy of Medicine set up the College of Surgery of San Carlos in Madrid in 1787, they used the works of Boerhaave as basic texts.[5]

But though the theorizing framework came from abroad, much of Spanish medicine continued to operate within a long tradition based on practical experience. Arab surgeons in western Europe had kept alive this empirical approach throughout the Middle Ages. In Spain, the emphasis on the clinical in certain schools had never completely disappeared. It remained important in Valencia, Seville, and, to a certain extent, Barcelona. Despite the fact that faculties of medicine in the universities were dominated by a book-oriented, Aristotelian-Galenic curriculum that stressed memorization of aphorisms of Hippocrates, there continued to be many 'outsiders' of Jewish or Arabic extraction practising medicine in Spain – practising in the fullest sense of the word. These surgeons, precisely because they were excluded from universities, functioned outside the stilted academic atmosphere that stifled originality in the *médico latino*.

Luis Granjel points out in his history of Spanish paediatrics that there was little interest in child care in the first half of the century. But it must be granted that developments in the second half marked a renaissance, rather than a genesis.[6] The first known book on obstetrics and care of the new-born had been written in Córdova in 950 by Arab Ibn Saib: *A Treatise on the Generation of the Fetus and the Treatment of Pregnant Women and the Newborn.*[7] There were numerous clinical descriptions of diseases and many of these concerned childhood illnesses. In particular, diphtheria was the subject of much interest in sixteenth- and seventeenth-century Spain, though it was not described in France before the works of Caron (1807) and Bretonneau (1826).[8] Ruth Hodgkinson points out that statistical records in England did not differentiate between scarlet fever and diphtheria before 1861.[9] Spain had a history of clinical expertise in childhood diseases long before other countries in western Europe developed an interest in them.

Nor did medical literature suffer from the kind of restrictions and censorship we tend to associate with the import of scientific ideas from abroad. From the first years of the century when the new Bourbon monarch Philip v arrived with his court surgeon, *comadrón* (male midwife), and physician, Spain was open to the advances in medicine occurring in France and the rest of Europe. Most standard medical treatises were available in translations. For instance, Ballexserd's prize-winning *Dissertation sur l'éducation physique des enfants*, which won the prize of the Société Hollandaise des Sciences in 1762, was translated and published in Spain only three years later.[10] The doctor of the Inclusa was himself responsible for making available in Spanish the work of Antoine Petit based on his course in the Faculty of Medicine in Paris on obstetrics and the care of the new-born. The Royal College of Surgery in Barcelona possessed 562 volumes, of which 17 were the classical tomes of *medicina antigua* and the rest were mostly by French authors on matters of anatomy and surgery. When the Royal College of San Carlos opened in Madrid in 1787, it possessed a library stocked with all the important treatises of the time devoted to child care including many from Great Britain such as Rush, *On the Asthma of Children*, in *Edinburgh Medical Essays* (six volumes), Sparrman's translation of Nicholas Rosen von Rosenstein's *The Diseases of*

Children and Their Remedies (1776), and numerous works on midwife-ry by Forster, Giffard, Hamilton, White, Smellie, and Deventer.[11] Even more interesting is that this library was open to the public.[12]

The contribution of Spanish doctors to the theoretical aspects of this literature on what the French called *éducation physique* was for the most part just a recycling of the general ideas of the time. These included works by doctors Pedro Dandais and Francisco Rubio and an archdeacon with scientific interests, Antonio Arteta. More simplified popular works aimed at educating the mother of the family were written by Bonells and Ginesta, while others such as those of Navas and Pastor were directed to improving the obstetrical skills of doctors and surgeons. But Spanish medicine made a special contribution in the field of clinical descriptions of diseases common to infants. Santiago García was awarded the prize of the Academy of Medicine of Madrid for his memorial describing hereditary *tisis* (pulmonary tuberculosis) in 1798. A surgeon of Barcelona, Francisco Sampots y Roca, won international renown for his description of *muguet* or thrush, and proposals for its cure, published by the Royal Society of Medicine in Paris in 1788.[13]

Women and children were closely associated in the minds of doctors, and medical treatises did not usually separate obstetrics from paediat-rics. Logically enough the two worked in tandem, and interest in the child was reflected by a new approach to obstetrics. Before 1750 this field had been left to midwives, and surgeons were only called in in cases of difficulty. In fact, from 1523–1750, the Royal Protomedicato in Castile had precisely forbidden doctors to have anything to do with childbirth.[14] However, the process modern historians have described as 'medicalization' was to change all this. In the words of one French physician: 'Now that childbirth has become a science it is too important to be left in the hands of ignorant women.'[15]

This new focus showed itself not only in the literature of the period but also in attempts to improve clinical practice. When the Royal College of Surgery of San Carlos was set up in 1787, part of its mandate was to instruct in obstetrics and child care. The ordinances proposed to study infants under three headings: (1) new-born; (2) infants of forty days until weaned; and (3) infantile diseases from birth to age seven. The college also sponsored public colloquia Thursday afternoons where doctors and surgeons could present some of their cases to be discussed and evaluated by the professors of the college.[16]

It was obvious that, for better or worse, the foundling hospitals were an ideal setting for observing the sicknesses of infancy first hand. Lorenzo Hervás y Panduro in a magisterial work entitled *La Vida del Hombre* had suggested that there should be special institutions devoted to the problems of infant care: 'The importance of the health and life of infants merits that there should be set up an academy devoted exclusively to their illnesses, to prescribe and make known to the public certain simple and easy methods to raise healthy children. This academy should train doctors destined uniquely to care for infants, and pay them good salaries with the condition that they charge nothing for their care. This would enable the poor to call upon them in cases of their children's illnesses.'[17] Inclusas were academies ready at hand for the medical men who had only to take advantage of the opportunity. Hervás y Panduro may not have had the foundling hospitals in mind, but the next logical step would be to associate the two problems in a way that would provide joint solutions to the problems of sick infants in general and foundlings in particular.

Foundling hospitals provided an opportunity to observe infants and their illnesses at close quarters and on a large scale. But science was not limited to observation. Inclusas provided a human laboratory for new techniques and experiments that could be justified because most foundlings were going to die in any event. One way in which the *expósitos* functioned as guinea-pigs was in the attempt to develop a suitable substitute for mother's milk. France, as the source of much of the literature on paediatrics, provided the model and inspiration for the doctor of the Inclusa of Madrid. Raulin, the French physician, whose work was one of the sources quoted by Santiago García, described an experiment in Rouen where thirty infants were set up in ideal conditions of cleanliness, fresh air, etc., and fed cow's milk. It was observed that the infants slept little, cried much, sickened, and died.[18] Experiments to cure syphilitic infants and their nurses by giving the woman mercury and than having her medication passed on through her milk were first tried out in the hospital of Vaugirard in Paris on a set of enfants-trouvés.[19]

Inoculation had been practised in some parts of the peninsula from the mid eighteenth century, and was given official sanction in 1792. The procedure of vaccination had to be demonstrated on a large scale in the foundling hospitals before the general public could be persuaded to take it up, though doctors were by and large convinced of its value by 1799. There were examples indicating that some medical practitioners expected *expósitos* to provide the kind of service to medical science that white mice do today. In 1803, there was an attempt to develop a new smallpox vaccine from goats. A royal order that proposed trying out this extract on the foundlings of the Inclusa was firmly opposed by the Junta de damas, 'because of the dangers that could come to the infants as a result of this [experiment], which, as of this point, has nothing to say in its favour.'[20]

Here we have an example of women's attitude toward the foundling differing from that of the male medical establishment, which tended to view the *expósito* as an expendable unit that could be sacrificed for the collective good. This particular experiment was subsequently performed on a boy from the Desamparados orphanage by Don Antonio Martínez and Don Pedro Hernández, with thirty doctors in attendance.[21] In contrast, the *damas* were eager to participate in a vaccination campaign planned for the Indies under the direction of the prestigious doctor Don Francisco Xavier de Balmis and involving many eminent professors. The project intended to immunize a series of infants, one from the other, as they made the stages of the journey from Madrid to the port of La Coruña, and thence to America. This would mean that on arrival in the New World, vaccination could be carried out directly from arm to arm, with fresh serum that had not been exposed to alteration or deterioration in the course of the journey. Seven infants from the Inclusa were donated for this project, which held more respectable credentials and seemed to the *damas* a cause worthy of the risks involved.[22]

Obviously, the foundling had become a means of progress for the medical profession as well as for political theorists. The *expósito* was exploited by those interested in the health care of the infant, but this was justified because it was assumed that the result would ultimately save lives. In the past, the function of the hospital had been more bureaucratic than medical – simply receiving infants and arranging for a wet-nurse to take them out. The *expósito*'s best hope for survival had always been directly related to the amount of time spent in the institution before some woman arrived to provide individual attention and a home, poor though it might be. But by the end of the century, as more infants were sentenced to longer terms, the Inclusa found itself turning into a primitive, clumsy, ineffectual, but nevertheless functioning, hospital for sick children.

There was another sense in which the Inclusa was beginning to function as a hospital. Any hospital before the end of the nineteenth century was considered, with justice, a health hazard. Townspeople lobbied to have them moved outside city limits because their effluence and contagion presented a source of infection to the whole area. Too often they were places where the suffering contracted diseases they did not have before, where slight illnesses became serious and serious ones mortal. On this ground as well, the Inclusa had become a hospital rather than a temporary shelter for the abandoned.

In the Inclusa could be found at first hand a plethora of cases to put to the test the best efforts of the doctor and his enlightened cohorts in the Junta de damas. One side-effect of the Enlightenment's focus on poverty was the attempt to cure the sicknesses of infants of the poor. Though serving more as caricatures than as models for infant health care, the attempts in the hospital to deal with large numbers of sick infants provide information about the science of paediatrics at a time when it was just beginning to establish itself as a separate discipline. The work done by the doctor and the administration of the Inclusa was evidence of the medicalization of the field of infant welfare that occurred under the pressure of circumstances at the end of the eighteenth century. The Inclusa pioneered in the field of health care – of necessity.

Some diseases the infants brought with them, some they caught from one another, others were the result of conditions within the institution itself. One that they brought with them was syphilis, which seems to have been very common. According to a report of the Council of Castile in 1772, among 18,000 admissions to Spanish hospitals, 12,000 had cases of syphilis.[23] Infants contracted it via uterine infection during the last months of pregnancy.[24] Apparently it could also be transmitted from the infant to its nurse. Pérez de Escobar insisted that it had spread throughout all the infants in one town from an infected *expósito*.[25] Because its presence usually could not be detected for the first few weeks of a new-born's life, the wet-nurse felt a certain fear and repugnance for the foundling. Despite the need to sell her milk, there was always the danger that she was bringing home to her family a source of contamination, even death. Infected eyes, mouths, or genitals were all sign of syphilis, though in many cases the eye inflammations, said to be endemic in these institutions, were probably due to gonorrhoea. Claimed one doctor: 'Ofalmias are the first disease they contract in these hospitals, and the cause is sometimes scrofulous, sometimes *herpético* or *psórico*, and often venereal.'[26] The treatment of diseases in infants in the past had often been the same as for adults. Mercury was commonly administered for syphilis, and the treatment, even for adults, was almost as bad as the cure; few infants survived.[27] An alternative was the aforementioned experiment in the Paris hospital of Vaugirard where the syphilitic nurse was treated and then given an infected foundling to nurse. This indirect dosage was apparently practised with some success.[28]

But perhaps the most deadly of infant diseases waited within the confines of the hospital itself. According to Lallemand, thrush, or *muguet*, was the cause of death of one-third of the foundlings in the Hôpital des Enfants-trouvés in Paris.[29] It made its appearance in 1739 and from that time no child who had to stay there more than two or three days escaped infection. Its symptoms were white spots starting at the corners of the lips, then spreading to the tongue and cheeks to form a white lining on the inside of the mouth. In serious cases this crust fell off to be succeeded by darker ones: 'Apthes can consume flesh down to the bone and in an acute form bring on fistulas, tumours and cancers.'[30] This, of course, made it very painful for the child to nurse and contributed toward weakening it.

Thrush was a fungal disease caused by *Candida albicans*, but other skin diseases were spread by an insect. *Sarna*, or 'the itch,' was common to jails, barracks, foundling hospitals, and 'the poor who share the same clothing and sleep in the same rooms.'[31] It was due simply to lack of cleanliness and the remedies were the common disinfectants of the period: saffron, vinegar and sulphur, and, of course, soap and water.

Another form of skin disease endemic to hospitals was a scalp infection called in Spain *tiña* (tinea or ringworm in English) – or 'leprosy of the head' or 'rust of the hair.' Prolonged cases (the severe form is called *favus*) could cause deep scars and, if glands became infected, even death. The remedy proposed by a doctor of the Faculty of Physic[k] in Paris was nothing if not drastic. 'Cut the hair close to the scalp and wash it with the child's own fresh urine as often as possible [other doctors suggested a strong concoction of tobacco and soap]. After two days cover with a bladder, or a urine-soaked linen plaster; follow this with a plaster of myrrh, aloes, pitch and turpentine and leave on for three days. Then pull off gently and all the skin will come with it.'[32] Probably this is the 'barbarous method used in the Inclusa of Madrid,' and referred to by Ruiz de Luzuriaga, that cured the scalp but left the child bald for life.[33]

Doctors of the day considered jaundice or *manchas amarillas* as a skin ailment of the new-born. This was so common that it was assumed to be a natural concomitant to the meconium present in the digestive tract of the new-born at birth. 'At three days,' we are told, 'the child appears yellow ... this will usually disappear within ten–twelve days, and if not, an emetic can be administered.'[34]

Skin diseases were common and could have been a relatively minor problem, except that in the atmosphere of the hospital they became almost uncontrollable. Certainly they were legion: *mal de rosas* (ulcers sometimes of the mouth), *costra* (crust), *lepras*, *sarna*, *tiña*, herpes, even *gangrena* were various ways of designating infections that attacked the delicate epidermis of the new-born.

Some doctors, influenced by the theory of humours, considered skin eruptions to be a healthy way for the child to rid its system of acids in its digestive tract. They deduced that the same crust lined the interior of the infants' intestines and produced redness at the anus. Therefore they encouraged purges, clysters (enemas), and emetics. The most popular purge, because it was most powerful, was antimony wine. This was a solution of a metallic substance that was exceedingly dangerous for the tender organism of a new-born. Underwood, a British doctor who wrote a very popular treatise on the care of children and the new-born, was aware of this problem and pointed out the evils of giving a child emetics for weeks at a time. He suggested, instead, a treatment of powders to absorb acidity and a salve of borax and common honey.[35] The fact that honey was commonly listed among the ingredients in the madre's *tandas* along with 'egg for a child with a sore mouth' would encourage the hope that the Inclusa favoured the milder forms of treatment. But whatever the case, thrush remained an epidemic in the inclusas as late as 1847.[36]

Of course, skin eruptions were only to be expected. The tender skin of a new-born is easily irritated. Coarse wrappings (the *talegas y quiebras* arriving from the textile factories) included serge and burlap, the usual cloth for the poor. The system of binding the infants in wrappings was time consuming and diapers were not changed often enough. It was difficult in the circumstances to separate sick from well or to employ adequate means of sanitation. The results were painfully obvious to anyone. 'They die covered with scabs and scales only eight days after having been born clean.'[37]

Inflammations on the skin ran second only to internal ones. In the words of one administrator: 'Indigestion is a common complaint when milk is in short supply and supplements in the form of animal milk or gruel too strong for the weak digestive systems of a new-born are prepared without sufficient regard for cleanliness.'[38] Boerhaave employed the technical terms dear to doctors to explain why the new-born was more susceptible to indigestion: the food had turned into acid rendering the humours vicious. 'It is caused by the weak texture of the fibres and vessels of the entrails, a condition common to children, the slothful, poor persons, maids [i.e. spinsters], and some tradesmen.' His remedy was to administer bleedings and give the patient lots of warm water to evacuate the causes of coagulation, then apply steam to loosen up the fibres, soften the humours, and allow the blood to circulate freely.[39] Underwood describes his successful cure for 'gripes': 'Give a puke and afterwards a warm purge with rhubarb. Follow this with a small dose of ipecuaca or a few drops of antimony wine and start a glyster [sic] two or three times daily ... If the child is very sick give as well a few drops of laudanum daily.'[40] These kinds of 'cures' were probably too elaborate for the hospital routine. In fact, simple stomach upsets were something that the administrator in the Inclusa of Pamplona, Uriz, felt could be handled by applying a little common sense and care in the early stages. He pointed out that the child's system should be given a rest. Doctors, however, were more likely to call for purges, emetics, and bleedings that only aggravated the condition, weakened resistance to serious infections, and eventually brought on death from dehydration. The term *extenuado*, sometimes given as a cause of death, may simply have meant that the child was worn out, exhausted from medicines as much as from the sickness itself. Indigestion and the complications from indigestion were sicknesses built into the hospital setting and routine.

As long as the foundling was being nursed it was relatively immune to digestive upsets, but weaning was a critical period. It coincided with teething around the age of eighteen months and the complications resulting from both were often attributed to the latter. Teething was taken to be a sickness in its own right, with its own set of symptoms. 'The infant drivels, slathers, its gums swell and become hot; there is redness in the cheeks and looseness in the bowels accompanied by griping and green stools, [sometimes followed by] coughs, breathing difficulties, fits, fevers, marasmas and universal decay.'[41] Along with the usual treatment of purges, pukes, bleedings, and blisters, the child was encouraged to chew on a hard stone or crust; gums were rubbed with gentle oils or, if it seemed necessary, lanced. Teething was listed as the most common cause of death of the infants with outside nurses (67 of 305 cases in 1802). Santiago García was sufficiently alarmed by the loss of life to think of bringing back all infants to the hospital at this stage and setting them up in a special room where their diet could be supervised during the sensitive transition to solid food. This was, of course, highly impracticable and expensive, with no guarantee of success because there was no possible way to set up a controlled environment that would not in itself lose as many lives as it saved.

Although doctors may not have been able to give either consistent or helpful advice to treat skin or digestive complaints, at least they knew what it was they were treating. Fevers, in contrast, were ubiquitous and accompanied any number of indispositions from the common cold to 'sudden death.' It is easy enough to distinguish tertians and quatrians among the 'intermittent' fevers. These were the malarial type occurring at three- or four-day intervals. At the same time, there were malignant, putrid, and continuous fevers as well as the all-encompassing *fiebres* and *calenturas* – all designations for what may have been the same or different ailments. Categorizing this medley of terms could be perplexing, even for the physician trained in Aristotelian logic. The ambiguity of the word allowed free rein to speculative instincts. It was one occasion where the penchant for theorizing in the abstract could be given full play. With a remarkable eclecticism, doctors amalgamated the traditional humours into the new mechanistic theories of the eighteenth century. The body of the new-born was described as a kind of machine with humours coursing through it. Too much acid caused the blood to thin and course too rapidly. Humours fermented and gave off gas or spirit, in the same way that wine produced vinegar. This brought on a certain 'commotion in the blood.' Or put in layman's terms, the blood boiled.[42] Brouzet explained that the pressure of restricted blood vessels that had become swollen almost to bursting by the impetuosity of blood running through the delicate veins of the new-born caused redness to mount to the face, placing the infant in immediate danger of suffocation. Fever was the way that nature relieved this pressure on the veins of the new-born that had been constricted in the birth canal or compressed by too tight wrappings that hindered normal circulation.[43]

It would seem that whenever the doctors found themselves stymied by symptoms they were unable to treat with any degree of success, they took refuge in highly abstract, logical constructs to explain their dilemma. Another popular explanation attributed fevers to the glandular excretions of the new-born. 'Their glands are much larger than in adults ... and constantly excreting their slimy contents ... which overloads their tender bowel causing most complaints, even death.'[44]

Whatever the variety in diagnosis, the treatment was more of the same: bleedings and purges designed to keep the system open and allow pressure from noxious humours to escape freely. Leeches were used for this purpose and were considered safer than other methods of bleeding because they were easier to control. Because humours were supposed to rise to the head, the usual remedy was two leeches behind each ear. During the early years of the century the *madre* often bought them herself. It is also possible that when she used 'wine for washing infants,' she was cooling the skin of a feverish infant in the manner of alcohol rub-downs today. Another way to allow humours to escape was to open up the skin and keep it open by causing a blister, or by rubbing the skin with Spanish fly – a caustic solution of grain beetle wings, better known as an aphrodisiac. Solutions of iron filings, wormwood, hot sulphur water, or a puke of rhubarb in beer were the basic techniques to expel noxious humours causing fevers. More success could be expected from quinine whose 'bitter, earthy, gently astringent and resinous-balsamic qualities' were seen as a corrective for the febrile matter causing the upset.[45] This remedy came into use in Spain earlier than the rest of Europe, after its properties cured the fever of the duchess of Chinchona.

In general, the treatises of the period show a penchant for elaborately constructed logical apparatus in order to explain in scientific terms why doctors were applying the same old techniques of 'purges, clysters, and bleedings' to any and all ailments. The underlying theory varied but the treatment in practice remained for the most part unchanged.

The new-born, frail and vulnerable, was particularly susceptible to the kind of infections that ran rife in the hospital. But some infants survived the disastrous decimation afflicting their comrades in the first days of life, and escaped, at least temporarily, from the confines of what had turned into a charnel house. However, for many of this group, the reprieve proved to be of short duration. Foundlings continued to sicken and die with their outside wet-nurses. For some of these infants, we have precise data on the cause of death. In the years 1802, 1803, and 1804, the administration of the Inclusa had a certain degree of success in extorting certificates signed by a doctor, surgeon, or clergyman citing the presumed cause of death. Listed in table 7.1 are the precise reasons given in the year 1802 for deaths of infants who had left the Inclusa.

The line between the foundling inside the hospital and foundling outside was often a fine one. Sickly infants in particular were often shifted back and forth between nurses and institution. This movement became more common as the century went on. In 1700 only 8 per cent had three or more nurses, but in 1790 the figure was 37 per cent. Because of increasing demand for their services, women could pick and choose

TABLE 7.1
Diseases causing deaths of *expósitos* in 1802

Disease	No. of deaths	Total deaths
Convulsions		59
Fevers		91
Calenturas	47	
Fiebres	24	
Tertians	20	
Colds		6
Catarrals	5	
Pleurisia	1	
Gastro-enteritis		93
Cursos	11	
Cólicos	1	
Inflamación colorín	1	
Inflamación interna	4	
Dentición (teething)	63	
Skin diseases		26
Costra	2	
Sarna		
Ulceras	16	
Gangrena	7	
Worms (*Inchada*)		4
Diphtheria (*Garrotilla*)		2
Measles (*Sarampión*)		8
Mumps (*Parotida*)		1
Scarlet Fever (*Tabardillo*)		5
Smallpox (*Viruelas*)		14
Syphilis (*Venéreo*)		35
Tumour, abscess		1
Whooping cough (*Tos*)		10

and simply exchange a foundling that was too much trouble. Others brought back the child on the verge of dying to save themselves any complications. Some of the same diseases from which children died within the hospital could have been contracted outside, and vice versa. For instance, thrush, the main culprit in institutional deaths, was also the major killer of those outside. As Lallemand pointed out, it caused the death of one-third of infants within the hospital in Paris, but another third died with the wet-nurse after having contracted it there.[46] Of course, they came and left with syphilis, often still undiagnosed. Coughs were considered an institutional problem by Santiago García, who blamed the dust stirred up by the traffic in the Puerta del Sol and the fumes from *braseros*, lights, and soiled diapers. But those who died of coughs outside were more likely to be suffering from pulmonary complications or whooping cough.

Other illnesses that afflicted the *expósito* but could not be blamed on institutional confinement were the usual childhood diseases of scarlet fever, mumps, and measles, plus a number that have disappeared thanks to modern developments in medicine, such as smallpox and scrofula (tuberculosis of the lymph glands). Two of the children, aged three and four, in the charge of Barbara Olivera were diagnosed as having this disease, which affected the glands of the neck.

The childhood disease that has been best documented in Spain is diphtheria. Variously named *esquinamcer gangrenosa, carbuncolo gangrenoso, morbo sofocante, angina maligna, ulcera anginosa, angina ulcerosa gangrinosa, maligna pestilente, difteritis*, and *crup*,[47] diphtheria was popularly known as *garrotilla* after that ultimate in sore throats, the gallows. Perhaps it was more common in Spain than elsewhere: 1613 was known as 'the year of the *garrotilla*,' and Pérez de Escobar describes epidemics in Castile in the years 1750 and 1762.[48] It has even been depicted in the art of the day.

If diphtheria was exceptionally well documented, other diseases are almost impossible to classify. It would be interesting to know what the symptoms were of *extenuado*, which literally means worn out, and *encanejado* (evil eye), which indicates bewitched. *Accidente* could, of course, mean any number of things.

The child who lived long enough to go onto a diet that included solids such as fruit, meat, and cheese was susceptible to worms. The infections were supposed to be caused by insect eggs that grew and reproduced in the intestine, causing paleness, weakness, constipation, and indigestion. Brouzet blamed solids for engendering worms because of thickened humours that blocked up particles of food in the folds of the intestines. He tells a horror story about a two-year-old who expelled a twenty-foot worm, and another about an eight-year-old in Adge, in the Languedoc, with a worm of eight or nine feet.[49] To destroy the insect eggs required a strong alkaline solution, usually mercury, dissolved in a syrup of ethiope and oils, or two ounces of mercury in one pint of water. Alternatives were steel, tin, copper, or pewter filings diluted in wine.[50] Mercury was actually prescribed as a preventive measure. It is scarcely surprising, therefore, to find that there were infants suffering from trembling of the hands – the same minimata disease that has afflicted Indians who fish from mercury-polluted waters today.

One of the most interesting of the childhood diseases from the viewpoint of both analysis and treatment was 'convulsion.' It was, after fevers and gastro-enteritis, the most common cause of death listed by outside nurses. Possibly brain damage was more common in the eighteenth century because of bungled deliveries; still, it seems most likely that these convulsions causing deaths were not epilepsy usually, but merely the final stage of some other illness. Because convulsion can be triggered by high fevers, it was associated with any number of diseases. J.P. Peter has found that in the eighteenth century convulsion was taken as a symptom of such illnesses as scarlatina, pneumonia, and diphtheria.[51] Convulsion also characterized tetany – an infant disease common to children in the southern United States in the nineteenth century – whose cause was malnutrition, specifically a lack of vitamin D. Whatever the cause, convulsion characterized many of the deaths of these infants because, in the words of Armstrong, 'convulsion merely closes the scene.'[52]

Doctors attempting to find some scientific explanation for the prevalence of convulsion were engrossed with the complexity of the problem. Ruiz de Luzuriaga in his comprehensive nineteenth-century inquiry into the causes of infant mortality paid particular attention to convulsion. He discussed the case of the Dublin hospital where nineteen out of twenty deaths of infants under fifteen days were attributed to 'nine-day convulsions.' He noted the following symptoms: fretful and crying from birth; gluttonous of both regular and nurses' milk; tendency to sleep deeply and twist upper extremeties when awakening; black and blue circles around the mouth (carp mouth associated with tetany); sudden change in colouring of face; wrinkling and puckering of mouth and moaning.[53] While he blamed any number of things – depression of the cranium in delivery, cold, indigestion due to constipation, acidic upset, or corruption of milk, lack of food or milk, teething, thrush, upsets from anger or fear, kidney stones, abuses of opium given to make them sleepy – the symptoms he describes strongly suggest that many of these infants were suffering from tetany due to malnutrition. Because they were being nursed by women whose milk may have been deficient in vitamin D, tetany would be a plausible diagnosis.

Convulsions were so common among infants that doctors assumed the child had a natural tendency to go into convulsions as a result of the extreme sensitivity and irritability of its finely tuned nervous system. As in the case of fevers, whenever the doctors dealt with an ill-defined and frustrating set of symptoms they resorted to an elaborate set of theories to compensate for their lack of solid knowledge. In this particular illness, the theorizing says a great deal about attitudes toward the child, particularly the way in which the infant was considered to be almost a subspecies of humanity. For this reason, I discuss convulsion in some detail.

The new-born was supposedly exceedingly frail, 'recovering from a nine-month illness.'[54] It should not be exposed to the light suddenly or blindness might result; rocking the cradle could derange the brain; pulling on an arm could break it; noses were crushed and flattened if a nurse held an infant too close when feeding it or wiped its nose too vigorously. Obviously the new-born was a very delicate plant. Parents were warned against allowing the infant to sleep with an old person, especially a sick one, because they could absorb from them unhealthy humours and exhalations.[55] If the external mechanism could be unhinged so easily it was hardly surprising that there should also be concern over the internal mechanism. A brain disproportionately large for the rest of the body was the seat of a set of nerves easily disturbed and prone to convulsion.

In analysing the physical make-up of the infant, the key words were 'fibres, glands, humours, and machine.' All these were brought into play to explain convulsions. The irregular flux of animal spirits affected the vibration of the fibres connected to the brain, explained Petit, and set off a convulsion.[56] Other doctors operating within a mechanistic framework saw convulsion as a result of instability within the newly assembled parts of the infant's machine that caused nerves to vibrate too quickly, so that glandular contents spilled out, blood sped through the veins, and excess humours evaporated and rose to the head. All these effects were attributed to a lack of harmony between different parts of the child's anatomy. In other words, convulsion was the result of an over-abundance of glandular excretions that caused acidic indigestion and sent off humours to the head.[57] This was a variation of the 'vapours' theory used to explain nervous upsets in women in the nineteenth century. Children were more moist than adults. As the new-born aged, it would harden and tighten up, and its fibres would dry out, becoming less lax and humid. Until then, the soft, moist character of the infant's nervous system made it (like women) exceedingly sensitive.[58] As a result, connections within the system could easily break down and the whole operation could go out of control. When this occurred, a convulsion was the result.

The remedy was relatively simple: allow the humours to escape before they built up pressure in the head and set off a convulsion. The quickest way to effect this exit was by bleeding. For a new-born, however, this drastic treatment was beginning to be questioned. Brouzet felt called upon to apologize for surprising his readers and suggested that the same result could be secured by inducing vomiting or hiccups. He recommended an emetic of tartar of ipecuacua or powders of frog's eyes, corals, magnesium, and eggshells to absorb the acidic humours of the intestines before they rushed to the head.[59] Petit, however, continued to defend the old system in the face of 'some wicked people who attribute the deaths of these infants to the bleedings rather than to the convulsions.'[60] As with fevers, Petit sought to prevent humours from rising to the brain by applying leeches behind the ears or between the shoulder blades, keeping blisters on the neck or bathing the feet with warm water, all designed to coax down the humours or forestall them from reaching and disturbing the seat of the nervous system.

In their concern for finding a cure, some doctors tried to attack the very root of the problem. Because the infant was a high-strung and very sensitive entity, steps must be taken to see that its nervous system was not deranged in any way. Obviously, the soft, impressionable cerebellum was the main organ of reception and the repository of the nerves. It was also the final receptor of the humours that circulated through the system. What were the external factors from which it must be guarded to prevent any over-excitement in its functions?

In a sensationalist and mechanistic framework, the mind as well as the body was formed by what it took in from the outside world. John Locke had explained that the mind of the infant ultimately was a tabular rasa, or blank slate, stamped by the environment. This theory was the basis for much of the eighteenth-century faith in medicine. It pervaded the speculation and practice of the doctors who had to deal with the problems of the new-born. It can be seen most clearly in doctors' approaches to the problem of convulsion. If external factors could over-stimulate the delicate organization of the new-born, close attention had to be paid to the relationship between mind and matter, body and spirit. The mind as well as the body was formed by the outside world. In the case of the foetus the connection was obvious, but once pushed out of the womb into a hostile environment, the new-born was still depending on nurse or mother for growth, development, and formation.

Milk made the formal connection between infants and their environment. Nursing was a form of transfusion – in some ways an extension of pregnancy. Milk functioned as a kind of 'white blood' half-way between the venous serum of the nurse and the chyle or nourishing element in the child's digestive system. Taking this logic one step further, it was assumed that milk provided not only physical nourishment, but also passed on the nurses' humours, which formed mental, psychological, spiritual, even moral traits in the recipient. In the humours could be found the basis for each person's individuality, and this individuality could be formed or deformed from the breast by way of the milk.

In this literal application of 'you are what you eat,' the preoccupation of doctors and administrators with the character as well as the physical attributes of the wet-nurse becomes comprehensible. An unhealthy woman with weakened milk might sap rather than strengthen an infant. Worse still, an immoral one might pass on traits that could frustrate any hope of the infant developing a strong character. Nero was supposed to have imbibed his drunkenness from his wet-nurse and Caligula his cruelty from his nurse's habit of softening her teat in blood before giving him suck.[61]

Mother's milk was obviously best and safest for the infant for many reasons. They were both part of the same network and their fibres vibrated at the same wavelength. But even here there could be problems. If the mother had taken in too much animal meat, strong spices, wine, or alcohol, these elements – passed on to the tender system of the new-born – could corrode the lymph or thicken the blood. More dangerous was the transmission of the mother's excitability and passions. Over and over, women were cautioned against nursing an infant after a violent emotional outburst or on any occasion that aroused strong feelings. Such events, they were told, could alter their milk, changing it into poison capable of disrupting the balance of the new-born – in other words, causing a convulsion.

Several proofs were offered in support of this warning. Underwood tells of one of his patients who had a visitor suddenly drop dead. The woman, naturally upset, nevertheless went ahead to nurse a six-month-old, who then fell into convulsions and a coma for thirty-six hours.[62] Armstrong recounts how a five-week-old suffered a convulsion when nursed despite the mother's surprise and joy at the unexpected return of her husband after an absence of several months.[63] However, the example most constantly cited had to do with a young woman who did indeed heed the dire prognostications of the medically learned.

After a fright, she gave nurse to a little dog so as not to upset her infant with altered milk. A moment later the dog suffered a violent epileptic attack. This story, originally attributed to Etmüller, recurs in Ballexserd, Bonells, and Raulin.[64]

Given these beliefs, could one consider even mother's milk to be good for the child? After all, as one author pointed out, 'women are, of all creatures, most subject to maladies and infirmities since, along with the qualities of air, water, fire, and malignant vapours from the air that affect all animals, they are most exposed to the effects of "*passions de l'âme*"' – passions that agitate and irritate the blood so that 'it lacks the balsam quality needed to make chyle.'[65]

The new findings of science put the doctor and the administrators of foundling hospitals in a quandary. If mother's milk was dangerous, what could be said about the milk of the wet-nurse? As a stranger to the infant, her humours could hardly harmonize with those of her nursling, even under the best of conditions. Moreover, how could the infant absorb the constancy needed for growth from a woman who was not only poor and unhealthy, but of the lower classes who were notoriously susceptible to emotional upsets and fits of passion – the very factors that brought on convulsions. In the words of Moreu de Saint-Elier, the misogynist author who expressed this theory in its most extreme form: 'The more the organs of the body of the nurse are excited by her restlessness and the influence of tumultuous passions, the more her blood acquires an acrid and unhealthy instability ... which she passes on to the child just as the saliva of a maddened rabid creature or the foam of a smallpox victim can communicate its properties to the healthiest of individuals.'[66] For this particular author, 'women of our century are so corrupt in morals and unhealthy physically that one should have as little as possible to do with their blood and humours.'[67]

Of all the disadvantages and disabilities the *expósito* suffered, one of the most serious was the shortage of an adequate milk supply. But for administrators like Uriz and doctors like Santiago García, aware of the theorizing on the relationship between milk and convulsion, the problem of nurses' milk took on a new and frightening dimension. Uriz tells us that the main cause of death of *expósitos* was the lack of care and seriousness on the part of nurses responsible for feeding them, women whose milk had become in his words 'a poison.' Santiago García used similar language, describing wet-nurses as women fit to kill rather than care for an infant. In this context, the rationale for such views is clear: these nurses were emotional, passionate women, and they did not use discretion but proceeded to nurse the *expósito* on any occasion, often with an 'altered milk' that brought on convulsion and death of the infant.

In the list of sicknesses submitted to the Inclusa, convulsion – associated with fevers and teething, or taken as a separate disease – ranked as a major cause of the deaths of these infants. For the doctors of the time, there was one major reason for the prevalence of convulsions: poor nursing on the part of poor nurses. In the mechanistic views of the medical profession of the eighteenth century, milk was the fuel that kept the motor of the infant in operation and allowed the child to grow and flourish. Nurses' milk was tainted by the passions of the undisciplined, unruly women who took out the infants of the Inclusa. Through lack of attention to the basic needs of their charges, they were responsible, doctors claimed, for causing the death by convulsion of at least 17 per cent of the infants they took out. For the man of science, keeping these infants alive meant preserving them as much as possible from the wet-nurses whose milk was more likely a to be a source of corruption and sickness than of health.

Convulsion can be taken as the prototype of a childhood disease. In terms of the anatomy and physiology of the time, some doctors concluded with inescapable logic that the key to its prevention lay in a form of artificial feeding. Foundling hospitals provided the ideal environment for setting up such a program. Nurses were in short supply, milk was needed, and the infants were dying in any case. The foundling hospital gave doctors the opportunity to experiment in finding a solution to an immediate problem that they envisaged as having long-range implications for the good of humanity.

The Inclusa, which had started out as a transfer centre to provide nurses for the infants, was beginning by 1800 to take on the rudiments of a centre for the treatment of infants. The aim of Santiago García was to develop a program of artificial feeding. Did he envisage the time when the hospital might take over completely, to isolate infants from any contact with the only too-human women who could pass on their only too-human weaknesses?

The doctors of the eighteenth century were the proponents of the philosophy of human betterment. Science was the key to producing a better future and better human beings. The eighteenth-century foundling had a key role to play in this scenario. We have no way of knowing how ambitious the doctor of the Inclusa was or how far he was willing to go in his attempts to improve the situation of the foundling and, perhaps incidentally, the future of all infants and the whole human race. However, it is clear that for many men of science, the infant held the solution to the problems presented by the obstinate human tendency to act in ways that were not 'scientific.' If the human being was a machine (though one not perfectly adapted to the environment as yet), the best hope for programming an ideal human being would be to find means to isolate the child from the corrupting influences that caused sickness, weakness, and death. Ironically enough, the hospitals where doctors hoped to put into practice these theories provided the worst conditions imaginable for any program aimed at improving the health and well-being of infants. For many doctors, the foundling hospital, which built into its structure a reliance on wet-nurses, set up a basically dangerous environment for the new-born. One of the major health risks – as doctors saw it in terms of the science of the day – was the milk provided by these women.

The sicknesses, diseases, and deaths that were the lot of the *expósito* had the ultimate effect of focusing attention on the child as patient, with the result that serious attempts were made to save the lives of these infants and those of following generations. Unfortunately, given the state of medical knowledge at the time, very little could be accomplished in these hospitals. Infants continued to die there. If anything, the mortality rose in the first years of the nineteenth century. Nevertheless, the Inclusa, its doctors, and its infants played an important role in the beginning of the medical aspects of care of the new-born. When the Royal College of Surgery set up its progressive curriculum, the care of the new-born was given a prominent place, evidence that the child had become a subject of serious attention for the medical profession in Spain. The Inclusa was one example of this attention.

To conclude, the foundling hospital in the eighteenth century had to deal with increasing numbers of infants. Many of these were sickly, frail, and weak before admission to the hospital. Some were half dead from the long journey in cart or on back of some porter who took them on as he would have any other package to be delivered. Many infants were syphilitic and some had been brain damaged in a bungled delivery – an occurrence that may not have been uncommon when the mother was unmarried and more concerned with a secret than a safe delivery. Others had been left by desperately poor parents who could not bear to watch their own child starve, a process that could have been already under way. Dropped off at an institution crowded with infants in which it was becoming increasingly difficult to provide adequate sanitation (even in the elementary sense of space, fresh air, and water), the infants were exposed to the most dangerous of contacts imaginable – each other. Skin diseases and gastro-enteritis were epidemic in the institution, to the point where the desperate administration acknowledged that the best thing that could happen to any infant in their charge was to discharge it. We have seen, however, that doing so did not necessarily improve the situation for many infants. Taken by poor women into their homes, the children still had to contend with an environment of poverty and disease. Sometimes the nurse was unable or unwilling to provide even the minimum in care – enough milk to keep the child alive. But even in the best of surroundings, childhood diseases took a heavy toll of the *expósito*. Fevers, smallpox, and skin and internal inflammations continued to afflict the infants even after they left the Inclusa. Finally, many of them succumbed to the nameless, unidentifiable illnesses that were classified as 'convulsions,' and that may have been associated with malnutrition. In the final stages of these diseases, the child died in a shocking, violent rage that seized its small frame and expressed – in a final miniature cataclysm – the revolt of its whole being against its sufferings, against fate, and against the system that made it virtually impossible for the *expósitos* to survive the experience of being abandoned to the Inclusa at the turn of the century.

The doctors of the period, helpless to cure most of these illnesses, nevertheless were beginning to take a new interest in infants and their diseases. Influenced by the Enlightenment's theories of progress, they tried to understand the infant in scientific terms and to apply this new understanding toward developing a better form of human being, one adapted to the environment and less susceptible to the diseases that had been taken for granted as the lot of humanity throughout the ages. In this context, the *expósito* had an important role to play. The sicknesses of the foundling, both within the Inclusa and with their wet-nurses, gave added incentive and impetus to the development of paediatrics as a separate and scientific field of study. Unfortunately, part of the search for improvement involved focusing blame upon the woman who nursed the child. Nevertheless, the Inclusa and the *inclusero* played an important role in the course of medicalization that was beginning to chart a path towards human progress. The death of so many infants was not completely without some redeeming value, if only evident in the establishment of the Royal College of Surgery by the government under the aegis of Charles IV and the college's explicit endorsement of the work of Santiago García. But despite the reforms attempted by the authorities of the Inclusa, government, and medical practitioners, the *expósito* did not demonstrate the victory of enlightened progress. We turn now to examine the reforms of the Inclusa under the Junta de damas to see how and why the children of the poor remained victims, and to consider the failure of enlightened reformers to conquer poverty and its concomitant illnesses.

8

Infanticide
and the Inclusa

The deaths of infants of the poor, their causes, and efforts at remedies have been a matter of overriding concern in this study. This chapter discusses how the issue was confronted and dealt with or evaded and obscured by the various groups involved with the Inclusa. These considerations bring to the foreground a problem that has flitted ghost-like behind the scenes: the spectre of infanticide must be given material form, faced squarely, and dealt with. The question is whether the parents who left an infant to the hospital, the rural or urban women who took out these infants as wet-nurses, and perhaps even the upper-class women in charge of running the hospital were all participants in infanticide to a greater or lesser degree. Did the state, the church, and society in general give tacit consent to the deaths of untold numbers of helpless new-born infants? Was infanticide a means of dealing with poverty in the eighteenth century?

The evidence assembled here and elsewhere is manifestly clear. Infants died in these hospitals – by the hundreds in individual institutions, by the thousands in individual countries. Abandonment to a foundling hospital was the equivalent of a death sentence. The circumstances of its exposure, the wet-nurses, and the institution itself presented hurdles to be overcome by the fragile new-born. Over the century an average of 58 per cent of infants died before leaving the Inclusa; of those who survived, close to 88 per cent sent out with nurses died.[1] That is, an overall average of some 11 per cent of infants who left with a wet-nurse eventually returned to the Inclusa at age seven to be transferred to another hospice or institution where their numbers again were decimated.

Numerous studies have documented how the foundling hospitals of

Paris, Dublin, Lyon, and Limoges funnelled infants to the graveyards. The same thing held true in less notorious towns such as Orvieto, Avila, Siguënza, and Ceuta.[2] Figures from institutions everywhere tell the same story: 'They die like flies,' 'their numbers are like the grains of sand on the beach' – even the similes are repetitive. There is no question about the magnitude of the slaughter. The slaughter is on record. What remains is to determine whether it can be termed infanticide. Were these deaths what we would call in theological terms sins, or in legal terms crimes, or were they simply, to put it in the terms of everyday life, a pity – a consequence of circumstances over which no one had control? In examining the public's awareness of the issues at stake and the relationship between abandonment, exposure, and infanticide, can we determine the role played by the foundling hospital in the deaths of these new-born infants?

THE PUBLIC AND INFANTICIDE

Infanticide is a crime that is difficult to verify. It is a crime performed by women, often alone, though sometimes with the collusion of a midwife. Traditionally it was associated with the single woman whose personal and family honour, job, status in the community, and whole future could be permanently blighted by a child wanted neither by her, its father, nor anyone else. Infanticide has a long history in the western world, going back to the Greeks and Romans when it was an accepted form of population control. In the Christian era and throughout the Middle Ages, the life of the new-born was protected, but infanticide was nevertheless punished with considerably less severity than was murder.[3] Barbara Kellum, who studied infanticide in England in the late Middle Ages, suggested 'that it may have been the very commonality of infanticide and child murder that allowed them to be condoned even in court.'[4] Nevertheless, evidence for the extent of infanticide during those early periods is hard to come by. Given the nature of the offence, it can be assumed that only a small proportion of cases ever came to the attention of the courts. It is only for two periods that the widespread nature of the crime, or at least the degree of concern on the part of authorities for what they saw as its extent, can be documented. These were both times of considerable social unrest and many countries witnessed attempts by governments to assert their authority and to impose a form of social control on unruly, undisciplined, and threatening numbers of poor by legislating harsh measures to punish bastardy, exposure, and infanticide. A recent study of Middlesex county in England has shown that infanticide made up 25 per cent of cases of those accused of murder in the early modern period. The authors concluded that the harsh terms imposed on illegitimacy by the poor law of 1576 had the effect of multiplying infanticides.[5] In France, legislation that made it a crime to conceal a birth may have had a similar impact.[6] Such laws can be seen as evidence of a reaction to increasing numbers of infanticides in these countries in the sixteenth century. In Florence, there were 181 cases between 1500 and 1540, and Nuremberg executed eighty-seven young women for infanticide between 1500 and 1750.[7]

In the case of Spain, Vicente Pérez Moreda, in a very detailed and complete demographic study of early modern Spain, has detected a pattern of increasing infanticide both in the early years of the seventeenth and at the end of the eighteenth century. However, if one takes the establishment of hospitals for abandoned children as a reaction to infanticide, then it could be argued that the opening of eight inclusas (including the one in Madrid) between 1504 and 1597 is evidence of a crisis in child deaths in Spain as early as the sixteenth century.[8] In other words, infanticide among the general population in western Europe was common enough, at least from the sixteenth century, and measures designed to punish illegitimacy may have encouraged rather than discouraged infanticide. Women were killing their infants in numbers that authorities could no longer ignore and thus implicitly condone.

The stigma attached to illegitimacy drove many single women to doing away with a new-born, often in a form of quasi-infanticide by exposing the child and letting circumstances take their course. Consequently, most women accused of infanticide were single women who had left a child to die or already dead in a deserted area such as a ditch or field, or, if more resolute, had thrown it down a privy or a well. Married women could both hide their crime and commit it more simply. Why expose an infant when it was easier to let it die of neglect? As a result, the exposed infant was usually assumed to be illegitimate. Foundling hospitals were set up for abandoned and illegitimate infants and it was taken for granted that the two were synonymous.

We have seen that by the end of the eighteenth century, not only the nature of the foundling, but the reputation of the hospital as a viable alternative to infanticide, had altered dramatically. Institutions had become so crowded that they were no longer able to provide effectively for the new-born. There is no doubt that foundling hospitals succeeded in preventing individual infanticides. Mercier points out that Switzerland, where there we no foundling hospitals, continued to prosecute numerous infanticides while Paris had none.[9] Nevertheless, there was a growing disillusionment among the administrators of these hospitals who were unable to cope with the numbers flooding their institutions. Hospitals were founded to prevent infanticides, but at another level they were themselves being used by the poor as an excuse and an escape-hatch for parents with infants they could not support. If the poor no longer did away with their infants directly, they did so indirectly by abandoning them to foundling hospitals that functioned more as an excuse than an alternative for infanticide.

The poor were well aware of what fate awaited their progeny: 'Tan, tan, tan / Angelitos al cielo van.' The little angels flying to heaven in the popular folk rhyme were *expósitos*. In the popular mind the association had been made and was common knowledge. Anyone, even the small child, knew, or found out early on, what went on in these institutions. 'A la Inclusa' was a powerful reminder to the naughty child of the perils lying in wait for those flaunting adult authority. One critic suggested an inscription should be limned above the doorways: 'Here die children at public expense.'[10]

But in fact the inscription that administrators blazoned above the portals in many of these institutions read, 'Abandoned by my parents, Charity welcomes me.' The image of Charity – the warm, welcoming woman, arms and breasts open to succour the needy – had turned into an image of Death, bony, grinning, and insatiable. Even more chilling is the inexorable conclusion that mothers, whether the infant was legitimate or illegitimate, knew this truth. That is, the poor knew what they were doing when they abandoned an infant; they understood it to mean almost certain death.

Nevertheless, the circumstances which brought them to such a recourse are understandable. Desperately poor, there were families physically incapable of supporting another child. Often such women left the child to the institution because they could not supply from their own undernourished frames enough milk to keep a new-born alive. These mothers were not faced with a viable choice: the child could die in front of their eyes or under the wing of public charity. But surely these were extreme cases, even in the worst of times. There were many others, fearing that they would become just as desperate as their indigent neighbours, who made the choice of sacrificing the family member with the lightest claim on their affections and sense of responsibility – the new-born. Religion, society, and the law forbade infanticide. But they did provide an alternative. The actual act, and the guilt for it, could be transferred to the institution. If the child died, it was not the fault of the family who brought an infant to its doors because they had nowhere else to turn. A charge of infanticide could hardly hold up against any considered judgment of the conditions that drove the poverty-stricken to abandon their own children, even when the sacrifice was made in full consciousness that it would cost the life of the new-born.[11]

Individuals abandoning their infants to the Inclusa can be categorized into three types. The first could be accused of committing deferred infanticide. They were women who would have killed the new-born anyway and who used the hospital to take the infant off their hands, realizing fully that it would probably die. The second group consisted of those who were desperately poor and whose infants might not have survived in any case. Their children swelled the ranks of the Inclusa during periods of famine and invasion, but during normal years their numbers declined. They were the poor who struggled along on the edge of indigence and who, during a crisis and for a short time, could not provide for another child. Though they were well aware that their infant would not survive in the foundling hospital, they also knew that they could not provide for it. Finally, there was a third group whose numbers are impossible to ascertain, but that we know existed. Rousseau is a classic example of the individuals who regarded the hospital as a kind of post-birth-control device. They were probably incapable of committing infanticide under normal conditions, but they found it easy to slough off the responsibility for the care of another charge, took no interest in its ultimate fate, and in the process undermined the credibility of the institution, the morale of its administrators, and the idealistic plans of government officials. How many of those were women like Rousseau's mistress, Thérèse Levasseur, is something we will never know. It is clear, however, that all three groups were doing essentially the same thing. The third category of the poor had been encouraged by the very existence of the hospital to abandon children that they otherwise would have cared for, grown to love, and accepted as regular members of a family. It is unlikely that Rousseau would have deliberately killed his children, but he was able to persuade Thérèse Levasseur to send five of them to the foundling hospital, and proceeded to take no more interest in their fate than in puppies left to the humane society. Infanticide was being committed by women who would have left a child to die in some deserted place anyway, by women who could not afford to feed a new-born, and by women who – with a struggle – might have been able to care for a new-born. The existence of the foundling hospital simply meant that the deaths of the infants occurred under official auspices.

When numbers began to rise at the end of the century and when they continued to rise year after year, cynics concluded that hospitals were contributing to, rather than solving, the problem by encouraging this third group. Some went further and claimed that hospitals were creating the problem by encouraging the poor to be improvident with the rationalization that they could leave infants to the state rather than raise them themselves. They claimed that the poor were committing infanticide, and that the foundling hospitals encouraged and institutionalized infanticide. Now, instead of charging individual, unwed mothers with child murder, or the poor in general with negligence, blame focused on the institution set up under the aegis of church and state to prevent the very crime of which it was accused. The hospital was thought to perpetrate the very crime it had been set up to prevent. By the mid nineteenth century, a Malthusian such as Lord Brougham in England could write: 'These institutions lead to an unchaste life and child murder.'[12] The circle had come completely around.

Given this situation, some historians have asked whether the foundling hospital was only one aspect of the phenomenon. Emmanual Leroi Ladurie discusses infanticide as a form of population control and refers to one small village near Paris where in the space of thirty months thirty-one babies were given to the same couple, one after another, and all died within an interval of a few weeks.[13] Nurses who killed (angel makers) have been documented for both Germany and England, where parishes sometimes paid a woman to take infants off their hands for a pittance, and nothing was heard of them again.[14] A contest held in German-speaking Europe for the best essay on how to prevent infanticide received 400 entries.[15] It can be assumed that these appalling conditions were a general phenomenon. The bishop's inquiry sent out in 1790 provides much of what we know of the extent of the practice in Spain. The responses received 'cannot be read without the greatest consternation.' In Santiago de Compostela the hospital compelled local nursing mothers to take a foundling for a pittance, and consequently most died. But, at the same time, districts without hospitals reported rampant and unchecked infanticides. One report from Lucena suggested that there had been 3000 infanticides in the previous thirty-year period.[16]

Although the poor made up most of the population in the Old Regime, and abandonment was usually done by the poor, to speak of the public only in terms of this sector is to over-simplify the issue. The authorities of church and state were well aware of the seriousness of the problem because they were involved with administering the hospitals. But we must consider also those well enough off to have no need for the services of foundling hospitals. Was there in any sense a 'public opinion' on this issue in the days before the media could be counted upon to raise the consciousness, if not the sense of responsibility, of society as a whole? At least one group of the public needed no convincing about the extent of the misery and seriousness of the situation of the abandoned infant. The members of the Junta de damas, *ilustradas* like their male cohorts of the Royal Economic Society of Amigos del Pais, took it upon themselves to act as a pressure group to bring public attention to bear on the plight of the *expósito* and to have something done about it. This formidable crew of enthusiastic, innovative, moralistic women made the cause of the foundling its own. These women spent years waging a campaign to secure control of the hospital. They pestered the officials for the right to check over the books of the admissions, deaths, and expenses. They harassed the hospital's protector for permission to inspect the premises. Armed with goodwill, intelligence, even political clout, they lobbied, manipulated, and finally convinced Godoy, the Prince of Peace, of the merit of their case. At the same time, doctors like Santiago García in Madrid, administrators like Xavier de Uriz in Pamplona, and concerned individuals like Antonio Bilbao y Durán in Antequera published books that were variations on the same theme of 'how to save the lives of the *expósitos*.' These were all facets of an active propaganda campaign to bring to public attention the conditions responsible for the deaths of so many infants of Spain. Much, if not all, of the educated public must have been aware of the plight of the foundling.

THE STATE AND INFANTICIDE

Forces bent on arousing public indignation were likely to focus on the hospital and its administration. But the institution could only work with the resources at its disposal – resources that ultimately depended on the twin powers of church and state. In Bourbon Spain the state was beginning to play a preponderant role in the charitable system; therefore, any attempt to understand the reasons for the deaths of these infants must consider the part played by the government.

Beneficencia or social welfare had a high priority with the enlight-ened reformers who made up much of the Bourbon administration, particularly under the rule of Charles III and Charles IV at the close of the century. The role of these reformers in calling for a rationalization of the system of social welfare has been discussed. The poor, sick, and unemployed, who were such a conspicuous and compelling constituency of the population of the Old Regime, were the focus of an overall plan to improve society. In this scheme the myriad of private, public, and religious groups were to be replaced by a coherent, centralized system of welfare. Support that had relied on religious duty, appeals to pity or guilt, the generous impulse of the moment, or some traditional sentiment that saw the poor as an integral part of the social structure was to become rationalized. The theorists, often referred to as *afrancesados* because of their debt to the French philosophers of the eighteenth century, had more in common with Enlightenment optimism than with the Christian message that taught that the 'poor we will always have with us.' Ultimately, they envisioned doing away with the poor completely. Education and training would transform the disadvantaged into hard-working individuals able to make a contribution to the state, rather than maintaining them as vagabonds and beggars draining its resources. The underworld of destitute men and demoralized women was to be replaced by a world where everyone had a part producing for the good of the whole.[17]

Those hoping to reconstruct the welfare system saw population as a key element in their grand scheme. Though *afrancesados*, they were also heirs to a long native tradition among the so-called *arbitristas* of the seventeenth century. These were writers who blamed almost all of Spain's internal and external difficulties on her 'population problem' or, more precisely, on a 'lack of population' problem. Deeply patriotic, perhaps even xenophobic, they attributed Spain's economic and social difficulties not to a lack of economic or physical resources, but to a shortage of human resources. Despite the hordes of unemployed and vagabonds, despite the numbers of poor beseiging them, they refused to see what was before their eyes – more people than the economy could support. Instead they took the opposite tack. Spain needed, they claimed, more people or – to be fair to their argument – more people utilized effectively as workers, farmers, soldiers, sailors, spinners, mothers of families. Given this obsession with population, it is only to be expected that some means to save the thousands of dying infants in the foundling hospitals had a high priority on the agenda of the reformers who were laying the groundwork for a new Spain. Their initiatives toward eliminating poverty at its source meant that they must deal with the *expósito*.

Those concerned with improving the lot of the *expósito* could depend on a strong reaction by touching the sensibilities of the government to the population issue. Campomanes, Cabarrus, and Jovellanos were among important reformers who had propounded such arguments for years. Xavier de Uriz pointed out that in Pamplona alone in the period 1792–98 the foundling hospital admitted 214 infants per year. Given a normal mortality, there should be 1498 alive with wet-nurses. In fact, there were one-sixth of that number – 243. Projecting this arithmetic over a thirty-year period with an average infant mortality rate of 50 per cent, one could expect, in time, 3210 adults – herding cattle, collecting the first shoots of esparto, developing simple artisan skills, and 'transforming the countryside.'[18] Bilbao y Durán estimated that if one counted six *expósitos* for each thousand *vecinos* in the kingdom (a moderate calculation, he asserted), and if one estimated the population of the kingdom at ten million, there resulted a total *expósito* population of 12,000 yearly. For any official lacking imagination he went on: 'How many strong arms would this secure for the country, how many workers, how many respectable farmers and grazers?'[19] Events after 1789 – wars and threats of wars with France and England – only served to add force to a theme that was likely to call forth a response from the administrators of the Bourbon government. The *expósito* as statistic was used to good effect by those who were well aware that it was a sensitive area among the powerful.

This theory of population nourished the attitudes of those planning a new order in Bourbon Spain. Men like Xavier de Uriz and Bilbao y Durán were in a sense handing back what they had absorbed. But what were the facts underlying these theories of population?

Demographers such as Francisco Bustelo insist that population growth in Spain in the eighteenth century does not fit into categories of 'modern' which involve 'a disappearance of catastrophic mortality, followed by a decline in ordinary mortality, and a decline in infant mortality, accompanied by some methods of birth control.' Nevertheless, thanks to a few good years of plentiful harvests, combined with relative peace and stability, Spain after 1720 experienced a demographic burst at least as great as that affecting other countries in western Europe.[20] In fact, her population increased even more rapidly than that of one of her rivals, France. Population growth, in conjunction with an intelligent economic policy on the part of the Bourbon administration, set Spain on the path of an agricultural and economic expansion that capitalized on an increased demand for foodstuffs and manufactured goods and provided some basis for optimism. However, the population theorists of the day continued to work in a time lag that persisted (in stubborn denial of the facts) in projecting a warped picture of Spain wallowing in decadence, which they associated with, or attributed directly to, a lack of population. This decline, they asserted, could be reversed by an intelligent use of physical, economic, spiritual, and human resources. Ironically enough, Jovellanos in 1794 began to offer a more positive prognosis. He spoke of 'the salutary fermentation of agricultural, industrial expansion, and population growth.'[21] But by this point, Spain had already peaked. A series of subsistence crises, continuing sporadically until 1816, conspired with the political tribulations at the turn of the century to usher in an era of genuine decline, thus justifying the underlying pessimism of the theorists.

For the politicians who took these theories seriously, the *expósitos* were an obvious waste of resources. One of the most direct ways to improve the prospects of Spain was to give the *expósito* a role in that future. Legislation at the end of the century encompassed a long series of acts to this end. In 1788, *corregidores* were instructed to forbid administrators of foundling hospitals to sell off property or income or to convert holdings to other uses. Administrators were also to see to it that boys and girls in their charge were trained in some skill and given instruction in the less practical 'grammatical' arts.[22] Other laws recommended that foundlings be given out for adoption only to individuals able to teach them skills and thus to provide a suitable future for them.[23] These measures were in preparation for a much more ambitious program. Foundling hospitals made up only one block, though an important one, in a bold project to turn beggars, indigents, needy, and helpless into productive citizens.

Helping the *expósitos* also served the interests of those seeking to curb the power of the church and bring it increasingly under government control. Church lands and church income would subsidize the plans for a state-run social-welfare system utilizing, in the most rational and progressive way possible, the human and economic potential of the whole country for the good of the whole country. With the support of many progressive prelates, Pius VI was pressured to institute a *Fondo pío beneficial* under the administration of Don Pedro Joaquín de Murcia y Córdoba as Colector General de Expolios y Vacantes. The funds to implement this policy depended ultimately upon the finances of the church. *Expolios y vacantes* were seats of canons or church appointees that no longer required the actual services of a cleric. This justified the appropriation of their income to support the government's set of charitable priorities. One of the foremost priorities was to be the *expósito*.

In the accepted bureaucratic tradition, Murcia prepared the ground by setting up an inquiry. On 6 December 1790, a circular went out to all the bishops and archbishops of the country asking for specific information on the following: (1) number of foundling homes in each diocese, including towns from which the foundlings come, means of transporting infants, and sums collected for their support; and (2) methods of administration – expenses, income, sources, and number of employees. Finally, the document went on to solicit the opinion of the prelates as to whether they considered present arrangements adequate, or whether they felt there was a need for additional institutions in some towns. It also called for suggestions concerning improvements in administration, care, and nursing.

Government inquiries have earned a reputation as excuses for putting off action rather than instituting changes. On this occasion, the government took what were for the time fairly prompt measures to support its good intentions. In a masterful feat of legislation, the king, in 1794, transformed the *expósito* into a citizen with full *hidalgo* rank. This meant an *expósito* could not be punished by the whip or the garotte. Moreover, he was shielded from that ultimate insult in Spain – the name of bastard – that impunged his honour and that of his family. The document itself formally admitted that hospitals were crowded 'because legitimate parents often expose [infants], usually when they see no alternative to saving their lives.'[24]

When the final results of the questionnaire appeared in the legislation of 11 December 1796, it was evident that the government had, in its deliberate if lumbering fashion, absorbed and come to terms with the essentials and even the details of the foundling problem. The legislation began by dealing with the long journey sometimes required before the infant could be deposited in a town that was large enough to support its own institution. Bishops and archbishops were charged with seeing to it that within a year houses be designated in intermediate towns where the infant could receive some minimum of care. Administrators had evidently belaboured the point that nurses of poor quality were at the root of the problem. The document read: 'Experience has shown that exceedingly low pay has been a reason for not being able to find nurses who could have saved the lives of many who have perished and continue to do so.'[25] Accordingly, the prelates were ordered to see to it that nurses were paid at the same scale as those who privately nursed families of the poor. This statement could be taken as no more than a pious sentiment on the part of the government, or a deliberate refusal to take seriously the complaints the inquiry had elicited. The whole point, as far as the administrators of hospitals were concerned, was that they did not have money to pay for good nurses.

However, there was an implication that might indicate some concession to the economic realities. It provided for economies at the expense of the older infant. Nurses for these infants were not to receive pay raises. Instead, administrators were instructed to choose, when possible, women who had *algo de que subistir ellas*, that is, women who were not completely destitute. The government evidently hoped that at least a few of these women would go on caring for an infant after the weaning period, even though the stipend must 'necessarily be much less than that offered for nursing.' Since it was true that the longer the child lived, the better chance it had to survive, there was some justification for this policy. In practice, though, it may have merely postponed rather than prevented the death of the foundling because in many cases the infant would be returned to an institution where its chances for survival were slight.

The inquiry brought to light many of the abuses of the system. Measures to regulate the practice of cheating the Inclusa stipulated that on the semi-annual pay-days, nurses were to bring with the *expósito* a certificate verifying identity from the parish and the *alcalde* of the town. In this way they hoped to deal with the practice of nurses substituting a different infant after the death of the *inclusero* in order to stay on the payroll.

Indeed, the terms of the document did try to take into acount almost any eventuality, even that of the child exposed outside the regular channels. For instance, a child left on the doorstep of some individual who was willing and able to care for it did not thereby lose its claim on the institution if by any chance the family could not continue supporting it. Perhaps because they felt they had covered most exigencies, the legislators took a hard line toward anyone who left a child in some deserted area where there could be serious danger of death. The act of abandoning a child, especially at night, at the door of a church or in some isolated spot was to be punished with the full severity of the laws. Some leeway was allowed only when information was given to the authorities immediately afterwards, so that the child could be found and rescued.

Infanticide was obviously very much on the minds of the members of the junta. Their wording was explicit:

In order to prevent many infanticides that occur because of fear of discovery and prosecution, for which reason infants are cast out and killed as is well known; justices of the towns who meet anyone in the countryside or town, day or night, carrying a child which they say is to be exposed in a hospital or hospice or parish of a nearby town are not to detain nor question them; if the justice deems it necessary for the security of the *expósito*, or if the person conducting it requests it, he can be accompanied so as to verify his purpose, but this is to be done without any questioning either officially or unofficially, and afterwards that person is to be allowed to leave freely.[26]

In general, the legislation reiterated in forthright terms a genuine concern for the lives of the foundlings and set out the means that would best meet this concern. There is nothing that could be taken as evidence that the protection of the infant did not have the highest priority in terms of the legislation of 1796. Certainly, the government showed itself petty in suggesting that the institution save money at the expense of the nurses, and its measures that cut back on the length of the weaning period were not likely to improve overall mortality figures. But to give the government officials the benefit of the doubt, the longer the child lived, the better were its chances. Both the king and Godoy were obviously sincerely dedicated to attempting to save the lives of their subjects, even such weak and powerless constituents as the *expósitos*.

The years 1794 and 1796 marked high points in social legislation. No country in the world had such an enlightened set of principles set out to guide its policy on the matter of the *expósito*. Only the legislation of the French Revolution made a comparable attempt, and its high-flown wording did not project the same sense of immediacy as that found in the concrete terms of the decree of 1796 in Spain.

It was obvious that the government felt proud of its accomplishments. The royal order was signed by Manuel de Godoy and sent out to the head of each diocese with the accompanying letter:

The King, not content with having provided for the civil rights of the numerous innocent *expósitos* of his domain, and being well informed as to the few of those who were ever able to take advantage of his decree of 5 January 1794, because so many of them die in early infancy; wishing to do away completely with the causes of this serious situation suffered by his subjects whose helplessness and tender age call forth his paternal consideration, has decided that the most suitable way to remedy this evil is to prepare this document after careful consideration and see to it that its terms be carried out.[27]

Seeing to it that the terms were carried out was where the document left off. The government earns full points for its concerned legislation; but when it came to actual implementation, this responsibility (and more important the funds for its implementation) was to remain with the church. The state can be acquitted, with some justice, of any charge of infanticide only because, after its exercise in fine words and lofty sentiments, the government handed the problem back to the bishops. The state then went on to institute legislation aimed at another set of priorities that would ultimately make it impossible for the officials of the church to carry out the well-meaning promulgations of the officials of the state. The government proceeded to cancel out with one hand what it undertook with the other.

THE CHURCH AND INFANTICIDE

While the concern of the state was bodies, the concern of the church was souls. Each infant possessed an immortal soul and it was the responsibility of the church to see to it that souls were saved. Essentially this meant that the infants had to be baptized, an event that was taken seriously. The *entradas* make it very clear: there is no page where date of baptism is not inscribed and the baptismal name noted. It was not sufficient to have the ceremony performed by the midwife or surgeon, or to have information attached to the child's wrappings vouching for its exposure to the sacramental waters before its admission. Unless a certificate with the name of the parish and priest was given, the infant was trundled off to San Ginés in order to make absolutely certain that it was eligible for the next life.

The records of the parish church of San Ginés witness the routine procedure that baptism had become by the end of the century. We can imagine the *madre*, accompanied by a couple of nurses, or a servant, appearing at the baptistry every morning with four, five, or six squalling infants – the night's usual yield. (Even after the guarantees provided by the legislation of 1796, many individuals took advantage of the privacy of darkness to leave the child at the courtyard fountain or *pozo del zaguan*.) The sacristan acted as godfather; the infants were given the name of the saint of the day in cases where there was no further information, and they were guaranteed eternal life before being shipped back to the Inclusa where most of them were to die.

Baptism, then, was a matter of routine, but it was not a matter taken for granted. Its importance is a matter of record: the books attest to its scrupulous observance. Other matters required legislation or attention, but this one was never mentioned because it was never questioned. Food, health, nurses, and finances were all problems, but baptizing was not. In this sense, the church did fulfil its responsibilities. It saw to the spiritual welfare of the infants in its charge. But was that all it saw itself as responsible for? Were subsequent steps in providing for these infants considered irrelevant by the church once it had fulfilled a basic obligation to save the souls in its charge?

It is not likely that even the staunchest anti-clerical could make such a claim. The church not only preached charity, it practised it. The whole system of welfare under the Old Regime was administered by bishops, chaplains, monasteries, and convents. Even the small groups of laymen or women who formed confraternities to carry out private works of mercy met in some parish chapel, had a spiritual adviser who was a religious, and operated under the patronage of some saint. The words of the Jesuit preacher Pedro de Calatayud summed up the policy: 'The rich have been charged by God as administrators of the goods that they have … to share them with the poor.'[28] Individuals may have become hardened, even cynical, under the deluge of infants. Witness the nun in the 'famous institution' described by Ballexserd, who horrified one *bien pensant bourgeoise* by telling her, 'It is just as well that all of them do not live because we would be unable to cope with the numbers,' and sent her off in a flurry of indignation.[29] But they went on to carry out their duties unquestioningly, because 'progress' or 'success' was not part of their attitude; they did not see their function in these terms.

The charitable system of the church functioned as it always had, and provided relief on an individual and institutional basis for growing numbers of the disadvantaged of the Old Regime without attempting to attack the root causes of distress. These institutions had accepted that they would always have the poor with them. For the traditional Christian, the poor were part of God's plan. They were to be loved for their own sake, but also as a means of grace. The poor served as objects of pity and generosity for the edification of the more favoured; they provided a constant reminder of the inscrutability of God's ways and the fragile base on which any human success and prosperity rested. 'There, but for the grace of God, go I' was the philosophical tenet on which Christians rested their indiscriminate alms giving.

However, progress was very much part of the ideology of the functionaries who formulated policy in the governments of Charles III and Charles IV. For the enlightened reformer of the eighteenth century, the poor played no useful role in society. They held back the coming of the millennium, throwing obstacles under the wheels of progress. Ideally poverty should be done away with completely and all transformed into useful citizens contributing to the material well-being of the whole. Not that those who preached the new gospel of public welfare were opposed to helping the poor, but they saw charity in completely different terms. The 'deserving poor' – the sick, the disabled, the old, and helpless children – were to be cared for in institutions where alms were sure to be put to good use. Money that had formerly been tossed off to beggars and vagrants according to irrational sentiments – the guilt or whims of the donor – was to be disposed of in an orderly fashion in state-run institutions. These men were willing to allow the church to administer charity, but the priorities would be determined by the preconceptions of the Enlightenment.

The attack on the traditional system of charity was based on philosophical grounds, but it was not completely altruistic. Some bureaucrats among the Bourbon Carlists hoped to expand the authority of the government at the expense of the church. One way to do so was to get control of the enormous network of hospitals, confraternities, asylums, and shelters of various sorts that composed an impressive financial investment in buildings, holdings, income on property, and mortgages. A campaign was mounted in the press and through the agency of members of the Royal Economic Societies who organized an open competition to give publicity to the issue. The weaknesses of the traditional distribution of charity – it was wasteful, inefficient, and haphazard – were exposed to ridicule. The societies pointed to soup lines at the doors of monasteries that brought in the poor from the surrounding countryside and the tossing of coins to beggars that discouraged able-bodied men from looking for work as evidence that the poor were thriving and their numbers growing. All this they claimed was the result of a system of charity based on outworn and ill-conceived premises that served to aggravate rather than resolve the problem of poverty.

The financial distress of the government at the end of the century meant that there were those in power with ears ready to hear a new message and hands ready to force the issue and grasp the potential monetary benefits. Increasingly, what had begun as an exercise in philosophical principles turned into economic and political coercion. Under the pressure of the war with France, and then with England, the government found itself desperate for funds. What better place to turn than to the resources of the church?[30] This undermining of the foundation of the church's welfare system took overt form in 1794 when the government set up a *caja de amortización* and ordered the various charitable institutions to deposit there 6 per cent of their income from agricultural property and 4 per cent of that collected from real estate held in the cities. The funds thus transferred were to be at the disposition of the government. At the same time, administrators were pressured to convert other income into *vales reales*, or government bonds, though the return at 3 per cent was becoming problematic. Of course, the inflation causing the government so many difficulties had eroded as well the income from real estate, *censos*, and landholdings of various types on which the church and its system of charity depended. Meanwhile, bishops were expected to make large contributions to the state in the form of forced loans, 'voluntary' gifts, and special taxes. These drains on the resources of the church occurred in conjunction with a set of factors that were making the lot of the poor critical. Welfare institutions were in a bind: they required more funds, but all circumstances combined to see that they received less.

Once embarked on this policy of encroachment, there was no going back. The government, pressured by its own set of exigencies, moved from subtle pressure to direct legislation and ordered, in September 1798, that the property of all hospitals and other charitable institutions be sold and the proceeds invested in *vales reales*. The return of 3 per cent on the capital produced was worth less with each day that passed. It could only be a matter of time before the income of the Inclusa disappeared into the maw of the *caja de amortización*. Though foundling hospitals were exempt for the moment, this legislation began the process that was ultimately to destroy a system of charity that had been one of the bulwarks of stability in the tormented society of the Old Regime. Enlightened reformers, who had envisioned the *expósito* as a vital element in a new utilitarian society, were now willing to sacrifice the welfare system in a short-sighted attempt to assert the claims of a unified state to absolute control in the name of this same principle of utility.

The outcome was, of course, predictable. A system that in the past had served to alleviate some of the distress of the poor in critical periods of famine and war was, for all intents and purposes, crippled. For instance, in 1808 at the height of the Napoleonic wars, the cardinal of the diocese of Toledo found himself forced to suspend all the charitable activities in his diocese for lack of funds.[31] Problems of caring for foundlings were placed on the doorstep of the church in 1796 by some of the same men who were busily formulating measures that could only make it impossible for their injunctions to be carried out.

In this macabre daisy chain we have moved from the poor, to the government, to the church. At each stage there were sets of individuals who claimed to have only the good of the infant at heart. Each set could defend its role in the network as a positive one. Each claimed to be doing its utmost, given the circumstances, to save the lives of the *expósitos*. The more we understand about the circumstances, the harder it is to disagree with them. The poor, who could not afford to support their infants, could not be blamed for taking them to an institution set up for just that purpose. Supposing they did realize that leaving their infant would probably mean its death, and that the hospital was a formalized means of infanticide, was it any more painful to have decline and death occur in the hospital than to have an infant waste away in front of one's eyes? The government had responded to a critical situation with a progressive and enlightened set of reforms; at last, the wealth of the church had been tapped with the excuse of providing for the poor in the long term by a more enlightened policy of welfare. There may have been a few cases where individuals themselves could be blamed for leaving a child to die, but at least both the government and church seemed to be doing all that could be reasonably be expected of them.

It was in the setting of the hospital, or in the care of those paid by the hospital, that the deaths of these infants occurred. It is ultimately the Inclusa itself that holds the answers to the questions: 'Was it infanticide?' It is in the Inclusa itself that we can see how decisions made by the poor, the state, and the church were to culminate in the deaths of the foundlings.

THE INCLUSA AND INFANTICIDE

The archives of the Diputación Provincial in Madrid contain a set of documents describing the meetings of the administrators of the Inclusa in the period February 1794 until it was taken over by the Junta de damas in 1799. These records chronicle the response of the hospital's administration to the problem of infanticide, though the word never was used.[32] Here can be seen firsthand the experience of a group of administrators riding out one crisis after another in an effort to keep the institution afloat. The newly appointed protector, Josef Vilches, a member of the Consejo Suprema, tackled his role with enthusiasm. He ordered that on the first Sunday of every month those responsible for running the hospital should meet in his quarters to study the problems. There, in his comfortable office, the three priests who were administrator, chaplain, and accountant, and the two treasurers, one of whom was a woman, got together to talk over what measures could be taken to improve conditions in the Inclusa. They looked realistically at the situation and agreed it was bad. The finances, the daily routine, the nurses, the building itself, all were examined critically. As one of his first actions, Vilches petitioned on 21 May 1794 for the privilege of raffling off two goats, a right that had formerly belonged to the defunct community of Antonio Abad. He also received a favourable and a surprisingly prompt response to a request for additional funding from the income of the Lenten Indulgences. These concessions, by a royal order of 27 May 1794, added to the income of the Inclusa as much as 20,000 reales yearly from the raffle, and a subsidy of 15,000 yearly from the funds collected for exemptions from Lenten fasts. Vilches also secured a concession from the Corporation of the Five Major Guilds, which held some of the capital investments of the Inclusa. It agreed to allow a 3 per cent return instead of the 2.5 per cent that had been paid up to that point.

But as the years went on, the success of the administration in finding new sources of income waned, and so did its enthusiasm. In 1796 hospital's administrators met only eight times; in 1797 only four. This was not because the problems had been solved, but because the problems seemed insoluble. By 1797 the situation was desperate: 130,000 reales were required for the salaries of nurses at Pentecost, and the treasury held 25,000 reales. The tone of panic was evident in the letter to Murcia begging for funds to forestall 'what could be the greatest disturbance ever seen in this hospital – even the thought is intolerable.' The petition was reinforced by statistics showing record-breaking admissions of 452 infants since January. The reply was tardy. The date of Pentecost was 4 June; the sum of 100,000 reales was not allocated until 3 June. On 7 June a royal order followed, advising Vilches 'to immediately come up with measures to increase the income of the Inclusa ... because the funds from *expolios y vacantes* are earmarked for other ends.'[33] Whether the injunction was not taken seriously, or whether the protector had run out of new ideas, Pentecost next year saw the same crisis. Urgent letters to Murcia, funding at the eleventh hour, but this time only half as much was forthcoming from the recalcitrant government and the treasurer was forced to withdraw funds from his deposits with the Five Major Guilds. Once these reserves were tapped, bankruptcy was only a matter of time.

At this point the story turns from a horror tale to a fairy tale. The fairy godmother was Queen Maria Luisa. Her daughter Amelia died in childbirth on 27 July 1798, and in her memory a donation of 352,000 reales replenished the coffers of the Inclusa. Moreover the *canastilla* of the princess's son who had died with his mother – two trunk loads of the finest linens and laces – were placed at the disposition of the hospital, which sold them to realize a sum of 17,918 reales, plus 800 for the two trunks. A year later a similar windfall of 325,963 reales in bank holdings, silverware, diamonds, watches, and metal came from a legacy of Francisco Xavier Castán, an important retired bureaucrat.

In fact, data supplied to the Junta de damas when the Inclusa was finally ceded to the ladies of the Royal Economic Society indicate the hospital had come into possession of a respectable accumulation of assets in the form of investments and real estate: 30 *acciónes* of 10,000 reales each from the government loan of 160,000 *millones*; 2 *vales reales* of 300 pesos from grant *creación* (1 July); 25 *vales reales* of 600 pesos from grant *creación* (15 March); 8 *vales* of 600 pesos of the Real Canal de Tauste (15 July).[34]

Saved at the last moment from a desperate situation, the protector fought to keep control of the Inclusa. Those who had borne the heat of the day, the hours of despair, viewed with some bitterness the decision of the government to hand over the hospital to a new administration. While it has not been possible to clarify exactly what the total income of the hospital amounted to, it seems to have been the case that, in 1799, the financial position of the Inclusa had considerably improved.

But the preoccupation with finances had taken its toll. It had sapped the staff's energy and dominated its mind. Infants themselves took up little or no time in the deliberations of the *junta* of the Inclusa. These officials acted as if they could have been running a domestic industry where infants were sent out to be processed and returned at the age of seven in a different form ready for the orphanage or hospice. The minutes of their meetings can be scanned unsuccessfully for any sense that these serious, concerned individuals were presiding over a holocaust. In 1796, 87 per cent of the infants who entered the Inclusa died.

But in the meetings there is no reference to mortality figures. Perhaps numbers on that scale have a numbing effect. Perhaps these administrators saw improvement in finances as the primary, if not the only, way out of the web in which they, the infants, and the nurses were enmeshed.

If finances were at the root of the problems facing these institutions, then we have reached the last link in the chain of responsibility. It means apportioning blame to the government, which for understandable reasons did not come to the assistance of the hospitals, and to the church, which for understandable reasons was not able to provide the funding needed to run these hospitals efficiently. With a sense of relief we can end the story here. The infants died because of circumstances, mainly financial, beyond the control of those responsible for the administration and support of the foundling hospital.

But, in fact, as we have seen, the finances (at least in 1799) were no longer the problem for the Inclusa. The problem had become a matter of the application of these finances – the way in which the hospital was run. Again the meetings of the *junta* are a source for understanding the priorities of the administrators. There we see very little interest in the routine of the hospital. Preoccupied first with income, then with staving off the incursions of the Junta de damas, there was little or no attempt to deal with improving the functioning of the institution. The administrators were content to concentrate on finding ways to allow the Inclusa to continue to go on as it had in the past. The challenge of how to deal with the increasing numbers of abandonments, and particularly with the increasing numbers of deaths of these infants, was the tenor of the book of Santiago García, the doctor of the Inclusa, who had never been included in the deliberations of the *junta*. He did not keep silent, perhaps from frustration or perhaps to force the issue.

The administrators of the Inclusa had pushed their talents and capabilities as far as they could go. More by dint of good luck than by innovative measures, they had succeeded in re-establishing the finances of the Inclusa. The biennial crises facing the institution each time the nurses from outside arrived for their pay had been resolved, at least temporarily. But even financial stability did not have an impact on the mortality figures. Infants continued to come into the hospital, their growing numbers keeping pace with the supply of nurses, and to die there. The governing body remained bankrupt when it came to dealing with conditions within the hospital. When Godoy and Murcia finally acceded to the importunities of the Countess del Montijo and her cohorts, it was in recognition of the fact that the Inclusa badly needed new blood to bring about any permanent improvement. It was the women members of the Royal Economic Society of Madrid who were to face the issue head on, and to institute measures aimed directly at saving the lives of the *expósitos* of the Inclusa. This group of women was dedicated to putting an end to the horrendous loss of life associated with the Inclusa. Here, for the first time, we have a group of women in complete charge of the hospital. Here we have an opportunity to see maternalism in action – in contrast to the traditional paternalism I have described as dominating the welfare system of the Old Regime.

If any hospital anywhere had the possibility of saving the lives of the infants in its charge it was the Inclusa of Madrid. Situated in the same city as the court, it was in a position to importune the sources of support directly. The need was evident, it was evidently just, and the evidence was before the eyes of the powerful. Moreover, the cause was popular and had friends at court. The king himself, his highest minister, Godoy, who was the real power in the state, and the reformers who influenced them were all concerned about the *expósito*. Where could this concern better show itself than in the Inclusa of Madrid? Finally, an administration of intelligent, enthusiastic, idealistic, and capable women had taken upon themselves to see to it that the Inclusa of Madrid functioned as a credit to the enlightened views of Spain and its Catholic king.

The Junta de damas set about effecting a complete reorganization. It was not for nothing that the Countess del Montijo had been educated in France. She seems to have modelled herself upon Madame Necker who was taking similar steps in Paris on behalf of the foundling. Although the rector and chaplain remained, the priest who had been the head administrator was replaced by twelve Sisters of Charity from France – the society that had been responsible for the countess's own education. *Gastos*, the record of expenses, tells the whole story. Gradually everything about the hospital was revamped. Staff doubled between 1799 and 1805. A second doctor was added, then a second surgeon. Separate quarters were set up for the sick infants. Furnishings of new linens, beds, and cribs culminated in a completely new building on the calle del Soldado, removed from the noise and dust of the traffic of the Puerta del Sol, in 1801.

One of the obvious characteristics in the approach of the women was a sense of hard-headedness and practicality. Under the administration of the Junta de damas there was finally an acceptance of the reality that the Inclusa was an institution full of sick infants. The early years of the

1800s saw a medicalization of the Inclusa. In order to deal with this situation, the women abdicated much of their authority to the doctor. Clearly, the women of the Royal Economic Society had as much faith in the progress as did their male confrères. In an attempt to save the lives of the infants, the Inclusa became progressively a medical as well as a foundling hospital. The *señoras* took the publication of Santiago García, *Breve instrucción sobre el modo de conservar los niños expósitos*, as a kind of rule book. Fresh air was one of the few concrete measures doctors utilized against the spread of infection. Windows were to be opened and rooms swept out at least once a day. Then the rooms were to be sprayed with vinegar as a form of disinfectant. Anything that could cause putrefaction was to be removed promptly; cooking and washing facilities with their strong fumes were to be set up at some distance from the sleeping quarters of the infants. For the same reason there were to be as few lights as possible, since the gases emanating from the cheap oil were harmful.[35]

The *inclusero* had become a medical rather than a social or a religious problem. Ironically, this was to mean signing over of much of the authority of the Junta de damas to the doctor – the new priest of progress. This change gradually affected all aspects of the care of the new-born, and one of its first consequences was an attempt to control the women on whom the health of the infants depended – the wet-nurses. In this instance, the common sense we associated with the Junta de damas was undermined by unrealistic expectations on the part of the doctor. Santiago García was convinced that the nurses needed a strong hand. Their schedule was to be strictly regulated and their conduct closely supervised. They were to rise at 5 AM in summer and 6 AM in the winter, wash the infants all over in warm water, change diapers three to four times daily, and nurse the infants in the presence of the *madre* six times a day. They were to keep their rooms clean and utilize any spare time making shirts and dresses for the infants. When allowed out for exercise and fresh air, they were to walk in groups of four, accompanied, of course. They were allowed to converse only with husbands or relatives or someone known to the supervisors.[36]

The regulations advocated by Santiago García were ideally suited to a reform school for wayward girls. Did the doctor really expect to be able to put into effect such rules? Could he be taken seriously when he went on with his list of characteristics for the ideal wet-nurse? She should be brunette, have had one child nursed successfully, and have good teeth, good disposition, etc. – qualifications we have discussed elsewhere, and which, given the context of the Inclusa, seem ridiculously out of touch with the realities of the situation. No one was in a better position than the doctor of the Inclusa to know that at the wages being offered, the best he could expect to find were women who were poor and un-healthy, and not likely to conform to standards of genteel behaviour. He admitted as much in reiterating that in his experience there had never been a nurse he would consider satisfactory. All needed to be treated, he claimed, as if they themselves were sick, because they had bad eating habits, drank too much wine and spirits, and were addicted to gadding about; as a result, their milk acted like a poison, giving the infants diarrhoea and convulsions.[37]

The doctor of the Inclusa was not a stupid man. He knew that nurses were the key to the success or failure of any program aimed at saving the lives of the *expósitos*. He was in a good position to know the basic flaw in any reform that had to depend on these women: the hospital could either lower its expectations in order to take into account the kind of nurses it had, or do without.

He opted to do without. His solution and ambition was to make the institution independent, insofar as it was possible, of the wet-nurses, thus allowing for some choice and a little flexibility. Administrators could afford to wait a few days for a good nurse, instead of sending an infant out with some woman who had had trouble with milk, or had mistreated a child in the past, or been dismissed for bad conduct. A program of artificial feeding could put the administration back in control of the situation. The hospital could then wait for someone who was, in his words, 'well-behaved and humble' – qualities notably lacking in the wet-nurses of the Inclusa.[38]

The attraction of a system of artificial feeding was obvious for an institution having troubles financially, but its attraction for members of the medical profession was particularly strong. This way doctors could take over almost completely. They could supervise diets, pick and choose nurses, in short, take control and make an intolerable situation tolerable.

Santiago García and administrators like Xavier de Uriz founded their suspicions and dislike on firsthand experience with wet-nurses in the Inclusas. They were an independent crew because they knew they could be. García claimed they deliberately made life difficult for the adminis-trators. While this may not necessarily have been the case, they certainly offered a challenge for the doctor trying to assert his authority.

García obviously considered them the main obstacle, frustrating his attempts to improve the hospital routine. He was determined to rationalize and systematize the organization; they represented the irrational, the disorganized. He was preoccupied with devising the healthiest diet possible, given the circumstances; they persisted in eating and drinking what they wanted, when they wanted. He wanted the infants nursed at regular hours and the remaining time profitably used to wash diapers, clean rooms, and care for the infant; they felt free to wander off with or without the infant into the Puerta del Sol, chatting and flirting and wasting time. No wonder that one of his first priorities was to see the hospital moved to a quiet, isolated area with adequate open space to walk the infants within its confines. In this he had in mind not just fresh air for the infants, but the peace of mind of the *madre* and the implementation of his own full-scale plan that began with control of the wet-nurses.

Technology that could do away with the wet-nurse altogether, or at the very least curtail dependence on this highly erratic factor, might help the finances as well. Animals were cheap and dependable and in plentiful supply. Wet-nurses fell short in all those categories. The doctors brought to the cause the added fervour of idealism. Artificial feeding called forth an instinctive response from the medical profession, which saw itself in the forefront of progressive, innovative experimentation – experimentation having as its end the ultimate improvement of the human race. Here was an opportunity to bring scientific expertise into effect and to do away completely with the human element; in the process, doctors would be enabled to save the lives of the infants.

Incidentally, of course, such a routine would be the responsibility of the medical staff and would require minute supervision and absolute control of the care and feeding of the infants. The doctor would be the key person, the important figure in charge of seeing to the success of the whole operation. In García's words, 'Method must be applied with patience, zeal and diligence.'[39] What better setting could there be to initiate such a program than a foundling hospital?

Of course, there had always been some form of artificial feeding for infants. The nursling of the country woman with a ready supply of fresh goat or cow's milk had often been given a gruel of bread crumbs that gradually prepared the way for weaning. Nor was it an innovation in hospital routine to give a new-born with syphilis or 'sore mouth' who was unable to nurse a *papilla* of eggs and honey, or a paste of bread in milk or even beef broth. However, in the days before adequate refrigeration, such a diet was risky, and the digestive system of a very young child rarely endured the ordeal. Certainly, before pasteurization was developed, any form of artificial feeding, especially one using milk, was dangerous, even deadly, for the newborn, and as a result had never been used on a wide scale.

But toward the end of the century, the idea of artificial feeding was discussed with a new sense of purpose. Earlier experiments were resurrected. Desessartz, writing in 1760, recalled that doctors and surgeons had been approached by the administration of the Hôpital des Enfants-trouvés in Paris as early as 1680. They had recommended water of wheat or a paste of bread crumbs and bouillon as a substitute for nurse's milk, but the proposal had been rejected by surgeons and doctors of the court.[40] In 1775 administrators of the hospice in Aix-en-Provence asked eight doctors of the Faculty of Medicine in Paris to draw up a paper on the best method of artificial feeding. It propounded 'goat milk cut with a mixture of rice water, then after four months a cream of rice or of bread made with water or meat broth.' This mixture was to be dispensed by a spoon rather than a bottle.[41] Brouzet, in 1754, described a number of choices. One was a mixture of bread boiled in beer, because milk spoiled too quickly, and honey or sugar added to form a gum-like substance. Some peasant women were said to give infants a soup of cabbage and lard, while in Iceland infants were left beside a pot of milk with a straw to help themselves as need be. Even the son of the queen of England was supposed to have been nursed with milk, bread, and bouillon.[42]

While there were doctors who declaimed that such mixtures were better suited to glue together the backings of books, there was a gradual acceptance of the idea that a system of artificial feeding was preferable to bad nurses. This revival of interest was related directly to the problems of feeding large numbers of infants in the foundling hospitals. An English doctor, George Armstrong, wrote a dissertation in 1767 entitled *Essay on the diseases most fatal to infants, to which are added rules to be observed in the nursing of children with a particular view to those who are brought up by hand*. He spoke of instruments such as a polished cow's horn with a perforated end to which could be attached two small bits of parchment, shaped like the finger of a glove and curved so that liquid could be sucked through it. Various tools such as boat-shaped bowls, sponges, wishbones (a type of plate?), pieces of wool cloth soaked in milk, or simply spoons were other means of injecting liquids into the infant without the intermediary of the nurse's breast. He personally opted for a shallow dish, a device that would allow more solid food to get through. Using it to administer a mixture of boiled water, crumbs of bread, honey, and cow's milk would make it possible, he felt, to support an infant up to the age of nine to twelve months.[43]

Santiago García was enthusiastic about an experiment he described, carried out by the Duc [Duque] de Hijar, who had succeeded in keeping a set of twins alive for fifteen days nursed by the same goat.[44] Why that should be considered a success rather than a failure is an interesting question. Xavier de Uriz described an experiment carried out by a certain Margarita Raller and her husband, Francisco Grayor of Astrain in Navarre, who nourished infants with rice water.[45] He himself duplicated the experiment in June 1800 in the Inclusa of Pamplona and reported that the child weakened a little but kept in good health, moderate strength, and vivacity.

Obviously, the subject was a live issue at the turn of the century. Doctors of the foundling hospitals had particular reasons for promoting the cause of artificial feeding. For others, it was only a second-best substitute to be used as a last resort when the real thing was unavailable for some reason. However, there were a few converts who became fanatics on the subject. They saw artificial feeding as a substitute not only for nurses' milk but even for that of the natural mother. For some doctors, artificial feeding generated the kind of enthusiasm that new techniques of reproductive technology arouse today. It appealed to a sense of control over natural functions that has provided incentive for much of scientific research.

Because milk was responsible for transferring physical nourishment as well as character and temperament to the infant, what better way to improve the human species than to manipulate the milk supply of the next generation? In this novel form of human engineering, Moreau de Saint-Elier advised that children be isolated completely from women and their corrupt humours.[46] For these writers, animals at least were innocent. Though most experts on the care of the new-born remained convinced of the superiority of mother's milk, the implications of the theory fired the imagination of such widely respected and influential authors as Ballexserd, whose prize-winning treatise on the care of the new-born was acclaimed throughout all Europe. He speculated that because milk affects the blood, humours, and fibres of the infant, it could be a means of altering national temperament. Those north of Germany could profit from goat's milk, which would give them more vivacity, more gaiety in both mind and body. In contrast, Italians should drink cow's milk, which would slow down the course of fluids, making them more robust, stronger, and less frivolous.[47]

The development of a system of artificial feeding may have had long-range utopian appeal to theorists, and for some doctors it may have justified a deep-seated misogyny, but presumably the Junta de damas had been convinced that it was a practical and perhaps even a necessary modus operandi. Santiago García had written in 1794: 'If I were convinced, as some seem to be, that there was no hope of finding better nurses than there are at the moment, then I would propose a method of raising the infants "by hand" [that is, using artificial feeding], and consider it preferable to such nurses as we now have. I am absolutely confident that there would be less waste [of life] than there now is.'[48] While for the moment he had to content himself with less dramatic improvements in the routine of the hospital, he did not give up on his ideal of a system of supplementary feeding based on goat milk. Convinced that new techniques of artificial feeding would not only produce healthier infants in the long run, he also hoped this method would reduce the hospital's dependence on women, especially poor women with their only too-human foibles and self-importance. Because of this possible alternative to the wet-nurses, he assured the damas, 'the day will come when they [the nurses] are well-behaved and humble, and [can] thus provide a better milk to their nurslings.'[49]

As enlightened reformers themselves, the new administration of the Junta de damas did not hold back on giving Santiago García the opportunity to try out his innovations on a large scale. The secretary had had on file since 1792 a description of a system of artificial feeding used in Austria. According to the Marquesa de Llana, it was a mixture of cow's milk, flour, rice water, and sugar, and the damas considered its composition appealing enough to send it on to the tribunal of the Protomedicato along with an enclosed drawing of the type of pottery flask to be used to administer it.[50] They also looked into the possibilities of another proposal that had been submitted on 28 February 1794 by Doña Polonia Sanchez.[51] In 1800 the damas called a special conference to discuss implementing the regimen of Santiago García. Personally, they did not need convincing, but they wanted official approval and so they sent on the reglamento to some of the leading professors of the Protomedicato, Manuel Pereira, Juan Bautista Soldevilla, Antonio Franseri, José Severo Lopez, and José Queralto, for their consideration. Finally, in 1803, the doctor of the Inclusa was vindicated. The Royal Academy of Medicine recommended that the system of feeding of Santiago García be instituted not only in the Inclusa of Madrid but in all other foundling hospitals of the kingdom.[52]

The señoras took up the project with their usual thoroughness. For the first four months the infant was to be on a program of breast-feeding, alternating with wheat paste or *papilla* of day-old bread dissolved in goat or asses' milk. Then the infants were to be weaned. At this crucial point the doctor would have liked all the infants transferred back into the Inclusa where their diets could be monitored closely, 'because many died at this point.'[53] In fact, he looked forward to the day when all the foundlings of the kingdom who were being weaned would be brought back at this stage to a central hospital. For the moment, a full-time goat keeper was added to the staff. The Countess del Montijo devised a kind of portable cushion whereby two infants at a time could rest under the mammae of the goat to facilitate the process. Those irritating wet-nurses were to be phased out and replaced as much as possible by docile and dependable goats.

Though the Inclusa never succeeded in doing away with human nurses altogether, the doctor of the Inclusa embarked on a program of artificial feeding that he hoped would eventually make that dream a reality. In a work entitled *Instituciones sobre la crianza física de los niños expósitos: obra interesante para toda madre zelosa de la conservación de sus hijos* (1805), he drew the outlines of his grand scheme. As part of an overall medicalization of the foundling hospital, the routine of the infant had to be very closely supervised. What he seemed to have had in mind was an institution that could function as a modern hospital for sick children. There were to be eighteen different rooms in all, under two main divisions: *salas* for the healthy infants, nurslings, and weaned; and *salas* for *niños enfermos* with separate quarters for the various types of illnesses. The former were to be subdivided as follows: infants under two days; infants from two to eight days; infants eight days to one month; infants, two months to teething; teething to weaning; weaning to three years; three to fourteen years, when term in hospital was over.

The rooms for the sick infants were divided into one for *males regulares* (ordinary illnesses), and then a separate room for contagious illnesses such as convalescents and colds, *gálicos* (syphilis), *sarnas* (scalp infections), *herpéticos* (skin diseases), *aphtas* (eye diseases), *glositis* (tongue disease), smallpox, and finally measles.[54] The doctor was to see each infant on arrival, check each nurse carefully, and give his permission before any child was weaned. The foundling hospital was to provide the model for a full-scale implementation of infant health care. Paediatrics as we know it was to be only the final stage in the ambitious program that had started out with attempts to save the lives of the *expósitos* in the Inclusa of Madrid.

While it never fulfilled the dream of Santiago García, the new institution, away from the noise, dust, and distractions of the Puerta del Sol, and supervised by twelve Sisters of Charity, allowed for a degree of organization and specialization that had been unthinkable before. For the first time in the history of the Inclusa, 'nurse' did not necessarily mean *ama*, or wet-nurse. The independent *madre* was replaced by a team of women under the direct surveillance of the doctor. Instead of all the nurses and all the infants under the charge of the *madre*, there was a separate room for sick infants supervised by a *hermana enfermera*. This nun kept a register where the doctor set down prescriptions and instructions as to diet, dosages, and so forth. She was expected to be able to administer laxatives and blisters, apply leeches, and act as a head nurse for the doctor.

But the *madre* of the past had performed these duties on her own. She had decided when to send out for herbs from the *farmacia*, or what medication to give the sick infant, and it was her decision to call in the doctor or surgeon. What skill she had was due to an inheritance of folk wisdom and the store of her years of experience. Now medical care was designated as the particular province of one of the nuns, but it was to be carried out under the strict charge of the doctor. Under the Junta de damas and Dr Santiago García, the long process of medicalization had begun. The hierarchy of the staff had altered to give the doctor a large share of control in the operation of the Inclusa.

The medicalization program of Santiago García was just one aspect of a complete overhaul of the institution aimed at bringing its facilities in line with the increased demands being made upon it. The move to larger quarters in the calle del Soldado in September 1801 and the dedication of a new chapel in 1802 were only the beginning of what was to be a complete restructuring of the Inclusa. This restructuring would change the hospital from a traditional hospice typical of the welfare system of the Old Regime into a modern hospital that would be a prototype of the paediatric hospital of the twentieth century.

The Inclusa seemed well on its way to becoming the institution that takes its place today, the Instituto de Puericultura. There were now two doctors and two surgeons, one of whom was charged with visiting *amas* of the *barrios* of Madrid and bringing back to the infirmary infants who were sick.[55] The ambitious program of Santiago García would require not only a dedicated staff, but a large one. *Gastos* that list the salaries show that the numbers of staff jumped in the year 1800 from twenty-five to almost double that. By 1805 there were fifty-four. Expenses increased accordingly. The cost of operating the Inclusa went from 52,832 reales in 1700 to 156,059 reales in 1800; by 1805, 264,415 reales annually were required. To complete the new building alone meant a mortgage of 121,000 reales. As in the past, finances had to be a major consideration if new medical and administrative measures were to have any lasting impact on the prospects of the Inclusa and its *expósitos*.

Here again the Junta de damas attacked the problem with originality and intelligence. They embarked on a campaign for funds by playing upon the susceptibilities of wealthy *madrileños*, whose names and contribution were published in the *Diario de Madrid*.[56] Volunteers took up a collection for the cause each Saturday in the churches. The Infanta, María Isabel, granted 1000 reales annually.[57]

But as early as 1801, the treasurer was writing to Murcia in almost the same words as her predecessor had used in 1798 and 1799. And, in fact, with somewhat less success. Murcia advised the ladies to redeem some of their present holdings to cover the emergency of Pentecost. The response to the crisis of December was even less sympathetic. This time Murcia's letter listed in detail the financial favours the establishment had already received: the concession to raffle two lambs; 15,000 reales in the income from the papal bull allowing meat in Lent; 80,000 reales from the income on mail; the income, furnishings, and building of the defunct order of San Antonio. The Inclusa was admonished to cut down on expenses and to start looking for other sources of aid rather than the perpetual calls upon the royal treasury.[58] There was nothing new in any of these admonitions except that the letter closed not with its usual grant as requested but with an exhortation to practise the virtue of thrift.

Despite the harshness of the rebuke, there was a certain justice in the recriminations of Murcia. The Junta de Caridad had indeed been generous financially to the Inclusa of Madrid, which enjoyed a patronage that few foundling hospitals of the time could duplicate. The official president of the Junta de damas was the queen, María Luisa. The group had the sympathy and support of Godoy, the single most powerful man in Spain. The administration was in the hands of an intelligent, enlightened, and beneficent group of women of high position and illustrious names. For medical care they could call upon the advice and experience of Santiago García. Finally, the hospital was situated at the court of the one king in Europe who had taken a personal interest in the plight of the *expósito*. The foundling of the Inclusa had to be the most fortunate of a crew of unfortunates.

Given all of the favours that had been shown toward the hospital and had made possible the impressive reforms undertaken by the Junta de damas, what was the outcome of all these measures the women had initiated at great expense and with considerable ingenuity? Had the administration of a group of enlightened women been able to solve the problems of the Inclusa? Was maternalism able to accomplish what paternalism had failed to do?

To find the answer to this question we must turn again to the mortality rates of the hospital after 1799, when the Junta de damas took over. There we find that despite all the improvements in physical and administrative aspects of the Inclusa – and even despite 'doctoring' of the mortality figures whereby the Inclusa disclaimed responsibility for the deaths of those under fifteen days of age, those who were returned to the hospital, and those sickly on arrival – we read the same melancholy story. In the disastrous year of bad harvests of 1804, mortality rates were the highest in the 300 years of the hospital's history. Finally, in another famine year, 1812–13, the fortunes of the Inclusa reached their nadir. Of all the infants admitted, each and every one died.[59] In 1844 the mortality rate was still 85 per cent.[60] It was not until the development of aseptic techniques at the end of the nineteenth century that bringing together large numbers of infants was not likely to be a serious risk to their health and well-being.

Mortality figures indicate that the administration of the Inclusa under the Junta de damas, despite the improvements in hygiene and medicine instituted by Santiago García, had been unable to have any impact at all on saving the lives of the expósito. Even the system of artificial feeding had been a failure. Xavier de Uriz explained that conditions in the hospital and the physical state of the infants made it almost impossible to sustain such programs with any degree of success.[61] Despite anything the doctor could try, hospitals justified their reputation as places where disease was spread rather than cured. Putting so many infants, sick or well, together could only bring about their deaths, rather than save their lives. While a method of artificial feeding depending completely on dry nurses of skill and good judgment could conceivably be worthwhile, ultimately it would mean replacing one set of poor women with another. In the considered judgment of the administrator, it was highly unlikely that conditions in inclusas could ever overcome the major difficulties involved in making such a system successful.

The failure of the Inclusa, however, can hardly be blamed on the administration or the doctor. It had as much to do with the general economic and political situation as it did with the hospital itself. The wars, bad weather, and the financial difficulties of both church and state in the critical years of the beginning of the nineteenth century made its success exceedingly problematical.

Finally, the political climate of the day worked against the *expósito*. Events brought about a strong reaction against the *afrancesado* element in power under Charles IV. Popular dislike of the foreign armies spilled over in animosity toward the many French sympathizers in high positions in government, beginning with Godoy. His spectacular fall in 1808 was foreshadowed by attacks on those who had prided themselves on his friendship. Some of this resentment made itself evident on religious as well as political grounds. The Countess del Montijo was exiled to her estate in Logroño, ostensibly on charges of Jansenism, in 1805.[62] It was a strong blow against the prestige of the Inclusa and her cohorts in the Junta de damas who had championed the foundling. Among those who would suffer from her loss were the *expósitos*.

In his *Memorias*, Godoy speaks with just pride about the role he personally played in supporting the *expósitos*, but it is clear to anyone reading between the lines how these well-meaning acts could be used against him. 'So many useful measures, so many projects in favour of these adopted children of the *patria*, and the noble, secret, and philanthropic steps that were instituted to enable disgraced mothers to preserve their honour and prevent infanticides – measures that brought down upon me censures on the part of some, doubtless holy and virtuous, who described these concessions as favours and called them a source of corruption, and an encouragement to loose living.'[63] In other words, his defence of the *expósito* had cost Godoy something in popularity among the more puritanical elements of the Spanish populace. Certainly the disgrace of Godoy, and the exile of the Countess del Montijo in 1805, followed by that of the Countess de Trullás (who had been president of the Junta de damas for eleven years), could be seen as a reaction against some of the progressive and expensive steps initiated in favour of the *expósito*.

In this context there was an interesting comment in the report of the meeting of the Junta de damas that described the transfer of the infants to the new hospital on the calle del Soldado. The secretary pointed out that the transfer had occurred without incident and without arousing public notice by sending the *amas* out two by two, each carrying two infants with her.[64] Is it possible that there was some apprehension that the move to more elaborate quarters might arouse contention? Was it the poor who were likely to be upset because they saw the new quarters as an unnecessary expense, or the conservative Spaniards who resented further 'favours' to the abandoned infant who may have been of low status, or even of sinful origin? Could these concessions to the disadvantaged, the deserted, and the abandoned be seen as an encouragement to women of lax morality, or even to married women who might be inclined to leave an infant to the Inclusa?

The attack against the leaders of the Junta de damas and Godoy could not help but undermine the morale and effectiveness of the hospital administration. Doubtless, it also had an impact on the ability of the institution to raise funds both from the government and from the public. It was a serious blow to the ambitious hopes and plans envisioned by the dedicated and enlightened *señoras* and the doctor of the Inclusa.

Neither medicalization, nor the enthusiastic efforts of the Junta de damas, nor the goodwill and support of the highest and most powerful of administrators, Joaquín de Murcia, with the backing of Manuel Godoy had been effective in saving the lives of the foundling of the Inclusa of Madrid. But can we generalize about the foundlings in Spain from the experience of the Inclusa of Madrid?

Undoubtedly the most perspicacious, thorough, and astute account of the foundling hospital situation in Spain, and perhaps anywhere before the work of Léon Lallemand in France fifty years later, is that of Joacquín Xavier de Uriz, archdeacon of the Cathedral of Pamplona. In two volumes entitled *Causas prácticas de la muerte de los niños expósitos en sus primeros años: Remedio en su origin d'un tal grave mal y modo de formarlos utiles a la Religión y al Estado un notable aumento de la población, fuerzas y riqueza de España* (1801), the author presents a careful and convincing analysis of all aspects of the foundling problem and sets forward possible solutions. As a member of the *junta* of the General Hospital of Pamplona, he shared with Santiago García firsthand experience in the complexities of running a foundling hospital. But because he was not a doctor, he could view the problem from a broader perspective, where medical solutions were just one set of conditions requiring attention. His analysis goes over, step by step, the variety of problems facing an administrator trying to save the lives of the foundlings in his charge.

What did this administrator, who qualified as an expert on the subject, have to say about the system of artificial feeding? He had no qualms about condemning its use. Acknowledging that it had been tried in

England, Rome, Florence, Bologna, and elsewhere, his personal experience had proved that it only caused more deaths. In the Pamplona hospital they had tried a *papilla* of fresh eggs, beaten with sugar and water, mixed with goat milk or asses' milk. But even with enough animals on hand, it was awkward to arrange their keep, and difficult to use them at specific times when the infants needed to be fed. The delicate state of the infants' digestive system, he pointed out, called for constant attention. Trying out one concoction might upset them, then substituting another would only aggravate the indigestion, until a series of upsets ended up killing them. Quite simply, 'the discernment, variety, and care absolutely necessary to the success of such a program as artificial feeding has to be considered in the present condition of our hospitals as impossible.'[65] Although he conceded that a method of artificial feeding depending completely on dry nurses of skill and good judgment could conceivably be worthwhile, under existing conditions it would just mean replacing one set of poor women with another. In his view, it appeared highly unlikely that inclusas would ever be able to overcome the major difficulties involved in successfully running a program of artificial feeding.

What the author proposed was a protector appointed by the king who would devote his total attention to the foundling hospitals of the kingdom. But for all practical purposes such a system was already operating. No one could have been more sympathetic to the plight of the *expósito* than Joacquín de Murcia, head of the Junta de Caridad of the whole kingdom, and there were protectors of the various institutions as well. Josef Vilches had been a very active intermediary between the government and the Inclusa of Madrid.

Obviously, Xavier de Uriz had pinned his hope for reform on another bureaucrat in a position of power in Madrid who would act as a liaison between the central government and the local authorities. This person would provide 'the practical implementation of the most noble ideas that otherwise cannot have any lasting impact.' He would ensure that the legislation set up by the government was actually implemented at the local level.[66] Bilbao y Durán had already envisaged himself in that role, and his credentials were excellent. He had written a book on the subject, summarized the returns from the inquiry of 1794, and was himself responsible for leaving an infant to the Inclusa at Antequera. Unfortunately that experience seems to have burdened a rather fragile psyche with a degree of guilt that ultimately deranged him completely.[67]

The experience with the hospital of the Inclusa in Madrid has coloured our reaction to the advice and suggestions of Xavier de Uriz. We listen to his pleas with a certain degree of cynicism and insensitivity. Not to denigrate his goodwill, intelligence, or perception of the problems, but we have already seen how far goodwill, intelligence, and an understanding of the realities of the situation had been able to affect the fate of the *expósito*. Although there was much ignorance and often neglect, still the problem was not one of ignorance or negligence. Nor was it simply a case of infanticide, conscious or unconscious, hidden or open. In the end, failure to help the *expósito* came down to an inability, at any level, to implement the solutions that men in power – the bishops or bureaucrats like Murcia and Godoy – had so proudly set out. In the social, economic, and political conditions of the period – and given the state of medical practice and theory – no amount of legislation and no increase in numbers of officials (whether medical, government, or ecclesiastical) were likely to make any difference to the life span of any infant left in a foundling hospital. The terms in which Godoy congratulated himself on the legislation concerning the *expósito* could not be more ironic, in view of the reality of the situation as it was described by Xavier de Uriz in 1801. The foundlings, the women who left the infants, and the women who cared for them were caught in the same web of circumstances woven by poverty. Nevertheless, the story of the *expósito* should be closed with the words of Godoy, as a fitting epitaph for the infants of the Inclusa in Madrid:

In the previous reign a beginning was made to give legal expression to Christian sentiments of charity in favour of the *expósitos* ... [but] *expósitos* died, and they died by the thousands; the few that remained lived a life of misery and ignominy sadder than death could have been. The two royal *cédulas* of Charles iv provided an efficient and permanent solution to all these evils. These unfortunate infants were provided with life and health and a suitable and fitting education aimed at giving them no less than the rights of citizenship, honour, and livelihood, since they were declared to be citizens with full rights to all privileges ... All this was assured in such a way that it has lasted up to the present time.[68]

In fact, all that these infants were assured was a quick baptism and a brief and tormented life, where death came as a welcome relief from pain and suffering. The demographic changes that produced a population expansion in the eighteenth century called for a dramatic restructuring of the economy to provide for this increasing population, but it was not until an industrial revolution presented such opportunities that the situation of the poor could begin to improve. In its dying years, the Old Regime was unable to provide for its poor, and that failure could only hasten its demise. The *damas* of the Royal Economic Society of Madrid, the *amas* who were charged with nursing the infants, and even the women abandoning a new-born to the Inclusa were no less victims of the system than were the foundlings. The dream of a paternalistic institution in a paternalistic welfare system had become a nightmare. Goya's unforgettable picture of Saturn devouring his children found a real-life counterpart in the *expósitos* of the inclusas of Spain in the eighteenth century. Before better medical knowledge was available, there was literally nothing that could be done. The most favoured of all hospitals for abandoned children – funded by the government, supported by the king, queen, and prime minister, and guided by the latest ideas of the Enlightenment – had tried everything that human ingenuity of the time could devise and had failed. The children of the poor were the victims of that failure.

Note on Sources

The primary source for this study has been the archives of the hospital of the Inclusa of Madrid, today Instituto Provincial de Puericultura de la Diputación Provincial de Madrid. These archives are at present being catalogued for deposition in the Archivo Histórico Nacional of Madrid (AHN). I have consulted the *Libros de gastos ordinario y extraordinario* 1700–1800 (expense accounts), *libros de entradas* 1700–1800 (admissions), *libros de salidas* 1700–1800 (records of wet-nurses taking out infants from the Inclusa), *libros de tandas* 1700–30 and 1746–1800 (expenses of madre), and *libros de missas* 1700–1800 (accounts of the masses). Supplementary sources on the Inclusa can be found in the Archives of the Disputación Provincial of Madrid (ADP), no. 59-1-2352, which contain records of the meetings of administrators of the hospital, 1794–98 (Libro de Juntas del Real Hospital de la Inclusa), lesajo 48, no. 2, and an inventory of 1782, lesajo 48, no. 1. The *libros de bautismos* of the parish of San Ginés also contain information on the foundlings of the Inclusa. Another important source has been the manuscript of Ignacio María Ruiz de Luzuriaga 'Estadística político-médica o estados comparativos de los Xenodichios, Derephotrofios y Horfanotrofios, o sea Casas de Amparo u Hospicios de Maternidad, Inclusa y Casas de Huérfanos o Desamparados de España, despuesta según el orden de Arzobispados y Obispados con la mirar de perfeccionar estos Establecimientos según las mejoras de la demás naciones de Europa.' 5 vols (1817–19) in the Biblioteca de la Real Academia de Medicina de Madrid, and two unpublished manuscripts by Antonio Bilbao y Durán, one from the Biblioteca Nacional of Madrid, 'Representacíon de D. Antonio Bilbao al Consejo sobre expósitos: resolución del Consejo e informe de muchos Prelados sobre la situación de los Expósitos en sus diócesis, 1790' (MS 11.267 [32]) and his 'Historia de un pecador convertido en la que se da idea de la perfección de la limosna y del ramo de niños expósitos o Inclusas,' AHN, estado 3235.

212 Note on Sources

Printed sources focusing on *expósitos* were discussed in the preface, but information on eighteenth-century attitudes toward poverty can be found in Bernardo Ward, *Obra pía: Memoria de remediar la miseria de la gente pobre de España*, his appendix to *Proyecto económico en que se proponen varias providencias dirigada a promover los intereses de España* (Madrid, 1787); Pedro Rodríguez de Campomanes, *Discurso sobre la educacíon popular de los artisanos y su fomento* (Madrid, 1775), Francisco Ignacio Cortines y Andrade, *Discurso político sobre el establecimiento de los hospicios en España* (Madrid, 1768), Leonardo Galdiano y Croy, *Breve tratado de los hospitales y casas de Madrid* (Madrid, 1676), and Fermín Hernández Iglesias, *Le Beneficencia en España*, 2 vols (Madrid, 1876). Modern authors include María Jiménez y Salas, *Historia de la asistencia social en España en la Edad Moderna* (Madrid, 1958), Jean Sarrailh, *L'Espagne éclairée de la seconde moítíé du xviiie siècle* (Paris, 1954), and William J. Callahan, 'Caridad, sociedad y economía en el siglo xviii,' *Moneda y Crédito*, no. 146 (Sept. 1978): 65–76. See also the study of European poverty by S.J. Woolf, *The Poor in Western Europe in the Eighteenth and Nineteenth Centuries* (London/New York: 1986) and E. Maza Zorrilla, *Pebreza y asistencia social en España, siglos XVI al XX* (Valladolid: 1987).

From the point of view of demography, María Carbajo Isla's article, 'Primeros resultos cuantativos de un estudio sobre la poblacíon de Madrid, 1742–1836,' *Moneda y Crédito*, no. 107 (Dec. 1968): 71–91, was useful for comparisons between the foundling population and the new-borns in general. Of particular value were the articles of Francisco Bustelo García del Real on the population of Spain in the first half of the century ('Algunas reflexiones sobre la poblacíon española de principios del siglo xviii,' *Anales de Economía*, no. 151 [July–Sept. 1972]: 89–106) and on the second half of the century ('La poblacíon español en la segunda mitad del siglo xviii,' *Moneda y Crédito*, no. 123 (Dec. 1972): 53–104; the book of Vicente Pérez Moreda, *Las crisis de mortalidad en la España interior (siglos xvi-xix)* (Madrid, 1980); and the article by David Ringrose, 'Inmigracíon, estructuras demográficas y tendencias económicas en Madrid a comienzos de la Época Moderna.' See also Claude Larquíe's description of Madrid parishes, 'Quartiers et paroisses urbaines: L'exemple de Madrid au xviie siècle' *Annales de Démographie Historique* (Paris/La Haye, 1974): 165–95.

There has been much debate on the question of how many of the foundlings were actually of illegitimate birth. See Edward J. Shorter's article, 'Illegitimacy, Sexual Revolution and Social Change in Europe, 1700–1900,' *Journal of Interdisciplinary History* 2, no. 2 (1971): 237–72. There are few hard data on this issue for Spain, but I have found that the conclusions of the eighteenth-century officials closest to the problems (Pedro de Murcia, commissioned by the government to prepare a report on foundling hospitals in Spain, Manuel de Godoy, first minister of Charles iv, and Pedro de la Vega, the administrator of the

Inclusa) accord best with the records of the Inclusa. They attributed the foundling explosion at the end of the century to worsening conditions among the married poor.

Eighteenth-century paediatrics has been discussed by Luis S. Granjel and Rosa Ballesteros Añon (see preface). A number of works by eighteenth-century Spanish doctors dealing with wet-nursing have been of relevance. See Antonio Pérez de Escobar, *Avisos de las causas de muerte de niños* (Madrid, 1778); Jaime Bonells, *Prejuicios que acarrean al généro humano y al Estado las madres que rehusan criar a sus hijos, y medios para contener el abuso de ponerlos en ama* (Madrid, 1786); José Iberti, *Método artificial de criar a los niños recien nacidos y darles una buena educacíon física* (Madrid, 1795); and, of course, the books of the doctor of the Inclusa, Santiago García.

The work of Paula de Demerson on the Junta de damas in her biography of the Countess del Montijo has been an important source for understanding the operation of the Inclusa at the turn of the century.

I have developed the figures in this volume through research on the Inclusa's records of admissions (*entradas*) and wet-nurse registration books (*salidas*), primarily for the period 1700–99. Also referred to were E.J. Hamilton, *War and Prices*, 246–57 (for figures 1.1 and 6.4) and Mario Carbajo Isla, 'Primeros resultados cuantitativos,' 81 (for figure 5.3).

Notes

ADP Archives of the Diputación Provincial de Madrid
AHN Archivo Histórico Nacional de Madrid
AI Archives of the Real Hospital de la Inclusa
BN Biblioteca Nacional de Madrid

PREFACE

1 Bernard Benoit Remacle, *Rapport à M. le ministre secrétaire d'état de l'interieur concernant les infanticides et les morts-nés dans leur relation avec la question des enfants-trouvés* (Paris, 1845)
2 Jean-François Terme and J.B. Monfalcon, *Histoire des enfants-trouvés* (Paris, 1840) and *Histoire statistique et morale des enfants-trouvés suivé de cent tableaux* (Paris, 1837)
3 Léon Lallemand, *Histoire des enfants abandonnés et délaissés: Étude sur la protection de l'enfance aux diverses époques de la civilisation* (Paris, 1885) and *La question des enfants abandonées et délaissés au xixe siècle* (Paris, 1885)
4 Jean-Claude Peyronnet, *Les enfants trouvés de l'Hôpital général de Limoges au xviiie siècle* (Paris, 1972)
5 Janet Ruth Potash, *The Foundling Problem in France, 1800–1869: Child Abandonment in Lille and Lyon* (Ann Arbor, 1979)
6 Claude Delasselle, 'Les enfants abandonnées à Paris au xviiie siècle,' *Annales (Économies, Sociétés et Civilisations)*, 30 année, no. 1 (Jan.–Feb. 1975): 187–218
7 Nicole Sergent, *L'Hôpital des enfants-trouvés de Paris et la reinsertion sociale des enfants-trouvés* (Paris, 1976)

8 Rachel Ginnis Fuchs, *Abandoned Children: Foundlings and Child Welfare in Nineteenth-Century France* (Albany, 1984)

9 George Sussman, *Selling Mother's Milk: The Wetnursing Business in France, 1715–1914* (Urbana, 1982)

10 Olwen Hufton, *The Poor in Eighteenth-Century France – 1750–89* (Oxford, 1974)

11 Jean-Pierre Gutton, *La société et les pauvres: l'exemple de la généralité de Lyon, 1534–1789* (Paris, 1970)

12 Cissie Fairchilds, *Poverty and Charity in Aix-en-Provence, 1640–1789* (Baltimore, 1976)

13 T.H. Nichols and F.A. Wray, *The History of the Foundling Hospital* (London, 1935)

14 Ruth McClure, *Coram's Children: The London Foundling Hospital in the Eighteenth Century* (New Haven, 1981)

15 Antonio Bilbao y Durán, *Destrucción y conservacíon de los expósitos. Idea de la perfeccíon de este ramo de policia. Modo breve de poblar la España* (Antequera, 1789)

16 Joaquín Xavier de Uriz, *Causas prácticas de la muerte de niños expósitos en sus primeros años. Remedio en su origen d'un tal grave mal y modo de formarlos utiles a la Religíon y al Estado con notable aumento del población, fuerzas y riqueza de España*, 2 vols (Pamplona, 1801)

17 Pedro Joaquín de Murcia, *Discurso politico sobre la importancia y necesidad de los Hospicios, casas de expósitos y hospitales que tienen todos los Estados y particularmente España* (Madrid, 1798)

18 Jacques Soubeyroux, *Pauperisme et rapports sociaux à Madrid au XVIIIᵉ siècle*, 2 vols (Lille, 1978)

19 T. Egido, 'Aportación al estudio de la demografía española: los niños expósitos de Valladolid, (siglos XVI–XVIII),' *Primer Jornadas de Metodología aplicada de las Ciencias Históricas, Ponencias y Comunicaciones* (Santiago de Compostela, 1973) III: 333–45. See also A. Eiras Roel, 'La Casa de Expósitos del Real Hospital de Santiago en el siglo XVIII,' *Boletín de la Universidad Compostelana*, no. 75–6 (1967–68): 295–355; Delfín García Guerra, *Hospital Real de Santiago (1499–1804)* (Galicia, 1983); and G. Santalo, *Marginación social y mentalidad en Andalucia Occidental: expósitos en Sevilla (1613–1910)* (Sevilla, 1980).

20 Rosa Ballesteros Añon, *La Historia clínica pediátrica durante el siglo XIX: análisis de la ciencia y práctica pediátrica a traves de la patología infantiles* (Zaragoza, 1977). See also Luis S. Granjel, *Historia de la Pediatría Española* (Salamanca, 1965).

21 Santiago García, *Breve Instrucción sobre el mode de conservar los niños expósitos aprobada por el Real Tribunal del Protomedicato* (Madrid, 1974) and *Instituciones sobre la crianza física de los niños expósitos: obra interesante para toda madre zelosa de la conservación de sus hijos* (Madrid, 1805)
22 Antonio Carreras Panchón, *El problema del niño expósito en la España Ilustrada* (Salamanca, 1977)
23 Paula de Demerson, *María Francisca de Sales Portocarrero, Condesa del Montijo: Una figura de la Ilustración* (Madrid, 1975) and 'La Real Inclusa de Madrid a finales del siglo xviii,' *Anales del Instituto de Estudios Madrileños* 8 (1972): 261–72
24 Valentina Fernández Vargas, 'Informe sobre el archivo de la antigua Inclusa de Madrid, hoy Instituto Provincial de Puericultura,' *Anales del Instituto de Estudios Madrileños* 5 (1970): 187–201
25 Claude Larquié, 'Les milieux nourriciers des enfants madrilènes au xviie siècle,' *Mélanges de la Casa de Velasquez* xix (1983): 221–42 and 'La mise en nourrice des enfants madrilènes au xviie siècle,' *Revue d'histoire moderne et contemporaine* 32 (Jan.–March 1983): 123–44
26 Joseph Robins, *The Lost Children: A Study of Charity Children in Ireland, 1700–1900* (Dublin, 1980), 26

CHAPTER 1: The Balancing Act

1 J. Alvarez-Sierra, *Los hospitales de Madrid de ayer y de hoy* (Madrid, 1952), 136, 137
2 Inventory of Tomás Prado, ADP no. 59-1-2352, legajo 48, caja 1, no. 8 (hereafter Prado, Inventory)
3 Alvarez-Sierra, *Los hospitales de Madrid* 136
4 *Libros de gastos*, 1700–1805, AI
5 Antonio Ponz, *Viaje por España*, 18 vols (Madrid, 1774), 5: 250
6 Prado, Inventory, caja 1, legajo 8, no. 1
7 Ibid., no. 3
8 Ibid., no. 7
9 Ibid., nos 4 and 5
10 Ibid., nos 11 and 12
11 Charles Kany, *Life and Manners in Madrid, 1750–1800* (New York, 1970; originally pub. 1920) 56
12 Julio Ramón Laca, *Nuevos itinerarios madrileños* (Madrid, 1961), 174
13 Prado, Inventory, caja 1, legajo 3, no. 9

14 Miguel Capella and A. Matilla, *Los cinco gremios mayores de Madrid, Estudio crítico-histórico* (Madrid, 1957), 79
15 *Gastos*, Oct. 1740
16 Ibid., Dec. 1780
17 S.L. Bensusan, *Home Life in Spain* (London, 1910) 10
18 García Guerra, *El Hospital Real de Santiago*, 333
19 *Gastos*, July 1710
20 'Report of the Commission of the House of Commons on the Management and State of the Foundling Hospital,' in K.H. Connell, *Irish Peasant Society* (Oxford, 1968), 68
21 Hufton, *Poor of Eighteenth-Century France*, 338
22 *Gastos*, Aug. 1800
23 Ruth Hodgkinson, 'History of Medical and Related Sciences,' lecture in Faculty of Medicine, Queen's University, 5 Jan. 1976
24 García, *El modo de conservar los niños expósitos*, 65
25 *Libros de tandas*, 1700–30, AI
26 *Gastos*, June 1799
27 Ibid., Sept. 1710
28 Ibid., Jan. 1760
29 Ibid., Sept. 1710, Dec. 1790
30 Alexander Laborde, *Voyage pittoresque et historique de l'Espagne*, 2 vols (Paris, 1806)
31 Fernand Braudel, *Capitalism and Material Life, 1400–1800* (London, 1973) 173
32 Ibid., 219
33 The *carro* was the standard measure for coal. Hamilton was not able to say its exact equivalent in *arrobas*, but in the twentieth century its equivalent is fifty kilograms.
34 *Gastos*, June 1760
35 Vicente Palacio Atard, 'Algo más sobre el abastecimiento de Madrid en el siglo xviii,' *Anales del Instituto de Estudios Madrileños* 6 (1970): 272
36 *Gastos* 1700–28
37 Palacio Atard, 'El abastecimiento de Madrid,' 272
38 Braudel, *Capitalism and Material Life*, 144
39 *Gastos*, Jan.–Feb. 1700
40 Ibid., Jan. 1765.
41 Ibid., Feb. 1785, Feb. 1790
42 David Ringrose, 'Madrid y Castilla, 1560–1850. Una capital nacional en una economía regional,' *Moneda y Crédito*, no. 111 (1969): 84

43 Cristobal Romea y Tapía, 'El escritor sin título' (1763), in E. Correa Calderón (ed.), *Costumbristas españoles*, 2 vols (Madrid, 1950) ii: 509
44 Earl J. Hamilton, *War and Prices in Spain, 1651–1800* (Cambridge, MA, 1947), 246–57
45 *Gastos*, Feb. 1780
46 Ibid., Dec. 1789
47 J. Vicens Vives, *Economic History of Spain* (Princeton, 1969), 528
48 *Gastos*, Sept. 1783
49 Ibid., 1700–40
50 Ibid., 1730, 1780, 1783
51 Ibid., Jan. 1800, Aug. 1800
52 Ibid., Aug. 1790, Dec. 1795
53 García, *El modo de conservar los niños expósitos*, 26
54 *Gastos*, Dec. 1770, Dec. 1778
55 Ibid., Nov. 1760
56 Ibid., Aug. 1790, July 1795
57 Jerónimo de Quintana, *Historia de la antigüedad, nobleza y grandeza de la villa de Madrid* (Madrid, 1954; originally pub. 1628), 137
58 Leonardo Galdiano y Croy, *Breve tratado de los hospitales y casas de recogimiento* (Madrid, 1676), 17, 18
59 Alvarez-Sierra, *Los hospitales de Madrid*, 136
60 Cosme de Abaunza, 'Informe de Junta de Hospitales,' 1693, AHN, Consejos, 51444, iii, 2
61 *Entradas*, June and Dec. 1700
62 Ibid., 1710
63 Ibid., 1700–99
64 E.J. Hamilton, *War and Prices*, 147
65 Annual summaries are provided in the *libros de entradas*, admissions (*entradas*), deaths within the hospital (*muertos en sala*), infants sent out to nurse (*salidas*), infants adopted (*entregados*), and alms (*limosnas*), AI, 1700–1800 (hereafter referred to as Totals).
66 Prado, Inventory. The inventory is organized as follows: (1) *juros*, 1639–1722; (2) *censos*, 1613–1781; (3) redeemed *censos*, 1606–1728; (4) *censos* against the hospital, 1654–1701; (5) foundations and legacies setting up chaplaincies or masses, 1630–1757; (6) municipal taxes, 1652–97; (7) wills, 1653–1707; (8–10) titles and deeds, 1579, 1699, 1701–24, 1769–72; (11) royal decrees, 1610–34; (12) royal grants, 1636–41; (13) various notes of little value, 1566–1765
67 Report of Julian de Barcenilla, Meeting of Administrators of Inclusa, 9 Aug.

1798, ADP, no. 59-1-2352, legajo 48, caja 2 (hereafter Meeting of Administrators)

68 Gaspar de Jovellanos claimed, 'There is scarcely another institution more repugnant to a wise and just legal system.' See 'Informe en el expediente de ley agraria, 26, april 1794,' in D. Candido Nocedal (ed.), *Biblioteca de Autores españoles des de la formación del lenguaje hasta nuestras días, obras publicadas é inéditas de D. Gaspar Melchor de Jovellanos,* vol. 50 (Madrid, 1898), 79–138.

69 Prado, Inventory, caja 1, legajo 5, no. 1

70 Ibid., caja 1, legajo 3, no. 6

71 Ibid., no. 8

72 Ibid., caja 2, legajo 6, no. 16. For instance, the dispute between the Inclusa and the heirs of José de Galera took ten years to resolve.

73 *Juros* listed in inventory of Prado, caja 1, legajo 8, no. 6: (1) 50 ducats per year on the sales tax (*alcabalas*) of Madrid, 1639; (2) 5602 reales on supplementary taxes (*servicio ordinario y extraordinario*) of Madrid, 1643; (3) 12,787.64 reales on import taxes (*servicio de millones*) of Madrid, 1657; (4) 12,117.64 reales owed to Inclusa by collector of the salt tax to be paid immediately by R.O. of Charles II, 1670; (5) 352.95 reales on salt tax, 1674; (6) 879.14 reales on import taxes of city of Cuenca, 1675; (7) 1800 reales on pepper tax, 1675; (8) 2,029.88 reales on taxes of city of Guadalajara, 1675; (9) two *juros* of 9117.84 reales each on import taxes (*almorifazgos*) of city of Seville, 1657.

Currency equivalents in eighteenth-century Spain (E.J. Hamilton, *War and Prices*, 38): cuarto = 3 maravedís; real = 34 maravedís; escudo = 340 maravedís or 10 reales; ducat = 375 maravedís or 11 reales.

74 Galdiano y Croy, *Breve tratado*, 17

75 José Luis Serda Carrión, *La hacienda castellana y los economistas del siglo XVII* (Madrid, 1949), 85, 86

76 Prado, Inventory, caja 2, legajo 6, no. 6

77 Letter of Josef Vilches to Countess de Trullás, *entradas*, 21 Sept. 1799

78 Cosme de Abaunza, Report protesting a law of 1712 concerning the rights of hospitals to exemptions from *sisas municipales*, AHN, consejo, 51444, III, 2

79 *Gastos*, June 1728

80 Prado, Inventory, caja 1, legajo 6, no. 3

81 Report of 6 April 1795 Meeting of Administrators, legajo 48, caja 2

82 María Carmen García Monerris and José Luis Peset, 'Los gremios menores y el abastecimiento de Madrid durante la Ilustración,' *Moneda y Crédito*, no. 140 (March 1977): 79. See also Capella and Matilla, *Cinco gremios mayores*, 240, where the authors point out that in 1798 the M. de Haciendo ordered the

Caja de amortización to deliver 2,500,000 reales in vales to the Royal Canal de Tauste so that the corporation could continue to pay interest.

83 Gonzalo Anes, *El Antiguo Régimen: los Borbones* (Madrid, 1975), 290
84 Vicens Vives, *Economic History of Spain*, 603
85 Report of 14 August 1798, Meeting of Administrators, legajo 48, caja 2.
86 Agustín González Enciso and José Patricio Merino, 'Public Sector and Economic Growth in Eighteenth Century Spain,' *Journal of European Economic History* 8, no. 3 (Winter 1979): 553–92
87 Jacques A. Barbier and Herbert S. Klein, 'Las prioridades de un monarcó ilustrado: de gasto público sobre el reinado de Carlos III,' *Revista de Historia Económica* 3, no. 3 (Autumn 1985): 473–95

CHAPTER 2: Human Resources of the Inclusa

1 *Gastos*, 1700–99
2 Ibid., May 1700
3 Ibid., 1769–99
4 Ibid., 1791–98
5 Ibid., 1720–70
6 J. Vicens Vives, *Historia de España y America*: IV, *Burguesía, industrialización, obrerismo* (Barcelona, 1961), 47
7 Vicens Vives, *Economic History of Spain*, 600
8 *Gastos*, 1760
9 *Libros de bautismos* of the Parish of San Ginés, 1700–1800
10 *Gastos*, 1700–50
11 Ibid., 1801
12 *Libros de missas*. These ledgers recorded the masses said, sums paid out and received.
13 Demerson, 'La Real Inclusa de Madrid a finales del siglo XVIII,' 261–77
14 *Gastos*, 1700–99
15 Ibid., 1792
16 Meeting of Administrators, 1794–99, Report of 8 June 1793
17 Ibid., Report of 2 Nov. 1794
18 Ibid., Report of 28 Aug. 1798
19 Jovellanos, letter of 14 Dec. 1798, quoted in J. Sarrailh, *L'Espagne éclairée de la seconde moitié du XVIII siècle* (Paris, 1954) 59
20 *Gastos*, 1700–99
21 Meetings of Administrators, Report of 25 Jan. 1797
22 Ibid., 29 Jan. 1797
23 *Gastos*, 1770

24 *Salidas*, 12 Aug. 1727
25 *Salidas*, 25 Dec. 1738. These cases, such as the baker and his wife who adopted the infant 'because of much love they bear her,' were rare. Only 2.2 per cent of nurslings were adopted by the wet-nurse who had taken them out (*entradas*, 1700–99).
26 *Gastros*, 1760
27 Ibid., 1770
28 Ibid., 1804
29 Ibid., 1720–50
30 Campomanes, *Discurso sobre la educación popular*, quoted in Kany, *Life and Manners in Madrid*, 242
31 María Dolores Marcos González, *Castilla la Nueva y Extremadura*, fasc. 6 of Miguel Artola (ed.), *La España del Antiguo Régimen* (Salamanca, 1971), 17
32 Diego de Torres Villarroel, *Visiones y visitas de Torres con Don Francisco de Quevedo por la Corte.* (Madrid, 1966; originally pub. 1746), 55
33 Arthur Hamilton, 'A Study of Spanish Manners, 1750–1800, from the Plays of Ramón de la Cruz,' *University of Illinois Studies in Language and Literature* 11 (Urbana, 1926): 337–428. Ramón de la Cruz wrote a number of entre-act skits or *sainetes* based on the customs of the working classes of Madrid that were popular in his day and are an important source of information for the social historian of eighteenth-century Madrid.
34 *Gastos*, 1761–87
35 Meeting of Administrators, Report of 2 Nov. 1794
36 *Gastos*, 1805
37 E.J. Hamilton, *War and Prices*, 185
38 Ibid., 1800
39 Ibid., 1700–1800
40 Ibid., 1740–83
41 Ibid., Sept. 1805
42 Meeting of Administrators, Report of 26 March 1802
43 *Gastos*, 1799
44 Ibid., 1770–99
45 Ibid., 1799–1805
46 Ibid., 1700–1805

CHAPTER 3: Rural Poverty and the Inclusa

1 E.J. Hamilton, *War and Prices*, 147–62
2 Miguel Závala y Auñon, *Discursos varios* (Madrid, 1787), quoted in A.

Domínguez Ortiz, *La sociedad española en el siglo xviii* (Madrid, 1955), 280
3 Gonzalo Anes, *Las crisis agrarias en España moderna* (Madrid, 1970), 345–67
4 E. J. Hamilton *War and Prices*, 185
5 Pierre Vilar, quoting the Census of Ensenada in *La formació de la Catalunya moderna* (Barcelona, 1970), 15
6 Marcos González, *Castilla la Nueva y Extremadura*, 28
7 Vilar, *La formació de la Catalunya*, 8. See also David Vassberg, *Land and Society in Golden Age Castile* (Cambridge, 1984).
8 María Carbajo Isla, 'Primeros resultados cuantitativos de un estudio sobre la población de Madrid, 1742–1836,' *Moneda y Crédito*, no. 107 (Dec. 1968): 71–91
9 Massimo Livi Bacci, 'Fertility and Nuptiality Changes in Spain from the Late 18th to the Early 20th Centuries,' *Population Studies* 22 (1968): 99
10 Anes, *Las crisis agrarias*, 197
11 Julio Caro Baroja, *El Carnaval: análsis histórico-cultural* (Madrid, 1965)
12 Vilar, *La formacío de la Catalunya* 24
13 Braudel, *Capitalism and Material Life*, 345
14 Torres Villarroel, *Visiones y visitas de Torres*, 132
15 Ponz, *Viaje por España*, xii, 323
16 Marcos González, *Castilla la Nueva y Extremadura*, 264 n1
17 Catherine Lis and Hugo Soly, *Poverty and Capitalism in Pre-industrial Europe* (Hassocks, Sussex, 1971), 139
18 Marcos González, *Castilla la Nueva y Extremadura*, 36, 37
19 Vicens Vives, *Burguesía, industrialización, obrerismo*, 138
20 Ignacio María Ruiz de Luzuriaga, 'Estadística político-médica,' i, 42, ms, Biblioteca de la Real Academia de Medicina de Madrid
21 Vicens, Vives, *Burguesía, industrialización, obrerismo*, 114
22 See Marcos González, *Castilla la Nueva y Extremadura*, 75, and also Agustín González Enciso, 'Inversión pública y industrial textil en el siglo xviii,' *Moneda y Crédito*, no. 153 (June 1975): 45.
23 Pascual Madoz, *Diccionario estadístico-histórico de España*, 18 vols (Madrid, 1845–50), i: 450
24 Ibid., i: 463
25 Ibid., vii: 58
26 Sebastian Miñano y Bedoya, *Diccionario geográfico estadístico de España*, 11 vols (Madrid, 1825–28), i: 368
27 Marcos González, *Castilla la Nueva y Extremadura*, 37
28 *Salidas*, 1750–99
29 David Ringrose, 'Inmigración, estructuras demográficas y tendencias econ-

ómicas en Madrid a comienzos de la Época moderna,' *Moneda y Crédito*, no. 138 (Sept. 1976): 21

30 Jacques Soubeyroux, *Pauperisme et rapports sociaux á Madrid, au xv111ème siècle*, 2 vols (Lille, 1978), I: 118, 119

31 Figures for Madrid are based on studies done by Pascual Madoz (1849), Martorell (1930), Matilla (1961), and Domínguez Ortiz (1961). See also David Ringrose, 'Madrid and Castilla, 1560–1850: Una capital nacional en una economía regional,' *Moneda y Crédito*, no. 111 (Dec. 1969): 107.

32 Francisco Bustelo García del Real, 'La población español en la segunda mitad del siglo xvIII,' *Moneda y Crédito*, no. 123 (Dec. 1972): 101

CHAPTER 4: Urban Poverty and the Inclusa

1 Ringrose, 'Madrid y Castilla, 1560–1850,' 71

2 Soubeyroux, *Pauperisme et rapports sociaux à Madrid;* the author points out that widows made up the majority of *pobres de solemnidad* in 1805 in Madrid (I: 90).

3 Laborde, *Voyages pittoresque et historique*

4 E.J. Hamilton, *War and Prices*, 215

5 Cristobal Romea y Tapía 'El escritor sin título' (Madrid, 1763), quoted in E. Correa Calderone (ed.) *Costumbristas españoles*, 2 vols (Madrid, 1950), I: 503–15

6 Antonio Meijade Pardo, 'La emigración gallega interpeninsular,' in *Estudios de Historia Social de España* (Madrid, 1960), 465

7 Ramón de la Cruz, *Sainetes I*, John Dowling (ed.) (Madrid, 1981)

8 Louise A. Tilly and Joan W. Scott, *Women, Work and Family* (New York, 1978)

9 Bustelo, 'La población española del segunda mitad del siglo xvIII,' 64

10 *Salidas*, June 1750

11 J. Kaplow, *The Names of Kings* (New York, 1972), 84

12 García, *El modo de conservar los niños expósitos*, 65

13 Demerson, *Condesa del Montijo*, 203

14 Uriz, *Causas prácticas de la muerte de los niños expósitos*, I: 11

15 A. Chamoux, 'L'enfance abandonnée à Rheims à la fin du xvIIIe siècle,' *Annales de Démographie Historique: Enfant et société* (Paris/La Haye, 85. The author found that when there were two infants sharing the same nurse, invariably one died.

16 Tenon, quoted in ibid., 285

17 Process of Barbara Olivera, AHN, consejo, sala de alcaldes, 1804, 793–814

18 Ibid., testimony of Teresa de Orche, widow of Antonio Galza, 793

19 Ibid., *indulta* of 13 August 1808, 812–14

20 Letter of Countess del Montijo to Alfonso Durán of the Junta de Caridad, 24 June 1805, *Libro Rector*, AI, June 1805
21 García, *El modo de conservar los niños expósitos*, 39ff. This description of the qualities of the wet-nurse had become a cliché. It is found in writings as early as the Greek physician Soranus, 98–138 AD.
22 The work of Claude Larquié has been of great assistance in clarifying the parochial organization of the city; see his 'Madrid au xvɪɪe Siècle: Quartiers et Paroisses,' *Annales de Démographie Historique* (1974): 165–95
23 Soubeyroux, *Pauperisme et rapport sociaux à Madrid*, ɪ: 129
24 Ibid., ɪ: 89
25 Ibid., ɪ: 232
26 Ibid., ɪ: 129
27 Ibid., ɪ: 337
28 Meeting of Administrators, 25 Jan. 1797. ADP, legajo 48, no. 2
29 Letter of Countess de Trullás, 9 May 1801, quoted in Demerson, *Condesa del Montijo*, 225
30 Soubeyroux, *Pauperisme et rapport sociaux à Madrid*, ɪɪ: 446. San Nicolás de Bari had been set up specifically to punish adulterous wives, without having them mingle with the prostitutes and other criminals of la Galera.

CHAPTER 5: The *Expósito* as Bastard

1 Jehanne Charpentier, *Le Droit de l'enfance abandonnée* (Paris, 1967), 114
2 Charles Louis de Secondat, baron de la Brède et de Montesquieu, *Esprit de Lois*, 2 vols (New York, 1900; originally pub. 1748), ɪɪ: xxiii
3 Peter Laslett, 'The Bastardy Prone Sub-society,' *Bastardy and Its Comparative History: Studies in Social Demographic Change* (London, 1980), 217–46
4 Soubeyroux, *Pauperisme et rapports sociaux à Madrid*, ɪ: 102
5 Evelyne Buriez-Henaux, *Pauperisme à Lille au 18e Siècle* (Paris, 1968), 160
6 Peyronnet, *Les enfants trouvés de l'Hôpital général de Limoges*, 210
7 Lallemand, *La question des enfants abandonnées et délaissés*, 163
8 Delasselle, 'Les enfants abandonnées à Paris,' 187–218
9 Pedro de la Vega, 'Computo necrolo[g]ico de la Real Inclusa de Madrid, 1765–1812,' in Ruiz de Luzuriaga, 'Estadística político-médica,' ɪ: 44–56
10 Murcia, *Discuro político* apendice tercero, ix
11 Vega, in Ruiz de Luzuriaga, 'Estadística político-médica,' ɪ: 45
12 Crane Brinton, *French Revolutionary Legislation on Illegitimacy, 1789–1804* (Cambridge, 1936), 72, 73
13 For a discussion of social welfare by contemporary writers, see references in 'Note on Sources.'

14 Murcia, *Discurso político*
15 José Lesen y Moreno, *Historia de la Sociedad Económica de Amigos del País de Madrid*, 2 vols (Madrid, 1863)
16 Edward J. Shorter, 'Sexual Change in Illegitimacy: The European Experience,' in Robert J. Bezucha (ed.), *Modern European Social History* (Lexington, MA, 1972), 231–69. See also his *Making of the Modern Family* (New York, 1975).
17 Domínguez Ortiz, *La sociedad española en el siglo XVIII*, 65n22
18 Dorothy Marshall, *The English Poor in the Eighteenth Century* (New York: 1969), 36
19 Duc de la Rochefoucauld-Liancourt, 'Rapport de la Comité de la Mendicité,' in Peyronnet, *Enfants trouvés de l'Hôpital général de Limoges*, 212
20 Royal order 11-xii-96, quoted in Murcia, *Discurso político* ix
21 Demerson, *La Condesa del Montijo*, 223
22 Ibid., 218n6
23 Carbajo Isla, 'Primeros resultados cuantitativos'
24 Galdiano y Croy, *Breve tratado*, 12
25 Totals, 1700–1800
26 Galdiano y Croy, *Breve tratado*, 19–21
27 Ibid., 27
28 Demerson, *La Condesa del Montijo*, 222
29 *Illegitimacy: Data and Findings for Prevention, Treatment, and Policy Formation* (New York, 1965), 41–3
30 Vega, quoted in Ruiz de Luzuriaga, 'Estadística político-médica,' I: 46
31 Frederico Carlos Sainz de Robles, *Breve historia de Madrid* (Madrid, 1970), 121
32 William J. Callahan, *La Santa y Real Hermandad del Refugio y Piedad de Madrid, 1682–1832* (Madrid, 1980)
33 Demerson, *La Condesa del Montijo*, 193
34 Larquié, 'Le mise en nourrice des enfants madrilènes,' 125–44
35 *Entradas*, AI, 1804
36 E.A. Wrigley, 'Marriage, Fertility and Population Growth in Eighteenth-Century England,' in R.B. Outhwaite (ed.), *Marriage and Society: Studies in the Social History of Marriage* (New York, 1981), 137–85
37 Ruiz de Luzuriaga, 'Estadística político-médica,' I: 50
38 Ringrose, 'Inmigración, estructuras demográficas y tendencias económicas,' 21
39 Carbajo Isla, 'Primeros resultados cuantitativos,' 81
40 F. Lebrun, 'Démographie et mentalités: le mouvement des conceptions sous

l'Ancien Régime,' *Annales de Démographie Historique* (Paris/La Haye, 1974): 44–50
41 E.J. Hamilton, *War and Prices*, 162
42 Ibid., 163
43 Delasselle, 'Les enfants abandonnées à Paris,' 200. See also Peyronnet, *Les enfants trouvés de l'Hôpital général de Limoges*, 171.

CHAPTER 6: The *Expósito* as Victim

1 Antonio Bilbao y Durán, 'Historia de la vida de un pecador convertido ... ' AHN MS, estado 3235 (Madrid, 1794), 201
2 Totals, 1794–99
3 J. Ballexserd, *Dissertation sur l'éducation physique des enfants* (Paris, 1780; originally pub. Paris, 1762), 17
4 Brouzet, *Essai sur l'education médicinale des enfan[t]s sur leurs maladies*, 2 vols (Paris, 1754), I: 86
5 Ibid., I: 357
6 M. Boerhaave, *Maladies des femmes et des enfan[t]s avec un traité des accouchemen[t]s, tirés des Aphorismes de Boerhaave commentés par Van Swieten* (Paris, 1759), 60
7 García Guerra, *El Hospital Real de Santiago*, 333
8 Michel de Montaigne, 'De l'instituciones des enfan[t]s, *Essais* (Paris, 1914), I: xxv, 108
9 Antonio Arteta, *Dissertaceión sobre la muchedumbre de niños que mueren en enfancia y modo de remediarla y de procurar en agilidad y fuerzas competentes* (Saragossa, 1802), 19
10 Lallemand, *La question des enfants abandonnées*, 50
11 Delasselle, 'Les enfants abandonnées à Paris,' 191
12 Uriz, *Causas prácticas de la muerte de los expósitos*, I: 52
13 Ibid., I: 53
14 Alvarez-Sierra, *Los hospitales de Madrid*, 137
15 Uriz, *Causas prácticas de la muerte de los expósitos*, I: 22
16 Report of Junta de damas, in Ruiz de Luzuriaga, 'Estadística politico-médica,' I: 47
17 Uriz, *Causas prácticas de la muerte de los expósitos*, I: 20
18 Ibid., I: 45
19 *Entradas*, 1790
20 Report of Junta de damas, in Ruiz de Luzuriaga, 'Estadística político-médica,' I: 59

21 Uriz, *Causas prácticas de la muerte de los expósitos* i: 46, 47
22 *Entradas*, 1700–99
23 Madoz, *Diccionario estadístico-histórico*, i: 463
24 Miñano y Bedoya, *Diccionario geográfico*
25 Madoz, *Diccionario estadístico-histórico*, i: 450
26 Ibid., xiii: 800
27 Ibid., vii: 58
28 Ibid., iv: 306
29 Kany, *Life and Manners in Madrid*, 412
30 Antonio Domínguez Ortiz, 'Una visión crítica de Madrid del xviii siglo,' *Anales del Instituto de Estudios Madrileños* 6 (1970): 303
31 José Antonio Martínez Bara, 'Problemas de policía urbana madrileña en el pasado,' *Anales del Instituto de Estudios Madrileños* 7 (1971): 383
32 Ibid., 376
33 Ibid., 342, 343
34 Kany, *Life and Manners in Madrid*, 412
35 *Entradas*, 1700–99
36 Charpentier, *Le Droit de l'enfance abandonnée*, 29
37 Norman Longmate, *The Workhouse* (London, 1974), 182–9
38 Duc de la Rouchefoucauld-Liancourt, Rapport de la Comité de la Mendicité, quoted in Peyronnet, *Les enfants trouvés de l'Hôpital général de Limoges*, 212
39 Wayne Dennis, *Children of the Crèche* (New York, 1973), 55
40 Uriz, *Causas prácticas de la muerte de los expósitos*, i: 73

CHAPTER 7: The *Expósito* as Patient

1 Richard Ford, *Gatherings from Spain* (London, 1906; originally pub. 1846), 243
2 Bilbao y Durán, 'Historia de la vida de un pecador convertido,' 201
3 William Buchan, *Domestic Medicine* (London, 1769), 297, 298
4 Ruiz de Luzuriaga, 'Estadística político-médica,' i: 59
5 Michael Burke, *The Royal College of San Carlos* (Durham, NC, 1977)
6 Granjel, *Historia de la Pediatría Española* (Salamanca, 1965), 38
7 M. Henri Jahier, 'Le Livre de la génération du Foetus et la traitement des femmes encientes et des nouveaux-nés, de Arib Ibn Sib, de Cordue (950),' *Asclepio* 8 (1956), 163–6
8 Carlos Rico-Avello, 'Los clásicos del Garrotillo,' *Congreso Internacional de Historia de la Medicina* 15 (Sept. 1956): 120

9 Ruth Hodgkinson, *Science and Public Health* (Open University Series, London, 1973)

10 Juan L. Morales, *El niño en la cultura española* 4 vols (Álcala de Henares, 1958), I: 270

11 Juan Riera and Juan María Jíminez Muñoz, 'Documentos sobre el colegio de cirugía de Barcelona,' *Asclepio* 28 (1976): 90

12 Burke, *Royal College of San Carlos*, 132

13 Juan Riera, 'Cirugía de España ilustrada y su comunicación con Europa,' ACTA *Historia-Médica Vallisoletana* 7 (1976): 69

14 Juan de Navas, *Elementos del Arte de Partear* (Madrid, 1815; originally pub. 1795), lxxxix

15 Antoine Petit, *Traité des maladies des femmes encientes, des femmes en couche et des enfans nouveau-nés*, 2 vols (Paris, an VII), I: 280

16 Burke, *Royal College of San Carlos*, 120

17 Abate D. Lorenzo Hervás y Panduro, *Historia de la Vida del Hombre*, 7 vols (Madrid, 1789), II: libro 5: 240–6

18 Joseph Raulin, *De la Conservacion des enfan[t]s*, 2 vols (Paris, 1768), I: 325

19 Charpentier, *Le Droit de l'enfance abandonnée*, 132

20 Demerson, *La Condesa del Montijo*, 236

21 Ibid., 237

22 Ibid., 237

23 Soubeyroux, *Pauperisme et rapports sociaux à Madrid*, I: 162

24 Elizabeth Lomax, 'Infantile Syphilis and Acquired Characteristics,' *Journal of History of Medicine and Allied Sciences* 33 (1978): 25

25 Antonio Pérez de Escobar, *Avisos de las causas de muerte de niños* (Madrid, 1778), 141

26 Antonio Moreno González, *Gaceta de Madrid*, 9 September 1844

27 Raulin, *Conservacion des enfants*, I: 340

28 Charpentier, *Le Droit de l'enfance abandonnée*, 132

29 Lallemand, *Histoire des enfants abandonnées*, 170

30 Boerhaave, *Maladies des femmes et des enfan[t]s* II: 277

31 Pérez de Escobar, *Avisos de las causas de muerte*, 220

32 M. Andry, *Orthopaedia or Art of Correcting and Preventing Deformities in Children*, 2 vols (London, n.d.), II: 10

33 Ruiz de Luzuriaga, 'Estadística político-médica,' I: 81

34 Navas, *Elementos del Arte de Partear*, 164

35 Michael Underwood, *A Treatise on the Diseases of Children* (London, 1784), 44

36 Pedro Monlau y Roca, *Elementos de higiene pública o el arte de conservar la*

salud de los pueblos, 2 vols (Madrid, 1871; originally pub. Barcelona 1857), II, 40

37 Bilbao y Durán, *Destrucción y conservación de los expósitos*, 12
38 Uriz, *Causas prácticas de la muerte de los expósitos* I, 47
39 Boerhaave, *Maladies des femmes et des enfan[t]s*, 29, 60
40 Underwood, *Treatise on Diseases of Children*, 80
41 Ibid., 94
42 T. Sydenham, *The Works of Thomas Sydenham on Acute and Chronic Diseases, annotated by George Wallis*, M.D., 2 vols (London, 1788; originally pub. 1685), I: 339
43 Brouzet, *Essais sur l'éducation médicinale des enfants et sur leurs maladies*, 2 vols (Paris, 1754), I: 89, 232
44 George Armstrong, *An Essay on the Diseases most fatal to infants; to which are added rules to be observed in the nursing of children: with a particular view to those who are brought up by hand* (London, 1767), 12. This theory is associated with a French physician of Montpellier, Théophile Bordeu (1722–76).
45 Lester King, *The Road to Medical Enlightenment, 1650–1695* (London, 1970), 197
46 Lallemand, *Histoire des enfants abandonnées*, 170 n30
47 Rico-Avello, 'Los clásicos de Garrotillo,' 121
48 Pérez de Escobar, *Avisos de las causas de muerte*, 225
49 Brouzet, *Essais sur l'éducation médicinale*, II: 59
50 Underwood, *Treatise on the Diseases of Children*, 160
51 J.P. Peter, 'Malades et maladies à la fin du XVIIIe siècle,' in P. Goubert (ed.), *Médecins, climat et épidémes à la fin du XVIIIe siècle* (Paris, 1972), 164
52 Armstrong, *Essay on the diseases most fatal to infants*, 32
53 Ruiz de Luzuriaga, 'Estadística político-médica,' IV: 318–20
54 Desessartz, *Traité de l'éducation corporelle des enfan[t]s en bas age* (Paris, 1760), 226
55 Brouzet, *Essais sur l'éducation médicinale*, I: 351
56 Petit, *Traité des maladies des femmes enceintes*, I: 290
57 R. Etienne, 'La conscience médicale antique et la vie des Enfants,' *Annales de Démographie Historique*, 116
58 Brouzet, *Essais sur l'éducation médicinale*, I: 357
59 Ibid., II: 15
60 Petit, *Traité sur l'éducation médicinale*, I: 121
61 Roger Mercier, *L'Enfant dans la société du XVIIIe siècle (Avant l'Émile)* (Dakar, 1961), 84
62 Underwood, *Treatise on the Diseases of Children*, 83

63 Armstrong, *Essay on the diseases most fatal to infants,* 72
64 Ballexserd, *Sur l'éducation physique des enfants,* 48. See also Jaime Bonells, *Prejuicios que acarrean al género humano* ... (Madrid, 1786), 131-4 and Raulin, *Conservacion des enfans,* 168.
65 Abbé Louis Malo Moreau de Saint-Elier, *Traité de la communication des maladies et des passions* (La Haye, 1738), 41
66 Ibid., 108
67 Ibid., 24-44

CHAPTER 8: Infanticide and the Inclusa

1 Based on *Entradas* for 1700-99
2 The basic source of information on the Inclusas of Spain is to be found in responses to an inquiry sent out by Joaquín de Murcia, member of the Consejo Suprema of Castile and head of the Junta de Caridad. The information is in the appendix of his work, *Discurso político* ...
3 Jean Louis Flandrin's 'L'Attitude à l'égard du petit enfant et les conduites sexuelles dans la civilisation occidentale,' in *Annales de Démographie Historique: Enfant et Sociétés* (Paris/La Haye 1973), 143-205, is a comprehensive examination for the medieval period. See also William Langer, 'Infanticide: A Historical Survey,' *History of Childhood Quarterly* 1 (Winter 1974): 353-6, and Maria W. Piers, *Infanticide* (New York, 1978).
4 Barbara A. Kellum, 'Infanticide in England in the Later Middle Ages,' *History of Childhood Quarterly* 1 (Summer 1973): 367-88
5 Peter C. Hoffer and N.E.H. Hull, *Murdering Mothers: Infanticide in England and New England, 1558-1803* (New York/London, 1981)
6 In 1540 Henri II passed legislation that all illegitimate pregnancies must be declared to the magistrates. An announcement to that effect was read from the pulpit twice a month.
7 Richard Trexler, 'Infanticide in Florence: New Sources and First Results,' *History of Childhood Quarterly* 1 (Summer 1973): 98-116
8 Vicente Pérez Moreda, *Las crisis de mortalidad en la España interior: siglos XVI-XIX* (Madrid, 1980), 171
9 Mercier, *L'Enfant dans la société du XVIIIe siècle,* 30
10 Monlau y Roca, *Elementos de higiene pública,* II: 656
11 One of the few documented examples of infanticide on an organized scale occurred in Baena where, when funds were short, authorities made arrangements to hand infants over to someone who would take them by night outside the town and leave them: 'Some are eaten by dogs of shepherds, devoured by foxes or wild pigs' (Valverde, *Historia de Baena,* cap. XIII, quoted in Domínguez Ortiz, *La Sociedad española en el siglo XVIII,* 64n22).

12 Lord Brougham, *Edinburgh Review* (1838), quoted in J.F. Terme and J.B. Monfalcon, *Histoire statistique et morale des enfants-trouvés*, 224
13 Emmanuel Le Roy Ladurie, *Mind and Method of the Historian* (Chicago, 1981), 19
14 Bogna W. Lorence, 'Parents and Children in Eighteenth-Century Europe,' *History of Childhood Quarterly* 2 (Winter 1974): 10
15 Ibid., 9
16 Murcia, *Discurso político*, apéndice tercero, xiv
17 Robert Sidney Smith, 'Spanish Population Thought before Malthus,' *Teachers of History: Essays in Honor of Lawrence B. Packard* (Ithaca, 1954), 23–257. Population theory has been discussed in chapter 3.
18 Uriz, *Causas prácticas de la muerte de niños expósitos*, II: 8
19 Bilbao y Durán, *Destrucción y conservación de los expósitos*, 137, 138
20 Bustelo, 'La población española, en la segunda mitad del siglo XVIII,' 53–104
21 Jovellanos, 'Informe en el expediente de ley agraria,' 81
22 AHN Sección Reales Cédulas, 15-V-88
23 Ibid., 2-VI-88
24 Ibid., 5-I-94
25 Murcia, *Discurso político*, apéndice tercero, xiv, article XVIII
26 Ibid., article XXIII
27 Ibid., Letter circulated to all the bishops and archbishops of the kingdom in conjunction with legislation, royal order 11-XII-96, articles XXVI, XXVII
28 Pedro de Calatayud, *Doctrinas prácticas que suele explicar en sus misiones*, 2 vols (Valencia, 1737–39), II: 122, quoted in Callahan, 'Caridad, sociedad y economía,' *Moneda y Crédito*, no. 146 (Sept. 1978), 70
29 Ballexserd, *Dissertation sur l'éducation physique des enfants*, 86
30 Richard Herr, 'Hacía el derrumbe del Antiguo Régimen: Crisis fiscal y desamortización bajo Carlos IV,' *Moneda y Crédito*, no. 118 (Sept. 1971): 47
31 Callahan, 'Caridad, sociedad y economía,' 75
32 Records of these meetings have been preserved in the ADP (Libros de juntas de la Real Casa de la Inclusa, 1794–98, legajo 48, no. 2).
33 Ibid., Meeting of 6 August 1797
34 Ibid., Meeting of 16 June 1799
35 García, *El modo de conservar los niños expósitos*, 27ff
36 Ibid., 41ff
37 Ibid., 50–8
38 Ibid,. 14
39 Ibid., 68

40 *Journal des Scavans* (August 1680, quoted in Desessartz, *Traité de l'éducation corporelle des enfants en bas age*, II: 149

41 Marie France Morel, 'Théories et Pratiques de l'Allaitement en France au XVIIIe siècle,' *Annales de Démographie Historique* (Paris/La Haye 1976), 423

42 Brouzet, *Essais sur l'éducation medicinale*, I: 159

43 Armstrong, *An Essay on the diseases most fatal to infants*, 107, 132

44 García, *El modo de conservar los niños expósitos*, 15

45 Uriz, *Causas prácticas de la muerte de niños expósitos*, II: 131

46 L'Abbé Moreau de Saint-Elier, *Traité de la communication des maladies et des passions*, 44

47 Ballexserd, *Sur l'éducation physique des enfants*, 73

48 García, *El modo de conservar los niños expósitos*, 15

49 Ibid., 35

50 Demerson, *La Condesa del Montijo*, 210

51 Ibid., 210

52 Meeting of 3 June 1803, quoted in ibid., 231

53 García, *El modo de conservar los niños expósitos*, 73

54 García, *Instituciones sobre la crianza física de los niños expósitos*, 49ff

55 Demerson, *La Condesa del Montijo*, 224

56 Ibid., 224

57 Ibid., 225

58 Ibid., 226

59 Ruiz de Luzuriaga, 'Estadística político-medica,' I: 56

60 Antonio Moreno González, *Gaceta de Madrid*, 10 Sept. 1844

61 Uriz, *Causas prácticas de la muerte de niños expósitos*, II: 26, 27

62 Demerson, *La Condesa del Montijo*, 243

63 M. Godoy, *Memorias y apologéticas para la historia del reinado del señor Don Carlos IX de Borbon*, 2 vols (Madrid, 1965), I: 212

64 Demerson, *La Condesa del Montijo*, 220

65 Uriz, *Causas prácticas de la muerte de niños expósitos*, I: 25

66 Ibid., I: 433

67 Bilbao y Durán, 'Historia de un pecador convertido'

68 Godoy, *Memorias*, I: 212

Index

abortion, 108, 109; attempts to limit, 128
Academy of Medicine, Madrid, 141, 154
account books, 5, 42. *See also gastos*
accounts, 37, 39
administration districts, 84
administrators: annual meeting, 37; attitudes to wet nurses, 82, 90, 131, 132, 169; hospital admissions policies, 103, 177; income, 37, 45; loss of enthusiasm, 192, 194; responsibilities, 34, 37–40, 183
admissions to hospital, 37, 103–22, 130, 146, 187
adoptions, 136
agrarian reform, 54
Alcala, 62–5, 85, 129, 136
Alcobendas, 135
Alcorcón, 64, 134, 135
alms. *See* parish alms
amigos del pais, 101, 180
Andalusia, 53
Aranjuez, 63
Archives of the Diputación Provincial of Madrid, 191, 211
Archivo Histórico Nacional, 211
artificial feeding, 200, 205, 207, 208

artisans, craftsmen, tradesmen, 61–3, 73, 88, 137–9
Asturias, 53

Ballexserd, J., 153, 169, 188, 200
bedding, beds, 17
bequests, 27; Luisa de Oliva, 9
Bilbao y Durán, Antonio, 125, 180, 208, 211
birth rates, 58
blankets, 29, 42
Boerhaave, H., 152, 159
bonds. *See juros*
Bonells, Jaime, 213
Borgia, Francisco: archdeacon Valencia, 27
Bourbons, 7, 153, 180, 182, 189
Britain, 7, 31, 102
Brotherhood of the Mortal Sin, 108
Brouzet, N., 161, 164, 167
bureaucrats, 5, 47, 156, 184, 189, 208, 209
Bustar Viejo, 65
Bustelo, Francisco, demographer, 67, 182

Campomanes, Pedro Rodríguez de, 101, 212

Carbajo Isla, María, 58, 105, 212, 213
Castile, 54, 56, 60, 61, 65, 66, 68
Catalonia, 53
censo, censos, 26–8
census: 1754, 44, 64–5; 1787, 66;
 1797, 63, 66; 1827, 64–5
charity systems, 3–4, 120, 188–9,
 191; destabilization, 190–1
Charles II, 7
Charles III, 18, 137, 180, 189
Charles IV, 31, 173, 180, 189, 206, 212
childbirth, 109, 127–9
Church of Santa Maria Magdalena,
 108
church resources, 190
church/state social welfare system,
 183
churchmen, 5, 151
clerks: pay, responsibilities, status,
 39, 40, 45
climate, 135
coal: supply, 5, 14; subsidies, 29
College of Advocates, 24
Company of the Philippines, 30
Confraternity of Nuestra Señora de la
 Esperanza, 108
Confraternity of Our Lady of Sorrows,
 9, 19
Confraternity of St Joseph of the Carpenters, 34–5
Convent of la Victoria, 35

day-labourer, 51, 55, 56. See also jornalero; peón
death rates: 1790s, 44, 58; 1799, 205;
 from illness, 133–5; gender, 139,
 142; urban, 85, 108
demography, 58, 67, 182–3, 209, 212
Desamparados, 17, 20, 107, 121, 148,
 156
diarrhoetic complaints, 79–80

Diaz de Cortina, Josefa, 132–3
diseases, 157–67, 170
doctor(s), 43, 79, 81, 82, 151, 168–70,
 172, 195, 200; authority, 196–8,
 202, 203
donated sources of income, 24, 27,
 28

England, 103, 115
Enkuïssen, 4
entradas. See admissions to hospital
Esquivias, 64
Extremadura, 53, 63

famine conditions: 1699; 51; 1723–
 95, 51–2
feeding/eating tools, utensils, 12, 199
finances, 7, 19–33, 39, 204
Five Major Guilds Corporation, 10,
 30, 64, 192, 193
France, 7, 31, 63, 71, 91, 102
furnishings, 10–12

Galdiano y Croy, Leonardo, 128, 212
Galicia, 102
García, Santiago, Dr, 79, 82, 152, 153,
 160, 163, 169, 170, 173, 180, 194,
 205; conflicts with nurses, 196–8,
 201, 203
Garcia del Real, Francisco Bustelo,
 212
gastos, 5, 8, 19, 24, 35, 36, 44, 45, 48,
 72, 77, 103
General Hospital: Brotherhood, 35.
 See also Desamparados; Sagrada
 Pasión
Ginesta, A., 152
Godoy, Manuel de, 180, 186, 194, 206,
 212
government bonds. See state bonds;
 juros; vales reales

grain costs, prices, 7, 32, 54, 61, 88,
114, 146
Guadalajara, 61–5

Hamilton, E.J., 15, 72, 213, 218n33
Hapsburgs, 7
Hernandez Iglesias, Fermín, 212
Hervás y Panduro, L., 155
hospital: administration morale, 207;
admissions, 105, 107, 111; expenses,
finances, income, 8–11, 19, 20, 28,
194, 195; function, 35, 36; mortality, 140–4, 150, 178, 179; reform,
196, 197; relations to church and
state, 189–91; social role, 123, 124
Hospital of Nuestra Señora del Carmen. See Desamparados
hygiene, 11, 205

Iberti, José, 213
illegitimate/legitimate births,
98–100, 102–4, 107, 108, 110,
115, 121–3, 176
income. See donated sources of
income; finances
independent farmer. See labrador;
vecinos
Indies, 7, 123, 156
infant abandonment increase, 95–102
infanticide, 4, 109, 128, 175–80, 186,
192
inflation, 31, 32, 36, 48
Instituto Provincial de Puericultura
de la Diputación Provincial de
Madrid, 4, 203, 211
inventory: Tomás Prado y Ovejero,
24, 28, 219n66, 220n73
investments, 193

Jesuits, 108
Jewish quarter, morería, 84, 85, 87

Jiménez y Salas, María, 212
jornalero, 51, 55–8, 65
Jovellanos, Gaspar Melchor de, 40,
101, 183, 220n68
Junta de damas. See Royal Economic
Society of Madrid, Junta de damas
juros, 24, 28, 30

La Mancha, 63
labrador, 55, 57
Lallemand, L., xii, 99, 129, 163
Larquie, Claude, 111, 212, 225n2
Las Recogidas, 108
legacies to the Inclusa hospital, 193.
See also inventory
legislation re foundlings, infanticide:
1796, 184, 186, 187
Livi Bacci, M., demographer, 58, 67

machismo, 97
madre: pay, responsibilities, status,
41–4, 130, 187, 196, 198, 203
malnutrition, 164–6
Maria Luisa, Queen, 31, 109, 193, 204
maternalism, 195
matron. See madre
mayorazgo, 25–7, 61
medical care development, 151–71
medicalization, 156, 157, 196, 203
misogyny, 169, 201
Montijo, Countess del, 194, 195; exile
1805, 206
municipal and government bonds.
See juros
Murcia, Pedro Joaquin de, 90, 183,
192–4, 204, 205, 209, 212

nurses: origins, 63; pay, 35, 41–3, 58,
133, 184–5, 192; responsibilities,
37
nursing: non-hospital, 162–3; quali-

ty, 184–6; staff size, 47, 133; standards, 18th century, 170

obstetrics, 153, 154
official, royal hospitals, Madrid: reports, 105
Order of St Francis 3
Order of San Antón 136

paediatrics, 152–5, 157, 202; 18th century, 213
parish alms, 19–24
paternalism, 35, 40, 44, 46, 47, 100, 195, 210; economic, 101
peón, 67, 74
Pérez de Escobar, Antonio, 157, 164, 213
Philip II, 19
Philip V, 7, 153
population growth, 116. See also demography
poverty, 121–3; patterns, 55, 63
prisons, la Galera, 109
prostitutes/prostitution, 105, 108
psychology, 59, 60, 97–8, 123

rations, 41, 43, 47
real estate, 25–6, 30, 193
records of departures/discharges from hospital. See salidas
Refugio, 20, 21, 108, 109
religious/political demonstration by women, 1766, 88
road building, 1760s, 53
Rochefoucauld-Liancourt, Duc de la, 103, 148
Royal and Holy Brotherhood of Refuge and Mercy. See Refugio
Royal Canal of Tauste, share ownership, 30

Royal Economic Society of Madrid, Junta de damas: attitude to artificial feeding, 201; conflict with Inclusa head Josef Vilches, 37; dismissal of administrator, 38; hygienic measures, 11; Inclusa administration take-over, 191; opposition to vaccine trials, 156; pressure-group tactics, 180; recognition of parents' rights, 103; reorganization, transformation of Inclusa, 78–9, 195–6
Royal Economic Society of Madrid: policies, 101–2
Ruiz de Luzuriaga, Ignacio María, 141, 165, 211

Sagrada Pasión, La, 20, 105–7
sainetes, skits by Ramon de la Cruz, 44, 77, 85, 89, 222n33
salidas, 51, 55, 62–5, 67, 72–5, 82, 84, 88, 91, 120, 213
San Ginés parish records, 37, 121, 187, 211
sanitation: hospital, 11; Madrid, 136–7
Sisters of Charity, 47, 203; from France, 195
soup kitchens, 120, 189
state bonds, 7, 24, 28, 30, 190
street-name sources, 87, 88
subsidized supplies, coal and textiles, 29
surgeons, 43, 195
syphilis, 79, 99, 155, 157, 163, 198

taxes, 7, 20, 28–31, 59, 190; on wine, 29
tenants, 29; farming, 54
textiles: industries, 71, 77; subsidies, 29; workers, 71, 77

Toledo, 63, 191
Torres Villarroel, Diego de, 44, 60
traditions, 59
Trullás, Countess de: exile, 206

Underwood, Mr, 159, 168
utilitarianism, 102, 110

vaccination campaigns, experiments,
155, 156
Valencia, 53
vales reales, 7, 30, 190
vecinos, 64, 65
Vega, Pedro de la, 99–100, 108, 212
Vilches, Josef, 30, 37, 192, 208
volunteer fund-raisers, 204

wages, 45, 48, 60, 61, 69
Wars of Succession: Austrian 1740,
76; Spanish, 23, 51

water supply, 18
wet-nurse: trial for criminal negligence, 80–2, 164
wet-nurses: contagious illnesses, 168,
169; dislike by doctors, 82, 171,
202, 203; dislike of foundlings, 157;
jobs of husbands, 62, 125, 136;
places of origin, 63; poverty, 67;
registration books, *see salidas*; regulations, 196, 198; rural/urban
roots, links, 57, 69; supervision by
madre, 130–2; survival rates of
charges, 139
wheat prices, 6, 45, 114
women's unrest, 88–91

Xavier de Uriz, Joaquín, 180, 197, 205,
208, 209